CW00983024

Street Urchins, Sociopaths and Degenerates

Street Urchins, Sociopaths and Degenerates

Orphans of Late-Victorian and Edwardian Fiction

David Floyd

CARDIFF
UNIVERSITY OF WALES PRESS

www.uwp.co.uk

British Library Cataloguing-in-Publication Data.
A catalogue record for this book is available from the British Library.

ISBN 978-1-7831-6010-5
978-1-7831-6011-2

Typeset by Hewer Text UK Ltd, Edinburgh
Printed by CPI Antony Rowe, Chippenham, Wiltshire

Contents

I
Introduction

'Get thee gone. Get thee gone. Thy mother dwells not in this city.'

Oscar Wilde, 'The Star Child'

Intentions and definitions

The 'long nineteenth-century' might also be called 'the century of the orphan'.[1] From the notable emergence of orphan figures in late eighteenth-century literature, through early- and middle-period Victorian fiction, and, as this book argues, well into the fin de siècle, this potent literary type is remarkable for its consistent recurrence and its metamorphosis as a register of cultural conditions. The remarkable ubiquity of orphans in the literature of these periods encourages inquiry into their metaphoric implications and the manner in which they function as barometers of burgeoning social concerns. Despite the consistency of their appearance in works of these periods, the cultural elements to which they are literary responses alter significantly towards the century's end. The overwhelming majority of criticism focusing on orphans centres particularly on the form as an early- to middle-century convention, primarily found in social and domestic works; in effect, the non-traditional, aberrant, at times Gothic orphan of the fin de siècle has been largely overlooked, if not denied outright. This oversight has given rise to the need for a study of this potent cultural figure as it pertains to preoccupations characteristic of the turn of the century. This book examines the noticeable difference between orphans of genre fiction of the fin de siècle and their predecessors in works including first-wave Gothic and the majority of Victorian fiction, and the variance of their symbolic references and cultural implications.

I have chosen to examine genre fiction specifically, for it offers non-traditional depictions of orphans that are not present in domestic and social narratives, which tend to express a preoccupation with the 'feminine' concerns of the home, the concept of the nuclear family and parental influence. Furthermore, orphans of realistic social and domestic works typically allude to economic concerns and notions of social class that are not an issue with the fin-de-siècle orphan. Likewise, realist and domestic texts predominantly present the ideal family as the reliable emblem of stability to the orphan aspired for its promise of security both financial and psychological. Late-century genre fiction, however, whether in the form of second-wave Gothic, science fiction, imperial romance or children's fantasy, instead is disruptive and anxious, offering orphan narratives bereft of the stable home and dealing with 'male' concerns of action and adventure, and is notable for its allusions to cultural factors particular to the fin de siècle such as degeneration, sexual ambiguity and imperial enterprise, which were notable threats to notions of patriarchy and masculinity.[2]

These variations in conception and depiction of orphanhood were the result of several factors. For one, deviations emerged in literary representations of the family, that unit to which the orphan is intrinsically linked; the ideal family, that attrahent to which the orphan drifted so frequently and naturally in earlier texts, gradually declined as a realistic notion, and even became targeted and maligned by some authors. In addition, the consideration of other previously marginalized figures, such as females, criminals and foreigners, altered the presentation of the different and outcast.

The years 1880–1911 form the parameters of this book for several reasons. 1880 marks the period when anxieties particular to the fin de siècle begin to manifest themselves, with genre literature of the period being particularly symptomatic of their development. The earliest text I examine is Robert Louis Stevenson's adventure novel *Treasure Island*, published in 1883, which reveals that those anxieties had already begun to loom on the period's psychic landscape. The decade examined in Holbrook Jackson's 1913 study of the fin de siècle, *The Eighteen Nineties*, falls into the centre of my own. Jackson notes that the final ten years of the decade were 'remarkable for a literary and artistic renaissance' and 'a new sense of patriotism' that degenerated respectfully into decadence and jingoism.[3] How portraits of orphans relate to these factors is part of this book's focus. It is important to consider the trajectory of this development of the orphan figure beyond the turn of the century as well; therefore, the book extends into the Edwardian period, where I place particular emphasis on the era's children's fantasy, in which renditions of the orphan are particularly salient and revealing. 1911 is the year of publication of the latest narratives I consider, Francis Hodgson Burnett's *The Secret Garden* and J. M. Barrie's *Peter Pan*. This year was chosen as well at the suggestion of Juliet Nicolson's *The Perfect Summer: England 1911, Just Before the Storm*. Nicolson discusses England in the summer at the end of the Edwardian period, just prior to the advent of the Great War, a period that compelled Ben Tillet to claim that the country was on the verge of collapse, and Winston Churchill to write in his diary, 'all the world is changing at once'.[4]

Colin Manlove states that the protagonist of the eighteenth-century novel 'often finds out what he or she is, while in the nineteenth-century novel the process is one of learning what one may become'.[5] This assessment applies as well to the role of the orphan, who in late eighteenth- and early nineteenth-century literature is often in pursuit of his or her true identity, or is in the service of a reform moral aimed at societal improvement, in either case signalling the fulfilment of some potential. Later versions of the orphan tend toward a more ominous nature, frequently portending some form of psychological malleability, degeneration both moral and physical, or the reality of an unreconciled orphan condition, a disquieting implication of 'what one may become'. The orphan of fin-de-siècle genre fiction becomes less a contrasting referent to ensure family validity or a convention speaking to social reform, as was often the case in earlier manifestations, and more a potentially wildly unstable entity or permanently unparented casualty. Whereas in earlier texts the orphan is a sympathetic character, parentless or abandoned, the late-century orphan is sometimes relentlessly autonomous, dangerously individualistic and capable of metaphorical and even literal acts of patricide. Orphanhood in earlier narratives is a result of wretched adult figures or of a mechanized and impersonal society, but in later texts it emerges instead to speak to crises particular to the end of the century. And, while in earlier fiction orphanhood often proves a temporary predicament capable of reparation, fin-de-siècle genre fiction often presents it as an unalterable state, a persisting and at times even desired condition.

While much criticism has been written concerning various interpretations of the orphan of the late eighteenth century and particularly the early to middle periods of Victoria's reign, virtually no consideration has been made of the way fin-de-siècle conditions produced portrayals of this figure, particularly in the later genre literature upon which this book will concentrate. Indeed, the majority of criticism concerning orphans focuses on the aspect of the secular moral that they provided, for instance, in regard to the oppression of women or the wretched conditions of the poor. But, once the urgency of that moral seems diminished, and emphasis shifts instead, for example, to the threat posed by the New Woman or the implications of the evident degenerative potential of the lower classes, the symbolic import of the orphan shifts as well. Perhaps it is the radical nature of this shift that has led some criticism to claim that orphans lose their significance, and virtually vanish, during the nineteenth century's final decades, only to resurface in the early twentieth century.[6] While this claim may be somewhat true for the late century's domestic and social literature, orphans remain relevant, vital figures of significant consequence well through the close of the 1800s as they are rendered in the period's genre literary forms; furthermore, with their unremedied orphanhood and troubling, even monstrous nature, they come to signal very different aspects of British culture than did their forebears.

By way of demonstrating the notable manner in which late-century genre fiction's treatment of the orphan differs from the same period's social and domestic works, I would like to consider first Thomas Hardy's *Jude the Obscure* (1895). While notorious for its modern examination of marriage and sexuality, the novel is nevertheless a typical social work in respect to its rendering of the orphan, addressing the class system, inequality of educational opportunity and effects of industrialization. Jude's lofty aspirations to study at Christminster are frustrated by his orphanhood, which decrees his station as stonemason. That relegation determines his class affiliation, 'a wall [that] divided him from those . . . men who had nothing to do from morning till night but to read, mark, learn, and inwardly digest. Only a wall – but what a wall!'[7] Similarly, in Oscar Wilde's *The Importance of Being Earnest* (1895), Jack's intentions of marrying Gwendolen are jeopardized precisely because of the revelation of his status as foundling and its attending questions of origin and class affiliation. Though he is not afflicted with the poverty typically experienced by the orphan, Jack's domestic happiness is threatened by Lady Bracknell's disapproval of the potentiality of his low birth.

Contrasting remarkably with these two examples is Mary Louis Stewart Molesworth's children's mystery *The Palace in the Garden* (1887), wherein the orphan functions to subvert typical perceptions of the family in ways that question traditional patriarchal paradigms. The child narrator, Spanish-born Gussie, orphaned at an early age and therefore unacquainted with the notion of the ideal family, provides an alternative vantage dissimilar to customary patriarchal assumptions and insinuative about the fragmentary potential threatening to undermine the family. Gussie's antithetic perception permits traditional types to achieve unaccustomed nuances, sanctioning what Frank Rigg calls 'new terms for family validity'.[8] In addition, there is the disturbing and destructive orphan of Wilde's fantasy 'The Star Child' (1888), whose mysterious protagonist is taken in by a poverty-stricken but virtuous woodcutter. Despite this adoption into an accepting and loving family, typically the remedy for the orphanic condition, the ethereal and beautiful star child is shockingly remote from sympathetic types such as Oliver Twist, spurning his biological mother and denying his surrogate parents, claiming, 'I am no son of thine to do thy bidding'; furthermore, he not only 'grew proud, and cruel, and selfish', mocking the afflicted and ridiculing the less fortunate, becoming 'foul as the toad, and loathsome as the adder', but he literally transforms into a reptilian creature due to his wickedness.[9] While Wilde's depiction is clearly a tale for moral instruction for children, the subversion of the conventions typically associated with the usually moving and pitiful orphan character attests to the metamorphosis portraits of orphanhood underwent in late-century genre fiction in a way they did not in social and domestic fiction.

Before addressing the criticism surrounding the Victorian orphan, I will provide an idea of the types of orphans discussed in this book. Whereas the notion of orphanhood typically evokes images of children, the majority of orphans discussed in this book are notably adults. Once beyond a certain age, even if one has lost both parents, one is not usually considered an orphan per se. However, one of the remarkable aspects of fin-de-siècle genre fiction is its adoption, and even subversion, of conventions associated with the child orphan's condition – lack of family, questions of identity, exile from social constructions –in a way that clearly emphasizes and perpetuates the adult's orphan status and underscores that status's particular resonance with fin-de-siècle anxieties. For a period wherein foundational and traditional paradigms were challenged if not altogether lost, the parentless adult served as a cultural emblem – an entity bereft of ancestral counsel, affection and guidance whose predicament represented the sense of loss, disorientation and uncertainty characteristic of the fin-de-siècle. The adult-as-orphan images the turn-of-the-century British psyche, severed from the ideologies and traditions intrinsic to a past from which fin-de-siècle culture found itself increasingly disconnected. Thus, for instance, the tragic nature of Renfield's fawning, even panicked, adulation of the parental Seward and the dread father figure, Dracula; Ignosi's constant demeaning appeal for Quatermain's patriarchal approval; the unsettling opposition and denial Hyde and Griffin exact against their respective sires; or Captain Hook's endeavor to make Wendy Darling a mother for him and his pirates in a land characterized by the desperate contrivance of alternate, substitutive domestic spaces.

Indeed, the term 'orphan' typically may initially elicit images of the 'Dickensian' type of popular imagination, the working-class child or the lower-class outcast waif so prominently featured in early- and middle-century middle-class fiction, and on which nearly all criticism focuses. It is, therefore, important to designate the peculiarities of the kinds of orphans with which this book is concerned. As the nineteenth century neared its end, the confidence and self-reliance of the mid-Victorian period were supplanted by anxieties concerning such topics as sexual ambiguity, moral and physical degeneration, and the practicality and ethicality of the imperial mission.

Attending this cultural shift was the waning of sentimental portrayals of childhood. According to Marah Gubar, Victorian and Edwardian childhood was constructed as an idyllic period offering escape from the complications of modernity. She also examines the bewilderment authors experienced insofar as how exactly to render the child when the notion of absolute innocence was no longer the only alternative, and that they furthermore were somewhat self-conscious about the issue of depiction of, engaging with and composing for children.[10] Children's fiction of the late 1800s became more introspective and less realistic.[11] The child protagonist of the turn of the century frequently displayed a notable incredulity and confidence, and tended to depend less on the intervention of a miraculous adult saviour figure and more on his or her own exertion of will and creativity. Seth Lerer notes at this time the simultaneous concern with children's welfare and a burgeoning preoccupation with 'the occult, the fantastic, and the supernatural'.[12] The child furthermore tended to formulate alternate realities or imaginative realms in collusion with other suffering children, ultimately affecting a kind of healing, order and assimilation notably without adult supervision.[13]

Orphans of the late period even tend towards a kind of aberration, even monstrousness, or are marked with a grotesqueness that is not present in earlier portrayals. Though a certain sense of exile and ambiguity is attached to all orphan forms, the types of orphans I discuss and which are noted below are distinguished by the extreme manner in which they deviate from earlier depictions and in ways particular to the fin de siècle: (1) the mimic; (2) the rebel; (3) the orphan of island literature; (4) the imperial orphan; and (5) the orphan of childhood fantasy. The mimic, the imperial orphan and the island orphan are types that rely heavily on inspiration from and imitation of others and the assimilation of various environments in order to survive. The rebellious orphan and the orphan of childhood fantasy, meanwhile, function within realms of their own creation, either for selfish aims or out of necessity. The mimic and the rebel typically function, whether intentionally or not, without parental guidance, and, like their ancestor the picaroon, must rely on wit, intelligence and even luck. The imperial orphan and the orphan of childhood fantasy are virtually defined by their relationships to either saintly or malign father or mother figures.

The mimic endeavours to exact some semblance of identity through the imitation of other, less fragmentary entities. Lacking the stability of a realized self, this type, an example of which is Stoker's Renfield, fully employs the orphanic attribute of malleability. Longing for some measure of inclusion, this type insinuates him or herself into diverse social structures, emulating the behaviours of more fully realized, stable personalities. His or her intent is to surmount the question of the orphan's intrinsic ambiguity and exile. The rebellious orphan, on the other hand, is characterized by immoderate levels of narcissism, seeking only to serve him or herself without any aspirations to assimilation. This type, like Wells's Griffin, pursues self-serving aims without regard for those with whom he or she comes into contact and even exerts a kind of malicious intent, at times causing harm to others. Rather than pursuing inclusion, this type not only rebels against but at times seeks the ruin of the social or family structures from which he or she is exiled. The orphan of island narratives, a figure like Stevenson's Jim Hawkins or David Balfour, is likewise removed from the comfort of his domestic space, usually after losing one or both parents, and is hurled into an unfamiliar realm where he is mistreated, abused and exploited for his labour or natural talent. His nemesis is often a malicious elder male, possibly a corrupt family member, who seeks to profit from that exploitation. The orphan's salvation initially appears to arrive in the form of surrogate father figures whose attributes he learns to emulate; ultimately, however, it becomes clear that these father figures are insufficient to remedy, and actually ensure the perpetuation of the orphan's fatherless condition. The imperial orphan, meanwhile, operates within the savage and sometimes fantastic worlds explored in imperial enterprise. Not only orphaned in respect to a lack of parentage, like Haggard's Ignosi, this type may too be orphaned by the empire itself; he or she may lose his or her familial affiliations due to inter-family violence, or he or she may be displaced by the actions of colonialism. The onus of this type is to address questions of personal and national identity, particularly when assimilation into his or her environment determines survival. This orphan type is typically depicted as somewhat childlike insofar as dependence upon and emulation of a more capable, notably British, imperial father figure. At the same time, orphans of British lineage, like many of G. A. Henty's protagonists, appear remarkably unaffected by their orphanhood, their heritage evidently sufficient to compensate for their lack of nuclear family that debilitates the native orphan. Finally, and displaying the trajectory of literature's treatment of the orphan into the twentieth century, the orphan of Edwardian childhood fantasy not only has lost one or both parents, but is introduced to an alternate realm wherein he or she assumes a creative, autonomous, even parental role. Within this fantastical space, he or she formulates a provisional family imitative of the paradigm of the Victorian ideal family rarely to be found in the period's texts otherwise. Whereas social and domestic fiction of the turn of the century challenged the notion of motherhood, Edwardian children's fiction retains the need for and even exaltation of maternal figures. This perhaps explains why the contrived environment of these texts is typically haunted by the presence, whether imagined, spectral or actual, of an influential mother figure who determines the success or demise of the constructed 'family'.

In each case, whether overtly Gothic or not, these orphans deviate from previous conceptions of orphanhood in that they exhibit the type of metamorphic alteration typical of late nineteenth-century Gothic narratives. This book's main focus, then, is on non-traditional orphan forms whose unusualness, apropos to the Gothic convention of irresolution and indeterminacy which, despite their genres, they emulate, makes them particularly effective as vivid emblems of the fin-de-siècle anxieties to which they correspond.

Considering the various definitions associated with the term 'Gothic', and taking into account the attention this book pays to literary categories extraneous of the Gothic, it is important to qualify the manner in which I will be employing the term. My approach focuses largely on the depiction of orphans as characterized by instability, malleability, uncertainty and an unclassifiable nature, in essence, their 'gothicity'. Some texts I examine, like *Dracula* and *Strange Case of Dr Jekyll and Mr Hyde*, have obvious connections with Gothic fiction, while others, such as *Treasure Island* and *Kim*, are not traditionally regarded as Gothic, but are peopled by orphans redolent with notably Gothic metamorphic and fragmentary qualities. The Gothic seeks to represent extremes of various kinds, and the severity of emotional and psychic trauma endured and even in some events effected by fin-de-siècle genre fiction's orphans are often portrayed in Gothic tropes of mutation, subversion, alienation, equivocation and unreality.[14] Other studies articulate the changeableness intrinsic to late-century Gothic literature and address the manner in which fin-de-siècle Gothic utilizes the human body as the locus of anxiety and transition.[15] Robert Mighall writes of the 'somatic aspect' of late-Victorian Gothic, of the monstrous potential for the physical being to be manipulated, degenerated or in some other way altered.[16] Kelly Hurley discusses the 'abhuman', representations of that which is only partially human, which imply the plasticity of physical constitution and which 'served to dismantle conventional notions of "the human"'.[17]

While acknowledging the insights of the studies preceding my own, I wish to go beyond them in considering other aspects of transition and variability as they relate specifically to the depiction of fin-de-siècle orphans. Mighall and Hurley focus largely on the material alterations of Gothic bodies in general, but I want to pursue the psychic applications of malleability as well as they pertain to orphanhood. Figures like Helen Vaughn or Kimball O'Hare display physical characteristics that either set them apart or permit their insinuation into a social structure, but the psychological facets of their incertitude interest me as well. The disruption of stable psychic states is consistently presented in the orphan of fin-de-siècle genre literature, featuring the mental extremes of desperation, defiance, instability and questions of identity that are so intrinsic to the Gothic. Furthermore, I would like to argue that the indeterminacy that typifies early portrayals of orphanhood is a quality equally present in later orphan forms. The typical homeless waif in the street is marked by namelessness, lack of association with a specific class and a disconnect from any familial or socially acceptable structure. I want to pursue this evasion of categories as it relates to turn-of-the-century orphans, but with an emphasis on pertinence to concerns less about economic difference and class affiliation and more about the degeneration, sexual ambiguity and imperial enterprise that characterized the fin de siècle. These are qualities that distinguish the orphan of the century's end from his or her predecessors in the earlier parts of the century.

In my discussion of these types, I do not wish merely to pursue vague interpretations of the concept of orphanhood, in the manner for instance of John Reed, whose analysis I address below and who grants equal treatment to orphans both literal and figurative. As I mentioned previously, my focus is on *non-traditional* depictions of orphanhood, and this at times engages characters not typically thought of as orphans. One type I examine, for example, is the adult who has either lost one or both parents, or who has, like Haggard's George Curtis or Wells's Griffin, intentionally orphaned him or herself by denying filial obligations and severing family ties through self-imposed exile. This type may tend to exhibit a condition of permanent immaturity, potentially wild ranges of emotional disturbance and in some cases either is incapable of or has a disinterest in assimilation. Stoker's Renfield is a 59-year-old who is never visited by family during his confinement in Dr Seward's asylum; furthermore, Stoker employs numerous conventions associated with orphanhood, such as the death of a parent, exile from a specific class and frustrated aspirations to inclusion, to portray the deranged aristocrat.

Stevenson's Hyde, if not yet an orphan, actually seeks to become one: his goal is to effect a state of orphanhood by destroying the tenuous provisional familial dynamics around him, and by establishing himself in the stead of his father-creator, displacing Jekyll in what is essentially an act of patricide regardless of their shared constitution.

Another type with which I am concerned are actually children; but, unlike characters like Dickens's Pip or Brontë's Jane, orphans who develop noticeably and incrementally, these fin-de-siècle orphan children are unsettlingly erratic, changelings who vacillate rather than mature, and seem to decry the incertitude of their time. In their exceptional Gothic instability, for instance, Kipling's Kim and Mowgli challenge categories of race and even species, respectively. Barrie's Peter and Hook elude classification and oscillate between the feminine and the masculine, strength and uncertainty, reality and fantasy, and never achieve the entirety found in the *bildungsroman*. Other Edwardian child orphans, like Burnett's Mary and Colin, are relegated to an orphan condition relieved only through their own creative impulses and the ironic adoption of parental roles. Each of these types is freighted with meaning corresponding to the period of transition that marks the turn of the century and that delineates them from previous portrayals of orphanhood. Evading specificity, refusing definition, even threatening to become dangerously unhinged, they are manifestations of the psychic effects of the fin de siècle's numerous cultural upheavals, which have not been examined previously in critical discourse.

Critical readings of the orphan

Criticism concerning nineteenth-century orphans typically focuses on the early and middle periods, and generally regards them as a convention speaking to class difference, economic disparity or social injustice, with the occasional regard for their symbolism as spiritual exiles. According to Reed, this convention was not a developed one. He cites, for example, its use by Dickens, whose view of the orphan does not seem to have been limited to a particular version. Indeed, one of the interesting aspects of Reed's study is the malleability of his definition of the term 'orphan'. He mentions 'spiritual' and 'psychological' orphans in addition to 'orphans of fact'; his use is pliable enough for him to refer to Dorian Gray as 'orphaned loveliness'. While some distinction might be made by Reed between the 'quasi' and 'genuine' orphan, the difference seems unimportant excepting cases where the real orphan was reared by malign guardians as well.

Much of Reed's treatment of orphans as a convention relates to their lack of material goods and their resultant perception of exile amidst the materialism that developed in nineteenth-century England, and furthermore reads the longing inherent in this sense of exile as suggestive of 'disinheritance and exclusion from society'.[18] He notes that many orphans typically suffer from a complex of belonging to the wrong class, stating, for example, that what George Meredith's orphans pursue is an ideal of material gain infused into them by either misguided guardians or by society in general. Having the onus of fate's decree or the machinations of others thrust upon them, orphans endeavour to work their way out of their destitution to either improve their social standing or to attain a manner of living consistent with their upper-class tastes.

Although Reed does address several late-century texts, with the exception of *The Picture of Dorian Gray* (1890–1) his focus is notably on domestic fiction, and typically with an emphasis on class orientation and monetary conditions. Although he does refer to Wilde's novel as a 'gothic fable', he hesitates to address the narrative's Gothicity, stating that Dorian's haunting of the story is 'not sincere', and he ultimately treats the novel as a 'romance', a 'melodrama', a 'drawing room fiction'.[19]

Reed locates other aspects in the orphans he discusses, noting that for many late-century writers orphans possess a symbolic potential either for man's spiritual alienation from a

God who had died or no longer seemed relevant, or man's precarious stance amidst the impending hazards of an indifferent Nature. Indicating perhaps the trajectory to which the orphan form was working, he cites Thomas Hardy's use of the orphan as signalling a period when the conventions associated with the orphan may have become no longer believable. In *Jude the Obscure*, for example, Reed locates the orphan as a symbol of spiritually orphaned mankind, a figure who is bereft of the old conventions, but with no new ones to contribute to his identity and fulfillment. While pointing to the orphan's potential to regard the malaise of modernity, Reed's treatment, again, is of social texts, and does not address fin-de-siècle anxieties specifically.

One of this book's primary concerns is the notion that the orphan must be considered in light of the family from which it is exiled, since depictions of the orphan noticeably change alongside perceptions of the family ideal. Kate Ferguson Ellis, focusing largely on productions of the early nineteenth century, sees the orphan as a target of the family unit's fear of the outsider. She examines, for example, the way Mary Shelley consistently formulates domestic structures in a manner that creates and sustains 'divided selves in the name of domestic affection'. This division, exacting a protective barrier around the home, ensures that unity and harmony of the family are preserved within, while the conflict and dissent epitomized in the orphan are kept without. Emphasizing the sanctity of the domestic space, Ellis notes that the insider departs this sacred space at his or her own peril, while the outsider is permanently ostracized. Ellis sees the orphan, who is outside the family, as a being that absorbs notions of dissention or revenge that members of the family cannot permit into their consciousness.[20] Using Shelley's *Frankenstein* (1818) as an example, she claims that Victor creates his monster to serve as a substitutive recipient of his resentment of Elizabeth's dependency. Similarly, she notes, Victor's refusal to speak damns the expendable orphan outsider Justine, while the wretch, orphaned by his maker, witnesses in Felix the vengeful potential of the domestic space when it finds itself threatened by outsiders.

Laura Peters, too, sees orphans as a type of scapegoat; their need for inclusion actually contributes to the family's legitimacy, particularly at a time when the 'unsustainable' concept of the ideal family was in crisis. For Peters, orphans function less as heirs of prejudice against the outsider and more as mediums of reassurance and validation. Both Ellis and Peters deal primarily with novels from the early to middle 1800s; with the exception of Rose Macaulay's 1924 *Orphan Island*, the latest book with which Peters deals is from the 1870s, her main focus being on texts like *Wuthering Heights* (1847) and *Jane Eyre* (1847), where, as in the case of the texts Ellis considers, the orphan's meaning differs from that of the late-century orphan.

Peters shifts emphasis from England streets to foreign soil in her discussion of the dispatching of orphans to the colonies. There orphans might not only leave their origin-less past behind them, but might forge new identities as well. Peters locates the paradox of orphans as colonial workers, who, doing the work of and thus representing the empire, are ensuring the preservation of institutions entrance into which they are denied; at the same time, they are lent a semblance of belonging to the empire and are, therefore, endowed with a kind of racial or class superiority they would be denied in England, over the kind of barbarism and savagery with which they would be associated back home. They are, in Peters's words, 'reconciled to symbols of British colonial authority while remaining alienated from and hostile to British internal social structures'.[21] Her focus, though, is on early- to middle-century treatments of British orphans transposed to other lands, and their subsequent endeavors toward self-realization as representatives of the Empire. Chapter 5 notes the manner in which orphans of British lineage are presented in adventure narratives of the New Imperialism of the fin de siècle as virtually unencumbered by their orphanhood precisely due to their affiliation with the Empire, but also considers the native orphan of such texts, who in order to regain position within their own familial or cultural structures must defer to the fatherly authority of British imperial entities, or must assimilate into imperial social constructions in order to alleviate their orphan state.

Nina Auerbach follows the development of the orphan form in her 'Incarnations of the Orphan', but only to a certain point. Beginning with the eighteenth century and progressing into the mid-nineteenth, with some mention of early twentieth-century manifestations, she clearly overlooks the period with which this book is concerned. Her first focus is on the eighteenth-century orphan's aspirations to gentility, and draws similarities between this first incarnation and the figure of the picaroon, the sharp-witted rogue who makes his way with his street-smarts. Along the same lines as Reed's consideration of economic determinants, for Auerbach it is money and class affiliation that defines orphans in their earliest versions. She does make distinction between various types; while Moll Flanders is defined by social standards, Jane Eyre is spiritually centred, and Dickens's Pip recreates himself by fashioning his own name. Auerbach states that the orphan 'stands supreme and a little monstrous, the great artificer, the self-made man'.[22] However, in the texts upon which she focuses it is ultimately class with which orphans struggle in their quest for identity. The actualizing of the orphan's self in each of these cases is linked more or less to his or her relationship to social rank, a distinction that ultimately determines his or her course of action. These are factors that do not bear upon the orphan of late-century genre fiction.

In addition to its general concentration on social position, Auerbach's treatment of the orphan differs from the present book in two crucial ways, namely, in the limits of her subject, and in her conclusions concerning late nineteenth-century orphans. She tends to focus on the rebellious, anarchic orphan who is a threat to the social structures from which he or she is exiled. She argues that the early nineteenth-century orphan is endowed with a spiritual aspect that belies the influence of a supernatural force. One of her arguments, for instance, is that Jane Eyre is motivated by a power that enacts its will through her; Pip, too, she sees as having a similar effect of purging the house he enters with a divine and cleansing fire; Heathcliff, meanwhile, provides the medium through which a supernatural being ensures its providence. The orphan becomes an instrument of divine intervention. Auerbach's concept corresponds to Peters's idea of orphans as *pharmakon,* beings whose disruptive spirits have a medicinal effect on the houses they enter; they are both 'bane and blessing', 'promise and threat', and perform a 'pharmaceutical function in Victorian society'.[23]

While Auerbach sees orphans as instruments of God, and Peters sees them more as vehicles for cultural purgation, both see orphans in this case as cleansing the home to some extent; orphans are entities that threaten the home as it stands, and effect a purification that, most importantly, results in a re-establishment of the status quo. Peters notes, for example, Heathcliff's purgation as resulting in the reunification of both family and the community in general, and that Jane's presence eventuates the expulsion of the Creole other, Bertha, so that the truly different is exorcised in order to permit a more traditional union to take place between Rochester and one of his own. Reed makes a similar acknowledgment of the eventual return to equilibrium within orphan texts, stating that very often orphanhood is reconciled with the convention of marriage. Martha Vicinus remarks that the conventional happy ending succeeded in bringing together the loose ends of a narrative, noting a Victorian preference not for what was necessarily possible or even realistic, but with what was desirable, citing a tendency in Victorian melodrama up until the 1860s to ensure the re-establishment of social stability.[24]

This book seeks to accomplish several things in light of this concept. First, it examines the manner in which the late-century orphan performs a function similarly as disruptive as the divine instrument or the *pharamakon*, but whose actions at times result in anarchy and chaos, not in a restoration of normalcy. In some instances, like the sociopathic escapades of Wells's Griffin or Machen's Helen, late-century orphans threaten domestic tranquillity, but their subsequent disruption instead results in vacancy, ruin and devastation of the spaces they alter. They do not re-establish the status quo; they attempt to disassemble it. These orphans epitomize the vexing yet seemingly unrelenting disintegration of tradition that marks the end of the nineteenth century. This study also considers orphans who are unlike those discussed by Auerbach in that they do not necessarily threaten the structure that denies them but, rather, indicate its importance. Instead, like Stevenson's Jim Hawkins, they demonstrate the ramifications of the familyless state; or, as in the case of Haggard's Ignosi, they pursue association with a cohesive social unit through deference and imitation; or, like Kipling's Kim, despite and perhaps even due to difference, they are assimilated into a larger familial organization. These orphans serve as emblems of a middle-class cultural desire for the entrenchment of the paradigm of the ideal family despite threats to that idea's fruition.

Auerbach's treatment differs from this book also in that it maintains that the orphan's significance diminishes as the century wears on. She claims that the form essentially disappears after the middle of the century, only to re-emerge in the early twentieth. This is an unfortunate oversight, as it does not take into consideration figures like Renfield, whose orphanic state embodies so many of the anxieties associated with the turn of the century; Stevenson's Davy Balfour, whose journey is nothing if not a quest for a father; or Burnett's Colin, whose invalidism and hypochondria are symptomatic of his motherless state. Stating that late-century orphans possess no power over the house they enter, Auerbach neglects examples like Stevenson's Hyde, who contributes to the death of the head of the household and that domestic space's subsequent emptiness; or the rash of suicides and the unstable social conditions begat by Machen's Helen; or the heartbreak and disruption of the Darling household effected by Peter's removal of the children from their parents' home.

This disregard of highly symbolically pertinent versions of the orphan limits Auerbach's argument, like Reed's and others', largely to domestic and social fiction. While giving a nod to Barrie's *Peter Pan*, Auerbach simply notes the novel's nostalgic 'yearning for the myth' of the orphan, and does not address the novel's allusion to fin-de-siècle anxieties.[25] Perhaps the closest Auerbach comes to approaching the orphan form in a manner similar to this study is in her description of the Victorian orphan as 'all the lost boys wandering through Dickens' London, embodying in their pathos all the Victorians' self-pity and terror in the mazes of the new world the nineteenth-century had inaugurated'.[26] Her focus, again, however, is on the pre-fin-de-siècle orphan of non-genre literature. In contrast, this monograph demonstrates that late-century orphans, within the pages of genre fiction, are just as potent an image and play as vital a symbolic role as their predecessors, continuing in modes differing from those established by late eighteenth and early nineteenth-century social critical dialogue, and evolving into a vigorous register of the period's doubt and instability.

Some criticism has focused on orphans as representations of various types of exile apart from those of a social dimension, particularly in regard to the theological anxieties of the age. Reed regards figures like Oliver Twist and Little Nell as spiritual exiles, 'emblems of the soul outcast from eternity', and sees orphans as signaling humankind's 'isolated, disinherited condition'.[27] Auerbach addresses their psychological aspect, calling orphans 'the primary metaphor for the dispossessed, the detached self'.[28] Christine Van Boheemen refers to orphanhood as representing an unavoidable severance from wholeness, 'a metaphor for the human condition as experienced in the modern era'.[29] Morse Peckam, focusing on the literal physical separation orphans experience, states that this literary form is useful as a symbol of the individual against society, utilized to display 'social alienation when the author is after the uniqueness of the self and its opposition to the social role'.[30] Orphans regarded in these examples, though, again, tend to be representative of early- to middle-century manifestations whose ostracism from society is contingent on their class identity. Late-century genre orphans are instead without society due not to class affiliation, but to differences ranging from mental illness, deformation and monstrosity, supernatural aberration or unalleviated abandonment.

Orphans are defined by their lack of family connection, and other criticism focuses on the impulse in orphans to discover their origins. Dianne F. Sadoff states that orphans in Dickens's novels seek 'to determine their origins and confirm their identities'. This identity, of course, is primarily found in a family structure. The Dickensian son demonstrates a desire for the paternal embrace, such as Barnaby's want of the robber Rudge's acknowledgement; the Dickensian daughter is possessed by a need of the father who spurns her, such as Florence's unrequited love for Dombey. Sadoff also cites the manner in which some Dickensian orphans, like Oliver Twist, are fated to locate their fathers; some, like Esther, acquire symbolic fathers; others, like Pip, have father figures thrust upon them and recreate themselves as a result.[31] In each case, the orphan locates identity upon the discernment of origin.

Of course, attending this preoccupation with origin is the idea of orphans' exclusion from the family structure, the social system into which they typically work to belong. *Oliver Twist* (1838), for example, is a novel of characters defined by their lack of a domestic space to call their own and by their need to discern and reconstruct a family-like situation to which they might belong.[32] This need to be included into the ideal is so strong that even beneath the malice and plotting of the melodramatic villain there exists an underlying compulsion to either exact retribution for, or acquire, a lost family.[33] In their discussion of Dickensian orphans, Baruch Hochman and Ilja

Wachs address the psychological aspects of the condition, and emphasize Dickens's attempt 'to master the passiveness and paralysis it entails'.[34] These considerations, while incisive about the orphan's exile from the family structure, are, again, limited to early- and middle-period novels. Not only does the present study consider the orphan of the turn of the century, it also addresses the remarkable inclination of certain orphan forms to resist inclusion altogether, revel in their own anarchic isolation and actually seek to dismantle the institutions from which they have exiled themselves.

There exists in some orphan texts the occasional shift from a preoccupation with the discovery of lost parents to unearthing instead a kind of self-generated coherence. The orphan Jan, in Juliana Horatia Ewing's *Jan of the Windmills: A Story of the Plains* (1876), for instance, eschews the inheritance extended by his found family in order instead to earn his own way with his art. Auerbach sees the tendency towards recreation as a method for reconstruction that appears in the late eighteenth century, then vanishes for a period, only to re-emerge with the twentieth century, however, in what she calls 'a less defined and durable manner'.[35] Concentrating on American literature of 1850–99, Suzan Bonifer examines the development of what she calls the female orphan's 'quest for rematriation', or reconciliation with the role of the mother, to a quest instead for an identity the freedom of which resembles less the matriarch and more 'the male canonical hero'. Bonifer discusses the modes in which the female orphan of early nineteenth-century American novels focuses on the separation from and eventual inclusion into mother-like roles and submission to paternal forces, and the orphan's development in later fiction into an entity desiring an artistic type of independence, and her ultimate need to choose between an identity determined by her culture or one formulated within her art.[36] Bonifer's study focuses specifically on female orphans of feminist American texts, but it nevertheless addresses the kind of alteration that characterizes the orphan myth as the century progresses. The orphans she discusses change from initially endeavouring to emulate their parental figures to seeking independence largely through artistic expression. These considerations are more related to parentage or self-definition through art; they are internal needs and practices. This book in part discusses instead how rebellious forms of the late-century orphan not only seek to define themselves as apart from, but actually accomplish the disruption of, their surroundings, the intentional desecration of traditional establishments and institutions, and the manner in which the turmoil begotten by their undertaking bears upon late-century restlessness. Bonifer's subjects attempt to define themselves rather than be defined by society; the rebellious subjects discussed in this book define themselves by attacking society.

A final attribute of orphans on which most if not all critics agree is their malleability, their 'capacity for rebirth'.[37] This ability to change implies a kind of progression in earlier portrayals of the orphan toward the ultimate fulfillment of his or her true identity, a journey from nameless outcast to integrated person of distinction. In contrast, turn-of-the-century orphans, while possessing this same malleability, often lack this developmental dimension, and instead often merely appear as turbulent, unstable entities. Rather than acquiring diverse incarnations in a kind of journey through numerous guises of convenience, each a progressive step toward the actualization of the self, the orphans of this study may leave one identity, only to regress to it later. If they evolve in some way, as in the case, for instance, of Renfield, it is often unclear as to what they are actually developing into. Or, more likely, their experience becomes less an endeavour to improve their social standing or gain the respect of their culture, and more a disturbing oscillation from one manifestation to another, and often back again. As such, their malleability proves less as a method of evolving and more a symptom of fin-de-siècle societal misgivings over both individual and nationalistic identity.

The fin de siècle as context

If the Victorian period was one of transition, the turn of the nineteenth century proved the shocking denouement of the age, marked by endeavours to reconcile the implications of that transition. Very much aware of their position in history as tenants of a pivotal age, late-century Victorians encountered anxieties particular to the fin de siècle. Conscious that changes of various aspects both social and cultural were not merely interjectional circumstances in an otherwise substantial and reliable world but, rather, the 'inescapable condition' of modern existence, late Victorians perceived their era as one distinguished by turmoil and exhaustion, a time marked by a momentum exceeding the ability of mankind to adequately adapt, and characterized by conditions of such 'overwhelming and adverse social conditions' that the human race was wearing itself out.[38] There emerged at the century's end an anxiety not so much from the process of change, but from the notion that the Victorians were no longer in control of the process.[39] Attending this was a sense of dispossession, of alienation in a culture the technological advancements of which had been 'exploited too quickly for the adaptive powers of the human psyche'.[40]

The fin de siècle was marked by a perception of British culture as waning on numerous fronts. Steven Arata discusses the decay of 'national, biological, and aesthetic' paradigms that bespoke the slippage of the Anglo-Saxon race; Nicholas Daly points out the 'monstrous anachronisms' of novels like Haggard's *She*, Stoker's *Dracula* and Stevenson's *Strange Case of Dr Jekyll and Mr Hyde* as serving to 'mirror a whole set of anxieties' particular to the century's final decades.[41] The period was fraught with the implications of sexual ambiguity, the challenge of the New Woman, concerns over the perdurability of the empire and the ethicality of the imperial mission, as well as threats to the traditional ideal family structure and the domestic space. All these concerns coalesced to engender a crisis of uncertainty for which orphanhood provided a striking metaphor. Prior, then, to examining the significance of the orphan figure to the fin de siècle, and to positioning the orphan as a register of the anxieties specific to the period, I would like to provide a brief overview of those issues followed by an examination of changing perceptions of the family and the domestic space as they pertain to this era.

If the prosperity of the mid-century embodied by the Great Exhibition of 1851 provided a watershed against which the remaining decades of the century might be gauged, the final years of the nineteenth century were characterized by decline of ethical, religious, artistic and even physical dimensions. In his infamous 1892 work, *Degeneration*, Max Nordau employs the phrase 'fin-de-siècle' to assess many of the definitive artistic and literary statements of the period, which he saw as characterized by a 'prevalent mental and physical degeneration'.[42] What Nordau termed 'ego-mania' was the cause of the 'diseased outlook and anti-social actions' of late-century artists and writers, the ego being 'synonymous with evil' and capable of inflicting indignity upon individuals and the community; he argued furthermore that it was physiological deterioration that engendered the period's dubious creative productions.[43] The 'decadence' in the fine arts and 'degeneration' of morality indicated an aggregate of 'physical lassitude' and 'psychological moral perversity', calling into question the stability and certainty of traditional intellectual and cultural paradigms.[44] In the Conclusion to his *Studies in the History of the Renaissance* (1873), Walter Pater had exhorted his readers to consider all modes and precepts as 'inconstant', an approach he claimed was 'the tendency of modern thought'.[45] Intellectually advanced as it was touted to be, this incredulity led to a 'mistrust of theory and system' with notably no distinct and articulate ideology or philosophy to replace what had been lost.[46]

In addition to doubts concerning philosophical and theological concepts was the emerging perception of the human being itself as a malleable form. Glennis Byron notes that 'the dissolution of nation, of society' was attended by that 'of the human subject itself'.[47] Previously regarded as a choate, fixed entity, humankind appeared not only to be capable of mutation and deviation, but also vulnerable to contamination by external forces. Hurley observes that a number of fin-de-siècle texts portray human beings 'that have lost their claim to a discrete and integral identity', so that categorical explanations previously employed to organize existence came into question and were no longer beyond reproach. Gothic fiction of the period, for instance, focused on the redefining of the human resulting from scientific discourses that examined 'the unpredictable strangeness' of nature and the inconstancy of the human being; Darwinian evolutionary theory proposed species, including humans, as not only metamorphic, but also capable of degeneration, devolution and even extinction, and furthermore that physical and mental disorders could be transferred or even inherited, so that conventional conceptions of all humanity – not merely the troublous, inconvenient or outcast – fell vulnerable to incertitude.[48]

A variety of paradigmatic shifts of the period scrutinized conceptions of gender roles and challenged the institution of marriage.[49] Ambiguity in regard to definitions and expectations of masculinity and femininity was perceived as symptomatic of the decline of society, and furthermore constituted an assault on the family.[50] This confusion jeopardized conventional considerations of the ideal family, contesting what Andrea Kaston Tange calls 'the troubling hierarchies' associated with traditional family constructions, particularly in regard to the male's position in the house.[51] The late-Victorian feminist, characterized by a masculine independence and a presumed undisciplined sexuality, seemed to defy the stereotypical husband and father and, in her relinquishment of her customary familial duties, came to be regarded as a monstrous figure endeavouring to challenge if not assume the place of the male.[52] Her defiant and autonomous demeanour, conflated with emerging social consciousness of alternative sexualities and incurable sexually transmitted diseases served as a 'most intimate and outrageous assault' on normative societal standards.[53]

As domestic spaces became sites of controversy, so too did Britain's status as an unchallenged world power. Gail Marshall notes that cohesion among the countries within the empire proved less assured than before, while that of Britain's self-perception held equally irresolute standing; in addition, she discusses the tendency of disjunctive texts of the period to portray the dissolution of identity intermingled with the cruel realities of imperialism, so that institutions, individual identities and even the narratives that detailed them reflected disunity and doubt.[54] The period thus saw various emergent discourses that proved applicable for the justification of the imperial mission. Advances in criminal anthropology, degeneration theory, psychology and other nascent sciences were particularly pertinent to imperialist ideologies concerning racial disparity and functioned to categorize 'abnormal human subjects' such as 'born criminals' and other atavistic, deviant types whose characteristics were narrativised as associated with those of native subjects in an effort to identify and thus better control less developed peoples and to distinguish British racial superiority.[55] Contingent on contemporary ideologies of racial difference, an emphasis exists, therefore, in imperial converse, and particularly in narratives of the New Imperialism, of the degenerative and atavistic qualities of non-European races, with British characters superior in every way to their 'savage', 'primitive' and 'uncivilized' counterparts. Even the British orphan is depicted as surmounting a condition typically defined by lack and incompleteness, while orphaned natives are shown to be chaotic, requiring leadership and ultimately deferential to imperial figures.

The progressiveness of the Victorian period served to propel Britain into modernity, but clearly at the cost of severance from the past and the comfort and reliability of traditions and paradigms attached to it. Such disruption compelled J. A. Froude, in 1883, to state that the most serious and foundational convictions 'have been broken up', that society was caught up in a current which it was useless to resist, and that both the wise and the foolish were 'equally ignorant where the close of this waning century will find us'.[56] The fin de siècle indeed proved a time of contradiction, so that 'the final decades of the century looked in two opposing directions'.[57] On one hand, advancements in science, technology and artistic expression begat a *zeitgeist* of development, a sense of forward movement; on the other hand, a sense of lament, even of mourning, of the loss of what had characterized the past seemed an unshakable spectre on the late-century psychic landscape. Perceiving itself as caught in this state of in-betweenness, Britain found itself lacking the surety of its forebears, questioning its institutions, unsure of its identity – in essence, in an orphanic state.

The importance of the family and the domestic space

As the French historian Philippe Aries observes, from the medieval period to the end of the seventeenth century, 'the communal model', which was comprised of members of various, sometimes non-related members, developed into the smaller, more intimate 'nuclear' family of more recent times; by the middle of the Victorian period, the nuclear family acquired an almost mythical status as the proper context in which a child should be raised, and furthermore came to be regarded as the cornerstone of a balanced, moral culture. Indeed, as Robert M. Polhemus states, it was within the context of 'stable, reciprocal family structures' that civilization 'could flourish and progress'.[58] Thus, the idealized home, with its attributes of acceptance, love and inclusion, came to be regarded as not just a space of physical comfort and safety, but one 'of full domestic joy'.[59] The determinants for this perception of the family are numerous, including a notable desire in Victorians for the stability of a permanent, loving environment to compensate for the gradual reduction in reliance upon or belief in a paradisiacal afterlife, a desire characterized by immersion into filial and parental obligations, what Polhemus calls 'familialism'.[60]

Frederic Jameson locates the combination of the Industrial Revolution's effects and Romantic philosophy and aesthetics as determining portrayals of the ideal family as a foundational emblem of social stability and a means of instilling the virtues of morality, fairness and justice.[61]

Because of the sanctity of the family, the domestic space that physically encompassed and symbolically represented it was particularly revered as an area of reassuring belonging and identity. Threats to the domestic space not only put into peril one of the pillars of society, but had the potential to deprive the orphan of the institution and its attendant attributes to which he or she traditionally aspired. Narratives featuring the disruption of the home were particularly relevant to the notion of orphanhood, a condition often rectified only by the acquisition of wealth or inclusion into some form of domestic union. While the family ideal is frequently seen as threatened as soon as it emerges in the popular consciousness, such threats in earlier literature actually seem to function to emphasize its necessity and importance, despite its tenuous nature, as a context for optimum psychological development and social stability. That is, threats to the ideal underscore its significance. Contrasting with the harsher, more materialistic climate of the outside world, the home provided a sacred, defensive centre of morality the preservation of which meant nothing less than the preservation of Victorian culture.[62] While in earlier Victorian literature the desolation of life on the street, the threat of death and the fear of homelessness are juxtaposed with the concept of the ideal home, such potentialities simply reassure the reader of the ideal's worth and necessity.[63]

For the first ninety years of children's fiction in England and America, the nature of the family remained largely unchallenged, home unquestionably the origin of children's religious and moral instruction; furthermore, the primary image of authority in the home was the father. Humphrey Carpenter states that, while belief in the 'father-dominated family as the source of moral wisdom seems to have become shaky by about 1850', curiously, the questioning of the traditional family structure does not appear in nineteenth-century English 'realistic' novels for children.[64]

However, late-century genre texts demonstrate a demythologizing tendency, proposing that the family ideal is no longer a possibility and might even be detrimental to the individual. Indeed, the family came to be assaulted on a number of levels, targeted as an entity of suppression, limitation and even corruption. The ideal to which the majority of orphans aspired and the mythic status of which endured throughout much of the Victorian period came under constant and increasing scrutiny and even eventual derision toward the end of the century. As Byron states, by the 1890s, Victorian Britain had become 'all too aware of the dark side of progress', one symptom of which was 'challenges to the traditional values and family structures upon which its much-vaunted superiority was based'.[65] Literary portrayals of the family in this period alter notably in reaction to these changing perceptions in regard to both families and children, 'an answering anxiety within the home as domestic structures, too, felt the force of change'.[66] The turn-of-the-century texts with which this book deals display the loss of an ultimately irretrievable notion, an unattainable fantasy to which the orphan is denied the recourse available in narratives earlier in the century. Literature has frequently depicted the domestic space as under threat of infiltration, betrayal, even physical ruin in order to exalt the importance of home and family; but the ultimate return to that sacred centre proves untenable for the fin-de-siècle orphan, who is often rendered in a condition of perpetual homelessness, an orphan state that remains unalleviated. These misgivings are notably marked by notions of deprivation, loss and insufficiency. Ultimately, then, the crucial function of the fin-de-siècle orphan is to address the crisis of the family's irreplaceability, the predicament of the individual without recourse to that fabled reconciling return.

The structure of this book

This book examines various non-traditional manifestations of the orphan condition as they appear in genre fiction of the fin de siècle. The term 'orphan' typically conjures images of children, perhaps most frequently the mid-nineteenth-century Dickensian waif, the poverty-stricken youth relegated to life in the streets of industrial England. Dickens's contribution is certainly an outstanding one, but there are others. Late-century orphanhood notably diverges from that rendered in early- to middle-century narratives, and the orphan condition speaks to various cultural anxieties specific to the end of the nineteenth century.

Inquiring as to what occurs when the institution into which the orphan has historically laboured to be incorporated is beyond his or her grasp or no longer even exists, chapter 2 discusses *Dracula*'s R. M. Renfield as emblematic of late-Victorian generational anxiety, a *zeitgeist* of loss of tradition and apprehension of an uncertain future. Renfield endeavours to construct his own provisional family in imitation of the ideal that Stoker consistently extolled in his fiction. In his attempts at assimilation, Renfield speaks to an inherent desire for inclusion into a family structure. His orphan condition correlates to a host of late-century anxieties, such as incredulity in regard to the Victorian professional, gender ambiguity, contrasts between the East and the West, and the notions of the colonizer and the colonized. In his orphanic irresolution, Renfield is a register of the uncertainty accompanying a period of cultural upheaval and transition; he ranges from insect-consuming, homicidal maniac to eloquent aristocrat, regressing and progressing at unpredictable turns. And yet, Renfield also endeavours to construct his own provisional family in imitation of the mythic ideal. In his attempts at assimilation, Renfield speaks to an inherent desire for inclusion into a family structure. His fragmentary personality mirrors more considerably stable characters with whom he comes into contact, and he exhibits a tendency to be attracted to and gravitate toward more well-rounded or self-confident personalities who embody the stability and certainty he lacks, attributes the Victorian world seemed to have lost.

In his own peculiar way Renfield exhibits the aspiration to familial inclusion typical of the traditional orphan; however, the turn of the century offered other incarnations less favorably inclined to that proposition, forms that brandish a defiant and dangerous vitality. Chapter 3, then, also examines one of the more unsettling products of the disintegration of, and disenchantment with, the family ideal: sociopathic orphans whose primary impulse is to disrupt the social structures from which they actually exile themselves, entities operating beyond the desire for belonging that characterizes conventional orphan forms. This type, exemplified in Stevenson's Hyde or Wells's Griffin, may possess erratic natures and refute any possibility of assimilation, or, like Machen's Helen, subtly insinuate themselves into the culture merely to corrupt it from within; in either case, this type seeks the fracture of those institutions formerly regarded as the identifying objective of the orphan. Moreover, unlike an orphaned figure like Frankenstein's wretch, that is arguably compelled by neglect and abuse to its ruinous actions, and remarkably contrastive with the pitiable, unjustly maltreated but morally virtuous figure of social moral narratives, the rebellious orphan is innately sinister, deviant and exceptionally violent. Such orphans, intentionally devoid of the normalcy and stability proposed by familial association, no longer provide a melodramatic illustration urging cultural reform or alluding to social injustice. By the 1880s, without the union whereby those previous forms located some sense of totality, this insurgent type embodied degenerative transgressions of traditional social modes and emerged fully defined extraneous of the parameters of normative family precepts.

Chapter 4 examines what is certainly the absolute orphanic space, the island, and how treatments of that space, particularly in regard to orphanhood, differ during the fin de siècle from those of earlier literary periods. Beginning with various interpretations of the island, psychological, metaphorical and otherwise, I emphasize the island's most remarkable characteristic, its dissociation from normalizing societal paradigms, that generates its literal and analogous associations with the orphan state. The chapter then proceeds to an analysis of the orphanic predicament the island imposes on those stranded upon its shores; the island imposes upon its unfortunate guest conditions conventionally associated with the orphan condition, namely a disjunction from civilization and the comforts and properties thereof that often validate identity. Lastly, sustaining my consideration of orphanhood in light of perception and portrayals of family constructions, I look at the remarkable variances in the island literature genre in regard to the portrayal of father figures. Whereas earlier island narratives present capable, inspiring paternal forms that remedy the protagonist's orphanhood, the tendency in turn-of-the-century island narratives is to present failed father figures whose villainy, neuroses and violence actually perpetuate the orphan's plight. I refer throughout to numerous examples from island literature, but the main turn-of-the-century texts upon which this chapter focuses are Wells's *The Island of Dr Moreau* Stevenson's *Treasure Island* and *Kidnapped*. Wells's novel is clearly a work of Gothic science fiction and, while Stevenson's texts are typically regarded as adventures, I read within these and other narratives the questioning and redefining of identity and the self common in the Gothic, inherent in orphanhood and symptomatic of the fin de siècle.

Centring on the divergence of portrayals of orphanhood in literature of the New Imperialism, chapter 5 demonstrates how, in the context of colonized space, orphans of British lineage are not debilitated by the inadequacies and psychic trauma that conventionally attended orphanhood, while native orphans are depicted as inefficient, incapable and lacking cohesion and identity. In the potentially chaotic and dangerous colonies, the native orphan's tribal and familial compositions are tenuous, traitorous and violent, while the British orphan's affiliation with the empire endows him with a sense of belonging and totality generally denied traditional orphan figures. British orphans Holly and Leo, of Haggard's *She*, are contrasted with the orphan indigene Ignosi, from *King Solomon's Mines*, while Quatermain is assessed as an imperial paternal figure to whom Ignosi constantly defers. In addition, this chapter addresses the malleability, hybridity and Gothicity of Kipling's Mowgli and Kim, and the manner in which these uncategorizable orphans morph contingent with the demands of their present conditions, transgressing social constructions, class and racial systems and even categories of species. Furthermore, both of these irresolute and unidentifiable orphans and their capacity for imitation, assimilation and infiltration are ultimately assumed by and put to the service of the empire. Thus, these potentially fragmentary and ungoverned orphan forms are brought into the broader family of the British Empire, perpetuating a kind of social paradigm imitative of and synonymous with the family ideal that had fallen under such suspicion and incredulity by the century's end. These observations and an analysis of Henry Seton Merriman's *Flotsam: The Story of a Life* (1896) attest to the New Imperialism's convention of portraying British orphans as reconciled by the intimations of their heritage and the native orphan as hindered by his.

In my final chapter I address a portentous shift in register of orphans of Edwardian children's literature and the manner in which the orphan simultaneously denotes the individualism of modernism as well as an appeal to traditional family structures. This chapter discusses the orphan who creates an alternative world in which he or she assumes notions of autonomy, but an autonomy that is characterized by endeavours to forge imitative, provisional family structures and is impelled or haunted by the specter of a maternal figure. My main subjects are J. M. Barrie's *Peter Pan* and Francis Hodgson Burnett's *A Little Princess* and *The Secret Garden*, which present either actual or perceived alternate worlds wherein the orphan possesses the potential to create his or her own contrived family system to serve as stabilizing mechanism for his or her own identity. Peter removes the Darling children from a functioning ideal family, insinuates them into his fantastic Neverland and attempts to create a mother out of Wendy. His denial of his need for the mother who shut him out and an unspoken desire for the substitutive motherhood provided by Wendy are both overshadowed by the maternal influence of Wendy's mother, Mrs Darling, whose unfailing devotion threatens the ramshackle family constructions of Neverland. The motherless Sara Crewe, of *A Little Princess*, re-envisions her miserable circumstances into realms of fantasy that permit the orphan to endure loss of family and fortune while assuming a motherly role for orphans Lottie and Becky. The unstable Mary and Colin of *The Secret Garden*, both psychically injured by their lack of a mother, find their own alternate space in which Mary assumes a maternal identity that is inspired and determined by the perpetually nurturing Mrs. Sowerby as well as the other-worldly machinations of the deceased Lilias. Chapter 6 also examines the malleable, imitative and Gothic nature of the orphans in all three texts and the catalyst that notably absent but nevertheless affecting mother figures exact upon them. These works hint at the trajectory of orphan literature in the new century, with its emphasis on the orphan attempting less to determine his or her past and more appearing to recreate him or herself; but it is a deceptive appearance of individuality, a process eminently directed and determined by maternal figures both actual and supernatural.

Conclusion

A great variance exists between orphans of the fin de siècle and their predecessors in the literature of earlier periods, particularly in regard to depiction, symbolic inference and the cultural preoccupations to which they were literary reactions. In addition to such recurrent distinctions as the absence of family, severance from society and an appeal to pathos, are the persistent presence of threats to, and an equal stress on the preservation of, the family and the domestic space, both entities to which traditional orphans travail to attain the identity and totality otherwise denied them. Furthermore, earlier orphan narratives almost exclusively allude to concerns about class affiliation, economic factors and social status, elements with which the turn-of-the-century orphan has little or no concern.

Late eighteenth-century and early to middle nineteenth-century orphans are characterized by consistent and recognizable qualities and allusions. Anxieties concerning social standing, aspirations to class transcendence and the critique of social conditions related to industrialism denote a cultural obsession with class difference and economic factors to which the orphan and the implications of his or her state were intrinsically connected, and that largely determined the period's depictions of the form. In addition, the orphan's necessary exclusion in large measure contributed to and perpetuated the notion of the ideal family, an institution that would find itself under attack later in the nineteenth century. Criticism of the family, including perceptions of it as oppressive and limiting rather than reliable and inclusive would alter representations of the orphan as the century ended, while older cultural concerns were displaced by anxieties associated with sexual ambiguity, degeneration and intensifying imperial tensions. These anxieties conveyed the sense of transition and its attending perception of unrelenting decline particular to the fin de siècle. The orphan form's pertinence to these changes is the focus of the remainder of this book.

2

Renfield's 'Agonized Confusion'

One of the persistent images in Bram Stoker's work is the portrayal of families in peril, with emphasis on the plight of the figure exiled from the family structure. Like Machen, Wells and other fin-de-siècle authors, Stoker endeavoured to articulate the experience of those orphaned from the family as emblems of late-century anxieties. Stoker in particular saw the family as an emblem of the fading traditional world rapidly being displaced by modernism. His concern was that the sceptical materialism of modernity threatened the spiritual and moral foundation associated with the traditional past for which Stoker had such an acute nostalgia and which to him was embodied in the Victorian myth of the ideal family. If the Victorian era was one of transition and progress, the fin-de-siècle was a period of conflicting paradigms, opposing philosophies and general uncertainty. Indeed, the late nineteenth century saw the Victorians in an orphanic state, severed as it was from the cultural certainties of its past and heading with increasing momentum toward an uncertain future. Stoker clearly perceived his generation as posited between two worlds, the traditional and the modern. And nowhere is this generational anxiety so demonstrated as in the orphanic state of *Dracula*'s R. M. Renfield.

What occurs when the institution into which the orphan has historically laboured to be included is beyond his or her grasp or no longer even exists? To engage this question, this chapter will focus on Renfield, arguably the most exemplary of Stoker's characters in regard to family, orphanhood and exile – and their connection to anxieties particular to the fin-de-siècle, and to late Victorian moral and psychic dissolution.

In rendering Renfield emblematic of an age of uncertainty, it is, above all, notably upon the conventions of orphanhood that Stoker relies. The 52-year-old patient is never visited by any family members, which indicates that he has either been ostracized from his family, or that he has no family at all. As I discuss below, his inordinate cleaving to Dracula as a terrible father figure and his obsequious fawning over and evident desperation for Seward's approval entrench the idea of Renfield's orphanic compulsion to acquire some type of father figure; furthermore, his notably asexual reaction to and subsequent affect by Mina belies his desire for a maternal figure as well. Lacking any connection with family and exiled from normal social structures, Renfield eludes categorization of class and identity, having lost whatever affiliations to aristocracy that he may have formerly held. Unpredictably malleable, he is a perfect example of the orphanic mimic, at turns mirroring most of the book's main characters.

Depictions of the fin-de-siècle orphan are often of disturbing, morbid, even malformed beings with an inclination to instability analogous to the dilemmas assailing the Victorian mind at the century's end. Renfield, a deceptively minor character, exhibits such instability. Gladden states that Renfield 'operates as a figure who stands between the vampire and its hunters' and refers to him as 'an earnest yet potentially untrustworthy bridge between good and evil'.[1] The range of critical reception Renfield has received is perhaps indicative of the instability demonstrated by his discrepant personality traits. He has been referred to as 'a relatively minor character', 'the novel's token idiot', a good idea that is unsuccessful and whose presence does little more than to bring together various aspects of the narrative, and the one character who could be considered boring.[2] Elsewhere, however, he has been called 'Stoker's most memorable minor character', 'the most complicated character in the novel' and lauded as being 'brilliantly realized'.[3] This 'undeveloped homicidal maniac' is invaluable in regard to a consideration of the cultural context from which the novel emerged.[4] I furthermore argue that in no other character in *Dracula* does the reader find a figure that embodies so well the anxieties particular to the fin-de-siècle in a manner so dependent upon the orphanic state.

Just as the aggressive progress of the Victorian period caused a severance from the surety of traditions, Renfield's disconcerting mutability offers no reliable constant by which he may be classified. Indeed, at times he appears 'to position himself *between* captivity and freedom'.[5] In keeping with the notion of orphanhood, he eludes proper categorization. He is presumably of aristocratic birth, yet he has been committed to Seward's asylum. He is capable of eloquent speech and even of academic and scientific allusions, yet he consumes insects and licks spilt blood from the floor. He is human and yet seems to aspire to some supernatural, suprahuman condition. Disconnected from his previous identity as an aristocratic and intellectual gentleman, he occupies various, often contradictory roles that challenge any attempt to categorize him. Portrayed with conventions associated with orphanhood, Renfield is emblematic of an age no longer sure of itself. Indeed, he resonates with the dualism typical of the late Victorian personality.[6]

Renfield suffers from an aspiration for some kind of pseudo-vampirism, a degenerative characteristic which results in his committal and the resultant excision from his previous aristocratic state. Either ostracized from his family or lacking a family of any kind and severed from a station in which he might have retained his true identity, Renfield acquires the status identical to that of the orphan. As a coping mechanism, perhaps in an effort to impose a kind of order to his existence, he subsequently develops what could be labelled Dissociative Identity Disorder (DID), a condition in which the subject displays various, distinct personalities.[7] Stoker portrays the patient, who has lost touch with his true identity, as adopting the orphanic imitative method, with Renfield mimicking the more stable personalities around him in an endeavour to assimilate into some social or provisional familial structure. This orphanic strategy, however, is complicated by Renfield's degenerative tendencies, manifested in his vampiric predilection for consuming lives. Attending this social descent, therefore, are hints of his former propriety confounded by alienating and antisocial tendencies. Renfield is an emblem of Stoker's generation's endangered and orphanic condition wherein the older, traditional world, demonstrated by Renfield's aristocratic state, is threatened by numerous degenerative issues embodied in the patient's neurotic tendencies.

Renfield's endeavour is to reconstruct his lost identity through the imitation of others, affecting a new reality through mimesis. In this Lacanian manner, his method attempts a refashioned self through the illusion of identification with other, substantial characters. His goal is to recover some semblance of wholeness to supplant his current, fractious self. Like the infant in Lacan's mirror scenario, Renfield locates within the object of his imitation a completeness to which he, as a yet unformed – or rather in Renfield's case disjunctive – ego aspires to attain. Seward, Harker and the other vampire hunters serve as unitary entities contrasting with Renfield's fragmentary self-concept. They become the imaginary self the emulation of which, in the process of *meconnaissance,* the false recognition, Renfield loses himself and at the same time tries to define himself.[8]

It is crucial here to recall that, while capable of simulating positive models, the orphan is ever in danger of patterning his or her self after negative models as well. This is exemplified by Renfield's frequent lapse into his degenerative, zoophagous state. There is always the threat of moral slippage due to orphanhood's conditional lack of familial stability or parental instruction. This threat is further complicated for Renfield due to his madness, the pseudo-vampiric nature of which compels him to submit to his baser desires. In this state, he is vulnerable to outside forces, which in collusion with that insanity make him just as apt to imitate Dracula as to imitate Lord Godalming. Renfield's oscillation between these two extremes epitomizes the treacherous potential of the orphan, who must often negotiate the moral geography of existence alone. As cultural exponent, vacillating between these polemic possibilities, the patient echoes Stoker's generational anxiety, the Victorian society grappling with its abandonment of the older, traditional order which promised identity and stability, and the potentially degenerative, incredulous and experimental system of modernism represented by the degenerative, sexually ambiguous and imperial aspects of vampirism.

Renfield's ramshackle personality demonstrates many of the symptoms of DID, including the expression of a number of mannerisms that are dissimilar to one another, the loss of memory, sudden fits of unwarranted anger and episodes of anxiety or panic.[9] He wavers from innocuous pensiveness to snappish distemper. There is a great disparity between the behaviour that belies his lunacy and the intellectual, ingratiating, even endearing loquacity of the 'normal' Renfield.[10] But that witty acumen is sometimes marred by childlike crudity. Seward writes that, at one instance, Renfield 'seemed as sane as anyone I ever saw' but, days later, that 'I mistrust these quiet moods of his [and] have a strait-waistcoat in case of need'.[11] The doctor later states: 'His moods change so rapidly that I find it difficult to keep touch of them'; Renfield is found at one point 'sitting in a corner brooding', only the next morning to be found 'up and humming a tune [catching flies] cheerfully and with a good grace'.[12] The same day Renfield attempts to keep track of his capture of flies by going to such extremes as to inscribe nail-marks on the edge of the door, he later brushes away the sugar crumbs from the window sill, empties his box and proclaims: 'I am sick of all that rubbish!'[13] Seward explains to Van Helsing: 'When our sane and learned lunatic made [the] statement of how he *used* to consume life, his mouth was actually nauseous with the flies and spiders which he had eaten just before Mrs. Harker entered the room'.[14] At another point, for an hour or more, he '"kept getting excited in greater and greater degree' but soon after 'grew quiet'.[15] Renfield's demeanour alters from servile passivity to violent hostility. At one point, 'he slid from the hands that held him, an inert mass' and then, a few moments later, 'stood up quite calmly and looked about him'; at another point he was 'perpetually violent', only later to 'grow quiet', then 'redoubled his efforts and then as suddenly grew calm'.[16] The same patient who scoffs at the attendants' mistrust by stating to Seward, 'They think I could hurt you! Fancy *me* hurting *you*!', is the same man who later attacks the doctor with a dinner knife.[17] His regard for others oscillates from mannerly deference to contemptuous insults. In relation to the asylum attendants, Renfield is 'usually respectable' and 'at times servile; but tonight . . . he is quite haughty'; Dr Hennessey writes that the patient 'is usually such a well-behaved man . . . except [for] his violent fits'.[18] And, yet, his gentlemanly regard for Mina is nothing short of impeccable. When frustrated that he is denied leaving the asylum, Renfield's response to 'the old fool' Van Helsing is an infantile 'I wish you would take yourself and your idiotic brain theories somewhere else. Damn all thick-headed Dutchmen!' After he is attacked by Dracula, however, Renfield states to Van Helsing: 'How good it is of you to be here'.[19]

Stoker depicts Renfield in a manner that is disturbing on numerous levels. In contrast to, say, Dracula, whose characteristic variances are in part determined by the diverse narrators' accounts of him and which serve to effect a multifaceted rendering of the Count, Renfield is presented through the medium of only one witness, Dr John Seward.[20] It is perhaps due to this myopic treatment of Renfield that the patient's inconsistent behaviours prove even more disarming. The variety of frameworks that result in a count who is at turns somewhat feminine, violently masculine, inherently evil and even pitiable does not exist in the depiction of Renfield. That is, the disturbing variety of Renfield's being is contingent not on numerous or conflicting accounts of several interpreters, but on his own actions documented by a single author. Furthermore, while Dracula's more disquieting attributes can more easily be projected onto a figure whose perpetual foreignness permits a certain comforting remove, Renfield's less appealing characteristics are demonstrated by an Englishman. Precisely because he is not a foreign body whose variances might be more readily expected due to otherness, the orphanic mimicry Renfield expresses is alarming because such behaviour by an Englishman is unexpected. Actions that by an Other might be typical nuances of foreignness, when displayed by Renfield instead speak of the English degeneration against which Stoker is cautioning. Renfield's imitation of someone like Seward is possibly more alarming than the Count's employment of perfect English or the ease of his assimilation into English society. For, while with Dracula, conflicting attributes and culturally othered classifications are embodied by an alien, foreign entity, Renfield, amidst his numerous idiosyncrasies, is unsettlingly English.[21]

I make this point to emphasize the disturbing implications this Englishness has with Renfield's troubling similarity to each of the vampire hunters, whose union forms a kind of representative Victorian congress.[22] As such, Seward the scientist, Harker the lawyer, Holmwood the aristocrat and Morris the adventurer collectively symbolize Victorian England, and provide Renfield with rational, western models the simulation of which he hopes will combat the irrational, arguably Eastern proclivities warring within him.[23] But, because Renfield's orphanic state and insanity are both indigenous to England, Stoker is able to suggest that the mysteries of the East are not necessarily requisite for the moral slippage, atavism or degeneration the patient at times demonstrates. In his mimicry of the Victorian emblem, Renfield becomes a representation of the order and rationality of traditional Victorian culture which found itself threatened by the dispossession characteristic of modernism, and thus more vulnerable to the simultaneous danger of the irrationality and supernaturalism perceived to be embodied by the East.

Renfield's dependence on the Count also has vexing implications, deriving as it does less from Dracula's mesmerizing influence and more from Renfield's defects that are particular to England. Just as the somnambulism Lucy inherits from her father renders her all the more vulnerable to Dracula, and her latent sexuality seems stimulated by the Count's attacks, Renfield's zoophagous nature pre-exists the advent of Dracula's influence.[24] Renfield, like Lucy, permits the Count's entrance into his space and is, due to these inherent, debilitating traits, to some degree a willing participant in Dracula's domination of him. While Lucy's somnambulism colludes with her supposed sexual nature to effect her vulnerability, Renfield's madness is compounded by his orphanic desire for a father figure that renders him virtually helpless against the Count as much psychologically as physically.

Kelly Hurley's discussion of the 'metamorphic and undifferentiated' physical representations found in the Gothic of the fin de siècle focuses on representations of physical metamorphosis and biological uncertainties; I would like to extend her ideas to include the psychological changeableness that is Renfield's primary attribute, his mimicry. Furthermore, Renfield's instability speaks to the rise of mental physiology and psychology of Stoker's time and the emergent anxieties produced by science's exploration of the mind.[25] This very Gothic condition of variability, which comprises what Seward calls the patient's 'agonized confusion', is indicative of the malleability that is a trademark of the orphan, and is symptomatic of the mimicry often demonstrated in the orphanic quest for identity and selfhood.[26] Without his previous societal associations, and lacking the identity granted by familial inclusion, the patient frequently lapses into the imitation of more stable personalities with whom he comes into contact.

He is ever in the process of mirroring others, acquiring their characteristics, imitating their demeanours. Through his multitudinous incarnations, he is at turns suggestive of each of the novel's main characters. He expresses overtly masculine as well as undeniably feminine qualities; he conveys a very western, systematic and rational intellect while succumbing to supernatural forces associated with the East; and he at once betokens both the avarice of the colonizer and the debilitation of the colonized. What his emulation registers is what sets Renfield apart from previous orphan imitators; in Renfield, Stoker utilizes the orphanic state to allude to late-century questions of Victorian identity, concerns over sexual ambiguity, conflicts between western rationalism and eastern mysticism, and the implications of the imperial enterprise.

The Victorian emblem

Renfield's likeness to both Seward and Van Helsing links him to the scientific and academic communities of the West. He is able 'to talk philosophy, and reason so sound'.[27] This 'so clever lunatic' is not only able to quote Shakespeare and pontificate on the ancients' symbolic use of flies' wings, but is also knowledgeable of Van Helsing's revolution of therapeutics and his 'discovery of the continuous evolution of brain matter'.[28] Renfield also shows knowledge of Harker's vocation, citing his inmates' tendencies toward *non causae* and *ignoratio elenchi*. He is able to discuss the adoption of Morris's home state, as well as the possible future ramifications of the Monroe Doctrine. It is clear that Renfield, like Arthur, has some connection with the highly educated upper class. The patient often bears the carriage and mannerisms of a well-bred Englishman, speaking with what Seward calls 'the manner of a polished gentleman'; upon meeting Van Helsing, Morris and Arthur, he is said to possess 'a certain dignity, so much of the habit of equality'; and Renfield mentions seconding Arthur's father at the Windham, a club founded for gentlemen interested in literature.[29] On a more humorous note is his insistence of 'tidying up the place' before Mina enters his cell.[30] That this tidying up consists of consuming his remaining flies and spiders is not as important as the implications of his insistence on some form of genteel propriety in the company of a lady.

While Renfield is perhaps not the embodiment of masculinity suggested by the Bowie- and Winchester-toting Quincey Morris, Stoker aligns the two by endowing Renfield with some notable similarities to the American. The patient exhibits at least adventurous enough a disposition thrice to escape the asylum, once even with the intent of attacking, and besting, three cart drivers. Seward writes that when he attacks the cart drivers bearing wooden boxes for Carfax, Renfield 'pull[ed] one of them off the cart and began to knock his head against the ground'.[31] But perhaps the most striking correspondence between these otherwise very dissimilar characters is the act of self-sacrifice that leads to their respective deaths. Morris's mortal wound by Szgany gypsies is acquired while scaling the cart bearing Dracula's box; Renfield's is received attempting to deter the Count's attack on Mina. Morris's parting words are the selfless proclamation, 'I am only too happy to have been of any service' and 'It was worth it for this to die!'; Renfield states after his struggle with Dracula that 'it made me mad to know that He had been taking the life out of her', his final moments characterized by penitential acceptance of his death in the service of defending Mina.[32]

Sexual ambiguity

Another concern of late Victorian culture to which Renfield alludes is that of sexual ambiguity. Of course, the confusion of gender roles in Stoker is not limited to Renfield, but it is in his particular case that the wavering between overt masculinity and latent femininity are symptomatic of the imitative tendencies bourn of his orphanic state. His desire for inclusion results, for example, in a servile femininity in deference to the masculine domination of Dracula, as well as an overtly masculine attempt to defend Mina. This ache for assimilation is problematized by his illness. He is at times aggressively defensive of his semi-vampiric notions, expressing a potential for alienating, masculine aggression. At one point, Seward notes 'a warning of danger [in the patient's face] for there was a sudden, fierce, sidelong look that meant killing'; when Seward and his attendants find Renfield for the second time at the chapel door, he writes that 'had not the attendants seized him in time, he would have tried to kill me'; Seward also mentions that the silent intervals between the chained Renfield's cries 'are more deadly still, for he means murder in every turn and movement'.[33] Indeed, despite being referred to as a 'feeble madman', this 'possibly dangerous man' is described as having 'great physical strength' and as being 'immensely strong'.[34] In one instance, 'he became so violent that it took all [the attendants'] strength to hold him', and even when struck with the butt-end of a whip, a blow that scarcely phases him, Renfield nearly bests three cart drivers, 'pulling [them] to and fro as if [they] were kittens'.[35] Perhaps most notable in this regard is the scene wherein Renfield bursts into Seward's office and attacks him with a dinner knife. In keeping with the patient's inconsistency, there is also his heroic effort physically to thwart Dracula from attacking Mina.

However, Renfield simultaneously reveals feminine characteristics as well, particularly in his loss of masculine agency and his submissive behaviours.[36] Consideration of his madness elicits notions of femininity. Rosemary Ellen Guiley diagnoses Renfield as suffering from 'homicidal and religious mania' and 'monomania'. Monomania was a common diagnosis of the times and was later replaced by the term 'hysteria', a condition considered during the nineteenth century as a female illness primarily due to the 'feminine' attributes of emotional imbalance and hypersensitivity associated with the condition.[37] In addition, Renfield's relationship with Seward posits him in a position of fawning and, therefore, feminized dependant. Seward notes at one point the notably feminine aspect of Renfield's eyes; they 'had something of their old pleading . . . and cringing softness'.[38] The Count's influence as well turns the patient 'into a coquettish and jealous masochist'.[39] Renfield's subservience to Dracula results in a loss of agency that effectively emasculates the patient. When confronted with the question as to why he wishes to be dismissed from the asylum, it becomes clear that Renfield is both mentally and physically bound by the Count. When Renfield escapes the asylum and presses his body against the door of the abbey in an almost sexually submissive manner, he exclaims, 'I am here to do Your bidding, Master' and refers to himself as a 'slave' who has 'worshipped' the 'Dear Master'.[40] Such sycophantic submission to another male relegates Renfield to a station at odds with Victorian concepts of manhood and masculine independence.

Rational West, supernatural East

One of the primary themes throughout Stoker's fiction is the contrast between the West and the East. This is demonstrated particularly in the difficulty the rational, scientific and systematic Western intellect experiences in comprehending supernaturalism and mysticism frequently perceived as associated with the eastern world. Renfield is emblematic of this contention in his mimicry of both the western Seward and the eastern Dracula, in personality shifts which represent the novel's oppositional ideological concepts of the logical and the wondrous.[41]

Much of the battle against Dracula is intellectual, manifested in the compulsive chronicling of events and the organization of documented information into a systematically presented study of the Count's activities and related ancillary occurrences.[42] The process of comprehending Dracula is crucial in the contest against him. The more western logic is applied to the vampire, the more he is classified and categorized, the more the band of heroes gains the upper hand.[43] Thus, one of the primary impulses of the novel's narrators is their penchant for writing things down. In their preoccupation with recording the minutest details of events, they employ the systematic method that writing imposes upon information, classifying and categorizing in an effort to apprehend and understand the bewildering implications of their nemesis.[44] Harker's journalistic depiction of Transylvania, for instance, is filled with 'facts [. . .] verified by books and figures, and of which there can be no doubt', while Seward's intent is to 'put down with exactness all that happened, as well as I can remember it'.[45] This kind of orderly and methodical approach is often contrasted in Stoker's fiction with the irrationality of superstition and the supernatural that is typically associated with non-western characters and the East in general. Superstition is often regarded by Stoker's narrators as an indication of intellectual inferiority, atavism or developmental immaturity; characters like the gypsies in 'The Gipsy Prophecy', or the 'picturesque' folk of *Dracula* and 'Dracula's Guest', for instance, are rendered merely as curious cultural artifacts for the entertainment of western scrutiny. Renfield represents, in unpredictable turns, both of these competing ideological approaches, by mimicking Seward's predilection for documentation while also expressing his supposed 'foreign' longing for a supernatural, vampiric existence in his consuming of lower life forms.

Renfield evokes the very western tendency to chronicle, for example, in his insistence to list the various forms of life upon which he feasts. There is an academic manner about his approach, but it is 'grotesquely "scientific"', a cerebration tinged with insanity.[46] Like Seward, whose case book 'was ever more full', the patient has 'a little note-book in which he is always jotting down something'.[47] With his 'masses of figures' which he 'added up in batches', Renfield expresses the same desire as the various narrators to impose onto events the structure of systematic application.[48] His methods are notably like those of the scientifically minded Seward, thought the content of their labour is dissimilar. And while Seward's is an endeavour to discern the data of his discipline's pursuits, Renfield's seems an inclination that borders on *furor scribendi*, something he cannot resist.[49] He remarks at one point that he has 'closed the account' of his notebook, only almost immediately to begin 'a new record'.[50] while being held in a padded room without his notebook, he persists in his tabulation by 'making nail-marks on the edge of the door between the ridges of padding'; only hours after claiming no more interest in flies and spiders, he spreads his sugar out and 'got a scrap of paper and was folding it into a note-book'.[51] Mock as it is, Renfield's own use of writing situates him in the category of the analytical methodology typical of western mentality.

Renfield also demonstrates resemblance to Seward in the erroneous application of knowledge.[52] Despite a determination for exactness and precision, Seward mistakenly attributes to the patient a 'sanguine' temperament, although Renfield actually falls under the category of 'choleric'.[53] Likewise, when Renfield assaults Seward, cutting the doctor's arm with a dinner knife and proceeding to lick the blood from the floor, the patient does so claiming: 'The blood is the life!'[54] While Renfield's statement implies notions of whatever life-giving properties he perceives conveyed by the ingestion of the fluid, his application is actually a misinterpretation of a biblical passage. The quote, which comes from Deuteronomy 12:23, is actually an exhortation from Yahweh for the Israelites to 'be sure that thou eat not the blood: for the blood is the life; and thou mayest not eat the life with the flesh'. Renfield's misappropriation of this text is analogous to Seward's misdiagnosis; both incidences are examples of a western mind's incorrect interpretation of elements associated with easternness. Seward's error shows the bewilderment with which his western categorical methodology deals with a patient whose illness is associated with the vampirism threatening from the East; Renfield's error is the misuse of an originally Middle

Eastern text. Both characters represent western intellects somewhat confounded by concepts associated in one way or another with the East.

In addition to his emulation of the western intellectual approach and its attendant compulsion for the documentation of minutiae and particulars, Renfield equally evokes idiosyncrasies which align him with mysteries affiliated in the Victorian mind with the eastern world. This association results in the bafflement of Seward's systematic methods; intent on 'making myself master of the facts of his [Renfield's] hallucination', Seward endeavors to categorize his patient, even coining the term 'zoophagous' to define Renfield's life-consuming actions.[55] But Seward's term fails to encompass matters such as the patient's incomprehensible dispositional inconsistencies. Renfield's manner, 'some fixed idea' that Seward 'cannot make out', evades absolute categorization, because one of the key aspects of his personality appears to belong to the supernatural realm that defies scientific tactics and the specificity of traditional classification.[56] The doctor, whose rationality is epitomized by his initial diagnosis of Lucy as suffering from anaemia, is confounded by the irrational concepts suggested by Renfield's condition. In a novel in which delineations are made between the rationality of the West and the mysteriousness of the East, between the discernable and the incomprehensible, and where those differences are related to humanity and super-humanity, Renfield's wavering between opposing extremes evinces his mental state, alludes to Stoker's generational predicament, man's potential for degeneration and furthermore is a literalization of the patient's mimetic orphanic condition.[57]

The colonizer and the colonized

Renfield's orphanic uncertainty speaks as well to broader cultural and political issues of the fin de siècle, relating to both the process of colonization and the experience of being colonized. His acquisition of living things in order to perpetuate his own existence is analogous to the imperial enterprise. He has, of course, been placed in the asylum because of his belief that what he gained from the consumption of living things 'was life, strong life, and gave life to him'; indeed, he 'used to fancy that . . . by consuming a multitude of live things, no matter how low on the scale of creation, one might indefinitely prolong life'.[58] As a colonizing entity, Renfield embodies an empire engaged in the procurement and exploitation of subjects that contribute to its development. Through Seward's entries concerning the patient's activities, Stoker emphasizes this in suggestive language. This 'God created from human vanity' negotiates 'some settled scheme' in a manner of 'selfishness, secrecy, and purpose'; he 'has laid himself out to achieve it [his plan] in a cumulative way'.[59] This scheme, of course, is to acquire pets 'of increasing size' and to 'absorb as many lives as he can'.[60] Indeed, Renfield's intention is to consume lives in an increscent manner, his notion being that in doing so, he will gain greater levels of the vampiric life they offer. In fact, Renfield acknowledges the worth of his acquisitions according to their own capacity for consumption of other species and seems notably concerned with devouring creatures that have devoured other creatures.[61] The patient's methods are akin to an empire's process of absorbing other, more vulnerable cultures in an effort to ensure its survival and affect its own increase.

Renfield also assumes the role of the colonized Other, a concept demonstrated on two levels. One is the literal subjection of the patient to various powers beyond his control which exact compulsion upon him to alter himself in some way. One might argue that he is subject to the constraints of the asylum, or that he is 'colonized' by his illness; both factors, in effect, impose some alternative identity upon Renfield, as might imperialism charge the subject with conforming to its standards. But it is perhaps Dracula's control of Renfield that most exacts the notion of the patient's subservience to a more powerful entity. In reference to the Count, Renfield repeatedly refers to a 'master', and claims at one point, 'I am not my own master'.[62] As such, the patient embodies Hughes's regard for *Dracula* as 'a fearful warning of the vulnerability of the Anglo-Saxon West to the seductive and infectious East'.[63]

A second manner in which Renfield represents the colonized is in the degenerate nature he reveals, which would have been associated in the Victorian mind with foreignness. For it is Renfield who perhaps most acutely demonstrates the characteristics and influence of the Other.[64] Renfield varies from a nigh convincing specimen of Victorian gentility to pseudo-vampiric ingester of insects and birds. Such a descent, variable as it is, from gentleman member of the Windham to grisly lunatic denotes the kind of evolutionary regression, atavism and degeneration associated in pseudo-scientific postulations of imperial ideology with colonial subjects. He is in this manner similar to the 'primitive' peoples whom Stoker often rendered as morally, physically and evolutionarily inferior, alluding to the prevailing Victorian concepts of racial disparity that associated otherness with, among other things, criminality.[65] Renfield's degenerative actions link him not only to the malfeasance to which Lombroso referred, but also to the otherness of the imperial subject thought to be intrinsically distinguished by similar forms of corruption.[66]

Renfield's provisional parents

Stoker's emphasis on the importance of the family and the maintenance of its ideal typically resulted in the orphans of his fiction somehow acquiring belonging in some either actual or contrived familial structure. One of the primary attributes of the family ideal is the reliable model father figure and Stoker often offers the surrogate father figure who serves as mentor, confidant or group leader, such as Van Helsing in *Dracula*, Treylawny in *Jewel of the Seven Stars*, and Rupert in *Lady of the Shroud*. In *Lair of the White Worm*, Richard immediately assumes the role of provisional father for the Australian orphan, Adam, to whom he refers as 'my son'; Adam likewise regards Richard as though he 'had been my own father'.[67] Maurice Richardson points out the 'father fixation' in Stoker's work.[68] Hughes notes Stoker's preoccupation with 'a father-figure who is both admired and feared'.[69] In the case of Renfield, Stoker employed conventions associated with orphans to exact the patient as a character symbolic of his generation's sense of itself as orphaned. He also developed the dynamic of a provisional family for this 'lost son' by establishing a father–son relationship between Renfield and Seward – which contrasts with the patient's unrequited appeal to the Terrible Father figure, Dracula – and a mother–son relationship between Renfield and Mina. In doing so, Stoker contrasts the tenuous, endangered association of the former with the self-sacrificial, redemptive relationship of the latter.

Lucy's choice of Arthur Holmwood as her fiancé denies Seward not only the familial unity marriage would have afforded him, but also prohibits him from fulfilling the role of procreative, biological father. Reeling from the dual loss of nuptial union and perpetuity, the doctor immediately redirects his energies, assuming a kind of imposed fatherhood, 'making myself master of the facts' concerning Renfield.[70] Joseph Valente remarks that Seward 'seems more concerned with maintaining his authority over "his lunatic" than with curing him'.[71] But, however Seward's interest in Renfield seems initially born out of the former's need for distraction, a receptacle for his own nervous compulsions perhaps, his regard for his patient develops rather quickly into one with paternal dimensions. Seward exacts a kind of protective ownership that exceeds the doctor–patient relationship, with Seward first coining the term 'zoophagous' in order to name the patient as one might a child, and afterwards by referring to him as 'my friend', 'my homicidal maniac', 'my poor mad friend', 'my patient' and 'my own pet lunatic'.[72]

There is a tenuous unity between the two which represents a provisional father-figure/lost-son dynamic. Indeed, Seward's treatment of Renfield tends to be fatherly, authoritative but sympathetic. The parental doctor urges his patient to abandon his flies and requests that he at least reduce his amount of spiders. He 'scolded' Renfield for consuming a blowfly and 'was firm' in denying him a cat; when approaching Renfield about the souls he consumes, Seward 'put my question quickly and somewhat firmly'.[73] The doctor notes that Renfield's notions 'might work out dangerously with strangers', inferring that his relationship with the patient assures his own safety, and admits that it is 'soothing somehow to the feelings' that he finds himself 'dissociated even in [Renfield's mind] from the others'.[74] At one point, Seward chooses not to invite Van Helsing to Renfield's cell, as the patient 'might not speak so freely before a third person as when he and I were alone'.[75] And Seward seems comfortable enough with his patient to allow him to whisper: 'They think I could hurt you! Fancy *me* hurting *you*!'[76]

Inasmuch as Seward enacts the role of provisional father, Renfield occupies the role of troubled son. Valente points out that the patient 'singles Seward out . . . for an expression of fealty that establishes the doctor as a kind of alternative master to Dracula'.[77] Renfield is at turns obedient and rebellious. Approaching Seward in one instance, he 'fawned on me like a dog' and 'threw himself on his knees before me and implored'; when Seward scolds him at one point, Renfield 'relapsed into his old servile manner, bent low before me, and actually fawned on me'.[78] But Renfield often lapses into behaviour similar to that of an irritant toddler, particularly when denied that which he desires. He sends Seward an 'urgent' message; the attendant delivering the communication states that if Seward does not see him immediately, the patient 'will have one of his violent fits'; at another point, a pained Renfield 'put his fingers to his ears and shut his eyes, screwing them up tightly just as a boy does when his face is being soaped' and soon 'fell from his high horse and became a child again'; Seward states that 'before me was a child' and 'it was useless to speak to him'; spitefully addressing Van Helsing, the previously mannerly and articulate Renfield adopts a childlike tone, referring to the professor as an 'old fool' with 'idiotic brain theories', and exclaiming: 'Damn all thick-headed Dutchmen!'[79]

Ultimately the father–son connection proves unsustainable. Renfield's knife attack against Seward, the patient's most extreme degenerative lapse, marks a turn in their relationship whereby the patient is relegated back to the status of mere clinical mystery. When Seward discovers the beaten Renfield on the floor of his cell, the doctor initially refers to him by name; however, as soon as Van Helsing arrives, Seward calls Renfield 'the patient' and 'the poor man'; and while Seward remarks that 'there was something pathetic [about Renfield] that touched me', overall the patient who once served as provisional son figure for the parental substitute quickly becomes merely a subject for analysis, objectified under 'a strict examination'.[80] Indeed, Renfield is all but forsaken by Seward and the other vampire hunters at this point.[81] He has overstepped his bounds, literally threatening the doctor's life, but also attempting to kill the tentative father who had endeavoured to help him, and Seward's interaction with Renfield after this incident is largely achieved through the intercession of attendants. The radical nature of Renfield's submission to his basest desires affects the dismantling of any suggested familial construction to which the orphanic Renfield may have aspired, and that may have afforded him some semblance of balance and even the possible retrieval of his former identity. In the context of Stoker's preoccupation with family, Renfield's attempted patricide provides a caveat against his generation's submission to the various atrocities suggested by modernity and an appeal to the traditions embodied by the family.

As a mimic, Renfield's failure to acquire a substantial sense of self may be contingent on Seward's anxious, uncertain and ineffectual demeanor, imitation of which would do little to alleviate the patient's orphanic incompleteness. Prior to his death, however, Renfield comes to a significant point of conversion, having encountered the capable and well-rounded identity of Mina, which provides him with a substantial, uniform completeness that compels Renfield to reclaim the stability of his former self. Under her moving influence, the patient is able to shirk the onus of an orphanic, fragmentary persona and retrieve a convincing semblance of his previous, true self. Of the book's main characters, it is Mina whom Renfield initially seems to resemble least. She is enterprising and productive; he is degenerative and ruinous. She is competent and altruistic; he is inept and narcissistic. However, in addition to their both falling to varying degrees under the sway of Dracula, the most poignant attribute the two characters share is the presence of disparate characteristics within their respective personalities. Like Renfield, Mina eludes categorization, although her acumen and capability result in a well-roundedness and integrity that, until his engagement with her, Renfield does not encounter, let alone possess.

Mina represents various potential classifications.[82] She straddles societal and gender roles much in the same manner as Renfield, but, unlike the fragmentary and irresolute patient, Mina's multiplicity renders her an example of the totality to which Renfield aspires. Contrasting with Renfield's self-interest and the squandering of his evident intellectual capabilities and thoughts of supernaturalism are Mina's selflessness, maternal nature and the prudent employment of her acumen and numerous talents.[83] Unlike Renfield's conversations that seem somewhat emulous and contrived, Mina's capabilities are applied for productive purposes. She reveals a desire to educate herself and has 'tried to be useful'; she works 'assiduously' at her shorthand and is 'practising very hard' the use of the typewriter; her 'knowledge of the trains offhand' surprises Van Helsing, whom she also impresses with her insight into Nordau and Lombroso in her discussion of Dracula's 'imperfectly formed mind'.[84] The Dutchman famously states: 'She has a man's brain – a brain that a man should have were he much gifted'.[85] Indeed, Mina proves just as competent and in many instances superior to Harker in composure and functionality. As opposed to her often effete husband, Mina assures the band that she 'would not shrink to die here', and by the novel's end is an armed accomplice in hunting Dracula down in the mountains of Transylvania.[86] She possesses the mental prowess and adventurous vitality of a male heroic figure while still embodying the chaste and maternal attributes of the ideal Victorian woman.[87] And it is in this role that Mina, who 'never knew either mother or father', demonstrates the tendency of the orphan to formulate provisional family structures to accommodate for the lack of real family affiliation, a method that for Renfield is problematized by his mental illness.[88] She serves in turn as mother and sister figure to the various vampire hunters. She frequently cradles the faint-hearted Harker, 'as though her clinging could protect him from any harm that might come'.[89] She asks Arthur, while comforting him, '[W]ill you let me be a sister to you in your trouble?', comparing his head to 'that of the baby that some day may lie on my bosom', and she strokes his hair 'as though he were my own child'.[90] She offers the same comfort to Quincey, whom she asks: 'Will you let me be your friend and . . . come to me for comfort'.[91]

Significantly, it is immediately following the establishment of her familial-type bond with Arthur and Quincey that Mina is compelled to request a meeting with Renfield; the proximity of this request to her forming of familial ties to the group seems to indicate her acquisition of him as another of her provisional relatives, situating her as a mother type which I argue Stoker intends to contrast with the refuted provisional fatherhood offered by Seward as well as the unrequited appeal to the narcissistic father figure of Dracula. When Mina enters Renfield's cell, it is with 'an easy grace which would at once command the respect of any lunatic'.[92] Seward notes her 'unconscious influence' and 'some rare gift or power' that she exudes.[93] The 'courage and resolution' Mina emulates encourages Renfield's contrition and even self-sacrifice.[94] There is criticism that claims the patient's redemption is induced by a renewal of his heterosexual passion for Mina.[95] I argue, however, that Renfield's defence of Mina is less an action based on sexual attraction, characterized as it is by 'such courtesy and respect', and more on the moral realization upon which he stumbles when confronted by the fulfilled potential of a multifaceted personality that is yet an integral and balanced entity.[96] The recognition of Mina's totality permits the mimic to reclaim his former, moral and uniform self. It is this that is 'some chord in his memory' that Mina evokes.[97]

The day following his encounter with Mina, therefore, Renfield has what Seward calls 'an unusual understanding of himself'.[98] His subsequent request for dismissal from the asylum is characterized by an immediacy that belies the crises brewing within him. His plea, 'Take me out of this and save my soul from guilt', and insistence that he is 'a sane man fighting for my soul' belie this renewed conception of himself.[99] The proximity of this statement with Renfield's introduction to Mina suggests that her 'unconscious influence', her completeness and surety, engenders his moral dilemma. His evident concern and admiration for the entirety that she represents reveals to him the horrifying reality of his neo-vampirism, the damnation of vampirized souls and the heretofore unacknowledged responsibility for his actions. His internal conflict comes to its resolution with this realization; he recoils from the madness the symptoms of which are analogous to those of orphanhood. Renfield's response to an insistent Seward, 'To hell with you and your souls', accompanied by the infantile behaviour akin to that which he displays earlier in the text, is attended by 'some process of mental disturbance' and some 'intense cerebral excitement'.[100] Here is evinced the anxiety he experiences with the revelation not only of the reality that his acquisition of souls implicates him morally, but simultaneously the recognition that his collusion with Dracula has imperiled the soul, and just as importantly for him, the coherence of Madam Mina.

This revelation permits Renfield's resignation at the point when Dracula, an emotionless, self-serving anti-father, disregards Renfield as soon as he gains access to the asylum, and dispenses with him violently in the instance of Renfield's opposition.[101] One significant and telling aspect of this incident is the relatively little emotional effect it has on Renfield; by this point, because of Mina's influence, he has acquired a sense of his former self, of his true identity. Ernest Fontana sees the patient as an incurable criminal according to Lombrosian standards.[102] However, I argue that by the time of his death, Renfield has clearly attained a state of lucid repentance and genuine conversion that indicates a cure of sorts: he has achieved the capacity to master the base desires that are inherent in his illness. Mina's influence encourages his sacrificial act, which is essentially a genuine, selfless imitation of the Victorian emblem and an assertion of his newly found totality. Renfield thus reconciles his orphanic state, shedding the characteristics of misplacement and loss, and at the moment of his death, returns to the state of belonging and entirety that is the goal of the orphan and Stoker's aspiration for his generation.

3
Rebellious Orphans

'Suffer me to go my own dark way.'
Robert Louis Stevenson, *Strange Case of Dr Jekyll and Mr Hyde*

Having examined the gradual erosion of the notion of the ideal family, I would now like to discuss the orphan as developing at times into an entity operating beyond the previously requisite clamour for inclusion, and look at the manner in which the orphan, devoid of the normalcy and stability proposed by familial association, no longer served as a sentimental convention generally alluding to class difference, economic disparity or social reform. Rather, the fin-de-siècle orphan often emerges as something quite different from his or her predecessors, acquiring new modes of symbolic resonance and appealing more to concerns particular to the century's end. By the late 1800s, without that familial union whereby he or she might have located some sense of identity, the orphan frequently evolves into a being who must construct a self outside of familial paradigms or criterion.

It is the orphan within this predicament who at times demonstrates a rebellious energy, who avoids familial inclusion and who actually seeks to destroy the family or social structures with which he or she is engaged. It is perhaps important here to note Mary Shelley's vengeful orphan, who seeks to destroy its maker's family due to its own deprivation;

but the rebellious orphan examined in this chapter should not be confused with the example of Shelley's wretch. While Frankenstein's creature is arguably compelled into its destructive behaviour and to some extent operates out of desperation, the orphanic rebel of the fin de siècle instead appears deviant from his or her very inception; he or she is *intrinsically* mutinous, predatory, even self-destructive.

This chapter focuses on three of these orphanic types: Edward Hyde from Stevenson's *Strange Case of Dr Jekyll and Mr Hyde*, Griffin from Wells's *The Invisible Man* and Helen Vaughn from Machen's *The Great God Pan.*[1] Hyde, Jekyll's 'bad son', 'rebellious son' and 'uncertain son', not only seeks to usurp the place of his father-creator and thus affect a kind of patricide, but also indubitably denies the provisional fatherhood offered by Gabriel Utterson.[2] Griffin virtually causes his own father's death, remorselessly steals his father's money and intentionally severs himself from his filial associations and obligations. The offspring of a blasphemous union, Helen, rendered an orphan by the death of her mother and by the notable absence of her supernatural sire, endeavours systematically to dismantle London society by undermining the foundational sacrament of marriage through maddening aberrant sexual misdeeds with society's well-born professionals. Each of these figures challenge, even threaten, the ideal with which the family had been affiliated, an ideal each unquestionably disdains.

There is a remarkable absence in these texts of a family ideal to which the orphan form would typically gravitate. By the end of the nineteenth century, middle-class sensibilities revealed a fear of the decline of the family, and the notion of the family ideal was largely ridiculed, rendered anachronistic and even considered repressive by some authors.[3] Stevenson offers no mother figures or effective father figures, Griffin ensures his own orphanhood through thievery and virtual patricide, and Helen's mother is rendered insane and her father is absent. The question then arises as to what becomes of the orphan who is not only denied but in no uncertain terms rejects the previously highly esteemed union with the family, particularly when the orphan is actually complicit in the dismantling of all for which that ideal has historically stood? Indeed, each of these figures is distinguished by a notable disregard for assimilation as well as a predilection for the disordering of their respective social and familial contexts. Irving Saposnik views Hyde as an emblem of 'uncontrolled appetites', and 'an amoral abstraction driven by a compelling will unrestrained by any moral halter'.[4] However, I view not only Hyde, but Griffin and Helen as well, as remarkably *deliberate* in their actions, less compelled by intemperate impulses and more motivated by a clear agenda of disruption and anarchy.

While previous orphan figures once insinuated the merits of traditional family cohesion, the rebellious type, self-sufficient, even ruinous, appears an analogue of the generational anxiety to which chapter 2 alludes. Indeed, there seems an intrinsic tension accompanying an aspiration to retain tradition and the evidently inevitable progress of modernity. And the rebellious orphan speaks to the haunting dualities that emerged with the contention between tradition and modernism, inclusion and individuality, good and evil. The late Victorians were vexed by notions of binaries and the interior conflicts that it is the nature of civilization to suppress. Hyde is emblematic of this idea of oppositional forces wrestling within mankind, the concept of good and evil coexisting in a single entity. Griffin's misappropriation of experimental possibilities stands as a caveat against the unchecked technological and scientific progress characteristic of modernism's advent. Helen represents the disastrous effects of modernism's attempt to sever the spiritual from the material, with the virtual denial of the former and an inordinate emphasis on the latter.

The rebellious orphan, then, is a dark representation of Victorian culture's painful separation from the past and its hurtling into what seemed a potentially destructive and degenerative future. The employment of Gothic motifs, for instance, expresses the middle-class conception that humanity was indeed undergoing a degenerative process, a concept that by the 1890s reached a level of panic.[5] That panic is embodied in the figure of the rebellious orphan. The indefinite quality characteristic of the orphan, the lack of name, of class affiliation, of place in society, in these texts is manifested in modes of somatic disruption. One may locate in the figure of the indescribably atavistic Mr Hyde, in the fractious and indefinite yet undeniably subsistent Griffin, and in the metamorphic and compositionally uncertain Helen the rebellious orphan's occupation of that discomforting space between the human and inhuman. All three allude to that uncertain space of being that evoked a demonstrative anxiety in authors like Stevenson and Stoker.[6] All three are startling incarnations of ethical and cultural elements perceived to threaten the Victorian world of the century's end. It is important to note, of course, that other, non-orphan figures possess the ability to address the anxieties of the day. What this chapter does is delineate these orphans from other characters by noting the necessity of their orphan states and the manner in which their respective authors utilize conventions associated with orphanhood with both traditional and subversive techniques.

Strange Case of Dr Jekyll and Mr Hyde: usurpation and patricide in the domestic space

Several critics have assessed Hyde's defiant and violent acts as merely random and meaningless, from 'stark acts' which lack motive or reason, to crimes that are 'petty, malicious, and self-indulgent'.[7] One critic states that the two incidences of violence of which we hear eyewitness accounts are merely 'brutal responses to accidental street encounters', while another emphasizes the apparent purposelessness of Hyde's 'motiveless malignity' that is all the more horrifying because it is absurd.[8] I would suggest, however, reading Hyde's misdeeds as serving very specific symbolic functions. While perhaps appearing resultant of haphazard encounters, these perpetrations, particularly the two cases of particular savagery, the stomping of the young girl and the murder of Carew, serve on a generational level to exact the isolation of the orphanic state that Hyde so aggressively pursues.

These acts function in a narrative manner similar to that which characterizes Stoker's previously noted generational anxiety, which posited his generation between two very diverse modes of existence. Hyde's trampling of the girl, a representation of the subsequent generation, is a disengagement from moral obligation or ethical responsibility for the prospect of posterity embodied in the child for whom he displays patent disregard. Similarly, his murder of Carew importantly challenges and eliminates a cultural patriarchal figure, an emblem of the traditional past from which the Victorian world was finding itself increasingly estranged in the fin de siècle. Indeed, Carew's 'old world kindness of disposition' and 'well-founded self-content' are the antithesis of Hyde's immorality and self-indulgence.[9] The murder exemplifies Hyde's absolute refusal of the traditional world, Carew's hierarchical implications and the mores and proprieties of the previous generation. Hyde effectively disengages from any bonds of sympathy with the generations prior and subsequent to his own circumstance. In his case, then, the medial generational condition is less one of potential valiant action and heroism, as often depicted in Stoker, and more the decisive declaration of egoism and insularity.

This detachment from emblems of previous and successive generations is part of Hyde's pursuit of an orphanic condition which is characterized by an increasingly narcissistic and misanthropic demeanour, compelling Jekyll to write in his final statement that Hyde's 'every act and thought centered on self'.[10] Enfield is as repulsed by Hyde's unfeeling response to the little girl's screams as he is to their jarring collision. As the text progresses, in fact, Hyde assumes an increasing apathy toward his atrocities, a remarkable pride in his harmful capacity. This conceit, which attends his increasing power over his father-creator, Jekyll, begets a sadistic predilection for accretive sociopathic violence, his 'drinking pleasure with bestial avidity from any degree of torture to another'.[11]

Hyde's assault on the society around him is intrinsically connected with his attempts at orphaning himself and with direct and indirect attacks on the notion of family. This occurs on numerous fronts, including his challenging of family-like associations, his insinuation into Jekyll's living space and his appropriation of sexuality from its natural context. Criticism of the novella often refers to Jekyll and Hyde in familial terms. Indeed, the doctor and his alter ego are labelled 'father-son'; Hyde is called 'the monster to whom Jekyll has given birth' and 'a schoolboy who attacks his father by destroying his portrait'.[12] Jekyll is said to have 'more than a father's interest', while Hyde 'had more than a son's indifference'.[13] Hyde, rather, asserts himself as a separate and autonomous entity with no interest in such familial associations. In a consideration of Hyde as the rebellious and homicidal son who, intentionally orphaning himself, seeks the disruption and usurpation of his father-creator's house, the stress that Stevenson places on the notion of the family and the worth of the domestic space becomes increasingly acute.[14] This may seem an odd statement regarding a novella that features no normative family constructions. Although the tale has been cited as one of 'sterile and self-consciously repressed' males, the homosocial constructions which its various Victorian professionals inhabit function to supplant this lack of traditional family configurations by offering a semblance of belonging and identity, however awkward and factitious.[15] As if to compensate for the obvious absence of actual close consanguinity, Stevenson repeatedly employs language that connotes familial associations. Utterson's closest friends 'were those of his own blood'.[16] Despite the evident lack of enthusiasm which characterizes his and Enfield's Sabbath jaunts, the fact that the latter is Utterson's 'distant kinsman' trumps the reality that their excursions are 'singularly dull'.[17] Utterson and Lanyon, though not related by blood, 'were old friends', and the lawyer is welcomed into the doctor's house 'subject to no stage of delay'.[18] Jekyll proclaims absolute trust in Utterson 'before any man alive'.[19] These social affiliations offer provisional family-like structures while underscoring Stevenson's emphasis on the belonging intrinsic to kinship. Contrasting with this telling and somewhat meagre attempt on the part of the story's protagonists are Hyde's efforts to dissociate from this created fraternal grouping, in essence, to orphan himself.

In addition to disengaging from these quasi-familial associations, one aspect of Hyde's modus operandi is the manner in which he assures the violation of these provisional associations. His intention is to effect the severance of Jekyll from his circle of friends, denying Utterson's offered assistance, endeavouring to corrupt Lanyon and eventually wholly consuming, and therefore eliminating, Jekyll. Essentially, Hyde seeks to dismantle the provisional family. There is a noticeable theme throughout the text of the severing of ties, of threats to familial relations the lack of which weakens resistance to Hyde's assaults.[20] Thus Stevenson's use of familial terms to describe Hyde's relationship to Jekyll; the evil that is Hyde 'struggles to be born' and Hyde is to Jekyll 'closer than a wife'.[21] Endowing Hyde with connotations of spouse and offspring, as well as making Hyde Jekyll's legal benefactor, Stevenson linguistically supplants the other, contrived relationships of Jekyll's professional circle, underscoring Hyde's disruptive intent: the destruction of familial bonds.

The most notable bonds that are severed in the novella are of a paternal nature. The theme of the treasure hunt emerges throughout Stevenson's work, typically in connection with the death of the father and the son's endeavour to acquire his inheritance.[22] What sets *Jekyll and Hyde* apart, however, is the son-figure's attempts to *affect* paternal death in order to stake his claim. Hyde's agenda is perpetuated on a number of other levels, not the least of which is the doctor's loss of his own home to his rebellious creation. Hyde's being the sole benefactor of Jekyll's will, an intolerable degree of access to the doctor's material wealth, permits Hyde to overtake the father's place, to 'step into the said Henry Jekyll's shoes'.[23] It also allows for the vulnerability of Jekyll's domicile to the seditious disorder of Hyde's machinations. Indeed, Hyde obtains 'full liberty and power' over Jekyll's house.[24] Stevenson's language effects Jekyll's gradual loss of his 'fortress of identity'.[25] Hyde, 'lurking in his victim's room', renders Jekyll alienated in his own home; the doctor finds himself 'a stranger in my own house' and feels he 'must flee . . . from a house that was no longer mine'.[26] When Hyde overtakes Jekyll without the administration of the serum, the doctor describes himself as 'houseless' and states that 'my own servants would consign me to the gallows'.[27] Jekyll is bereft not only of his physical dwelling, but also of whatever social affiliation his servants provide, Hyde again severing Jekyll from belonging, that he might assure his own orphanic isolation. Hyde's acquisition of the house is analogous to Jekyll's gradual relinquishment of his 'fortress of identity', whereby Hyde's ornamentation of the house is less the establishing of a warm, familial space and more the forging of a citadel of orphanic solitude.

The text consistently engages the notion of threats to and within the domestic area, that space so consistently under attack in the fin-de-siècle orphan narrative. Utterson imagines Hyde encroaching on Jekyll's bedroom, Lanyon dies in his own parlour and Hyde ultimately takes over Jekyll's house.[28] With three notable exceptions, the disruptive events that occur in relation to Hyde take place in living quarters. These anomalies are Enfield's account of Hyde's overrunning the little girl (which brings the girl's family forth from their home in her defence), the maid servant's observation of Hyde's murder of Carew (which she witnesses from her window, outside a gentleman's house) and Utterson's encounter with Hyde at the backstreet door (which is the latter's point of access into Jekyll's house). Even these exceptions, then, are proximate to homes. The narrative's events, including these exceptions which occur unsettlingly close to living spaces, notably take place within the domestic realm.

Stevenson associates the presence of domestic accoutrements with the tranquillity suggested by the domestic space, so that the ubiquity of creature comforts might subrogate non-existing familial intimates. Utterson's habit is to 'sit close by the fire, a volume of some dry divinity upon his desk'; Jekyll's home is 'warmed (after the fashion of a country house) by a bright, open fire'.[29] But contrasting with these somewhat feeble endeavours to contrive homely conditions that might compensate for the absence of matrimony or paternity are the disturbingly cheery surroundings of Hyde's living space. The area is 'furnished with luxury and good taste. A closet was filled with wine; the plate was of silver, the napery elegant; a good picture hung upon the wall . . . and the carpets were of many plies and agreeable in colour.'[30] Indeed, when Utterson and Poole break into the cabinet, they encounter an unsettlingly domestic scene the calming implications of which are contradicted and defiled by Hyde's presence. They observe the room

> in quiet lamplight, a good fire glowing and chattering on the hearth, the kettle singing its thin strain, a drawer or two open, papers neatly set forth on the business table, and nearer the fire, the things laid out for tea; the quietest room . . . the most commonplace [room] that night in London.[31]

In the midst of this serenity, however, 'contorting and still twitching' intrudes the form of Hyde, the very embodiment of disturbance of domestic tranquility.[32] Hyde's amassment of residential ornamentation seems a perverse imitation of the others' attempts at making their houses into homes. However, this profusion of domestic elements, despite their lending the appearance of hearth-and-home, is mere façade, implying something that is not actually present. The space is devoid of familial affection, its components instead a deceptive veneer concealing the self-serving individuation and isolation afforded by Hyde's orphanic state.

This sense of Hyde's isolation, of withdrawal from the society to which previous orphan figures typically aspired to belong, is present as well in the novella's undercurrent of masturbatory action. This is notable in regard to Hyde's dismantling of society and family due to its removal from the sexual act of any unitive or procreative function normative sexuality would otherwise contribute to a marriage and its potential for bringing into existence of new life, both of which are foundational to the perpetuation of society.[33] The setting of Jekyll's home becomes a metaphor for Hyde's self-indulgence, which is unsocial, uncreative, even pernicious. Despite Hyde's collection of finery and worldly goods, sterility characterizes the house's yard, which 'had once been a garden'.[34] The remark too that the morning, 'black as it was, was nearly ripe for the *conception* of the day' is a perverse inversion of its procreative implications, bearing as it does the likelihood of the perpetration of Hyde's said misdeeds.[35]

The implications of these misdeeds are epitomized in Hyde's use of the cane which he brandishes 'like a madman' and with which he 'clubbed him [Carew] to the earth . . . with a storm of blows'.[36] The cane, a gift that Utterson 'had himself presented many years before to Henry Jekyll', functions as a twofold symbol of Hyde's insurgent, patricidal comportment.[37] First, if we regard Utterson as a potential paternal figure, his bestowal of the cane is a metaphor for the conferring of reproductive potential from father to son. Hyde's acquisition of this phallic symbol can be read as a masturbatory abuse of sexual agency, a misuse that is not only non-procreative but, in this case, even lethal. Secondly, if we regard the cane as a cultural icon associated with the aristocracy, Hyde's misappropriation of this accessory for the purpose of murdering a representative of that social class further entrenches his abandonment of the propriety for which that class stands, and a sociopathic refusal of that society's laws and traditions.[38] With this single act, Hyde in effect purloins the father's generative potential, deprives himself of communal or reproductive opportunity and severs himself from the patriarchal social structure.

Jekyll is not the only father figure Hyde denies. He is notably oppositional to the potential father figure, Gabriel Utterson, who, being in possession of the will, while not enabled to alter its beneficiary, nonetheless is put in a position of concern for the doctor's affairs. Jekyll's creation of Hyde and his establishing of Hyde as beneficiary relegates the malicious character to a filial position, and the doctor's request that Utterson help Hyde 'for my sake, when I am no longer here' seems an appeal from one father to another for the welfare of the son.[39] But Hyde, whose initial courtesy quickly degenerates into contempt for Utterson, and who 'snarled aloud into a savage laugh' at the lawyer, refuses that help.[40] Other examples of Hyde's assault on paternal figures are the murder of Carew, the destruction of the portrait of Jekyll's father and the instigating of Jekyll's suicide; he furthermore exacts various destructive antics such as writing blasphemous lines in Jekyll's handwriting in the doctor's devotional texts as well as burning his letters.[41] Hyde constantly threatens to destroy Jekyll's text, so that in his final statement the doctor warns: 'Should the throes of change take me in the act of writing it, Hyde will tear it to pieces'.[42]

The disruptive nature of Hyde's effect on the professional community embodied by this circle of patriarchal figures is found as well in Hyde's encouragement in both Enfield and Utterson of unsettling imaginative speculation, an instigation of deviancy from Victorian propriety by inciting the two men to envision depravity that was typically extraneous of their class.[43] These creative conjectures are particularly encouraged in Utterson. The lawyer, whose imagination 'was engaged, or rather enslaved' with the idea of Hyde, is compelled by an arguably inordinate interest in Hyde, so that he transcends his role as lawyer and assumes a fatherly capacity instead that is comparable to Jekyll's 'more than a father's interest'.[44] This preoccupation, I argue, stems from Utterson's lack of an actual family, a lack whose need is projected onto the Jekyll/Hyde conundrum. If Utterson is overly concerned with protecting Jekyll, he is obsessed with Hyde. Hyde's exposure of Lanyon to 'a new province of knowledge' leaves the doctor's psyche 'shaken to its roots'.[45] With Jekyll, Hyde initially seems to offer the opportunity of indulgence devoid of consequence or guilt. This malignant influence, of course, ultimately offers Jekyll no recourse but self-destruction. The self-orphaned Hyde, in effect, partially dismantles the society into which he refuses to assimilate, in part by denying and even sabotaging emblems of familial belonging, and by provoking the moral dilemmas of society's patriarchal exemplars. Utterson and his similars, in their professions and in their repressive austerity, are the embodiment of acceptability and are emblematic of all against which Hyde rebels. Victorian professionals all, they stand for societal order and moral responsibility.[46] Hyde, however, through his pursuit of the orphanic state, intentionally exiles himself from the class of Victorian professionals that Utterson, Enfield and Lanyon betoken, and possesses the same rebellious propensity and intention to disrupt that Victorian culture as is demonstrated by Wells's Griffin.[47]

The Invisible Man: need and madness of the self-orphaned

Wells employs conventions generally associated with orphanhood to depict Griffin's condition, though with a somewhat inverted effect.[48] Certainly on numerous levels Griffin appears predisposed to a certain extent of exile. His ostracism seems foregrounded and complemented by his physical attributes; although albinism does not necessitate expulsion from society, his 'pink and white face and red eyes' naturally delineate him from others, while his invisibility distinguishes him from normative representations and assures that he is overlooked and neglected.[49] If perhaps his madness is initiated by the chemicals applied during his experiment, the orphan state Griffin acquires for himself contributes to his insanity and ultimately results in his demise. His description of the deficiency of his predicament is reminiscent of typical early to mid-Victorian portrayals of forsaken and destitute orphans. He relates to Kemp that he had 'no refuge, no appliances, no human being in the world in whom I could confide' and that 'the rows of London houses stood latched, barred, and bolted impregnably'.[50] The same sense of abandonment and deprivation that characterizes orphanhood is a hazard that attends the self-imposed exile that Griffin generates. However, although the orphanic state usually elicits sympathy, Griffin's wickedness deflects any pathos his condition might ordinarily entreat. When Griffin endeavours to exact his self-proclaimed reign of terror, he ostracizes himself, eventuates his criminal status and forgoes any appeals for sympathy that might usually be warranted for an orphan. His behaviour not only sets him apart from the Iping community, it bears disrespect for the mores of the society against which he will soon wage his private war; for example, in addition to his choice of 'the loneliest paths and the most over-shadowed by trees and banks', he 'indeed made no difference between Sunday and the irreligious days'.[51] Furthermore, while involvement in cultural observances or ceremonies may appeal to the typical orphan form for whom such formalities may offer a sense of inclusion, even Griffin's father's funeral holds no interest for him.[52] He bemoans 'the squalid respectability, the sordid commercialism of the place' and even claims that the funeral 'was not really my affair'.[53] What Griffin refers to as the 'current cant' of propriety necessitates his attendance at the burial of his father and epitomizes the societal construct from which he distances himself and against which he schemes, much in the manner that Hyde violates familial and societal mores in the service of his own intentions.[54] Furthermore, any confidence he seeks in another human being, as is evidenced in his conscription of Marvel and his attempted partnership with Kemp, is less a pursuit of companionship to reconcile orphanic seclusion and more the intended exploitation of another for the perpetuation of his anarchic plots.

Like Hyde, Griffin's endeavour is to actually contrive his own orphanhood. This not only involves the act of patricide, betraying the reliance and confidence implicit to family association, but also a radical disengaging from society and the premeditated disordering of that society. In essence, Griffin's scheme is contingent on an intentional abandonment of and even hostility towards the very institutions to which typical orphan figures usually gravitate in an effort to remedy their predicament.

Griffin steals from his father, causing a severance in family bonds, actually bringing about the very condition from which orphans normally attempt to extract themselves. Moreover, he retains an absolute moral detachment and disengagement from sentimentality not only in regard to the theft of his father's money, but to his father's subsequent suicide and funeral. He claims, for instance, that he 'did not feel a bit sorry for my father' and regards him merely as 'the victim of his own foolish sentimentality'.[55] So removed is Griffin from incidences unrelated to his own particular pursuits that he not only causes the death of his father, but rejects the guilt and responsibility associated with the act of patricide.

He admits that as he buried his father his mind 'was still on this research' and, as a consequence, 'did not lift a finger to save his character'.[56] Following the funeral, which he describes as being 'like a dream', Griffin returns to his room, which he states was as 'the recovery of reality. There [amongst his experiments] were the things I knew and loved.'[57] Like Hyde, whose amassing of domestic material items assists him in the construction of his refuge of seclusion, Griffin attempts a virtual implosion into self. Unlike ordinary orphan forms, whose primary impulse is to belong and through belonging to exact an identity, Griffin fabricates his own reality. This is a reality posited on 'the passion of discovery that had enabled me to compass even the downfall of my father's grey hairs', and within which, like

Hyde, he constructs his own identity extraneous of family or society, actually renaming himself 'Invisible Man the First'.[58] To some extent, this insistence on imposing some sort of order onto his existence, however perverse, actually serves as an ironic admission of the innate necessity of belonging to a social construction, a need that defines the orphan.

The assaults that Griffin perpetuates on Iping, that rural entity emblematic of what he considers the limitations and restrictions of the existing social order, frequently involve the disturbance or even destruction of domestic spaces. Like Hyde's, Griffin's aggression is often directed at the place that houses all for which the family ideal stands. He riots in the Coach and Horses, frightening and repulsing the Halls; he smashes the windows of the inn, thrusts a streetlamp through Mrs Gribble's parlour window, and breaks the windows of Kemp's house; he burglarizes the home of Revd Bunting; he insinuates himself into the home of the shopkeeper at Drury Lane, interrupting the owner's meal, pestering him with haunting, unexplained sounds and eventually rendering him unconscious and bound. At Omnium's, he 'had to tear down wrappings and ransack a number of boxes and drawers' to access the lambswool pants and vests he seeks.[59]

Accompanying and contradicting this predilection for dismantling emblems of domesticity, however, is Griffin's obvious need for the comforts they offer. Thus, when the self-orphaned insurgent finds himself in Omnium's, he proceeds 'to rob the place for food and clothing', and to 'prowl through it and examine its resources, perhaps even to sleep on some of the bedding' in an attempt to compensate for the condition into which he has cast himself.[60] In the little shop in Drury Lane he dons 'a wig, mask, spectacles, and costume', making of himself 'a swathed and bandaged *caricature* of a man', as though in imitation of the normalcy he has abandoned and against which he has rebelled.[61] His scheme of isolation, then, is confounded by a need of the very social structure he seeks to ruin. In Omnium's, he establishes a mock domestic setting, consuming food and drinking coffee and wine and resting on quilts. Tellingly, it is when Griffin is situated in these counterfeit lodgings and assumes his disguise that he 'began to feel a human being again'.[62] And herein lies his predicament; in his created severance from family and society, he becomes vulnerable to the cold, hunger and isolation typical of the orphan state, and which those very institutions keep at bay.

The scene in Omnium's perhaps most clearly exposes the intrinsic necessity of the orphan for reconciliation and alleviation of his or her dilemma, and lays bare the extreme desperation of the situation Griffin has made for himself. It is a desperation that is marked by a moral and psychic corrosion, a decline that seems a consequence of his severance from filial duty and his relinquishment of communal ties, that is, of his contrived orphanhood.[63] The more strenuously he exacts his orphanic state, the more despondent and volatile he becomes. Certainly, what begins as a kind of experiment gone awry degenerates into homicide and attempted anarchy; Griffin does undergo an incremental decline that begins with a betrayal of his chosen profession by a pursuit of power instead of knowledge, then leads to a rampage that is more slapstick than intimidation, but descends into an abject endeavour to stay alive and exact revenge, and ends in murder and insanity.[64]

Indeed, there is a gradual increase in the madness and violence that attend Griffin's actions. His immediate reaction to his new-found power of invisibility is 'a wild impulse to jest, to startle people, to clap men on the back, fling people's straw hats astray, and generally revel in my extraordinary advantage'.[65] But this initial notion of almost comical shenanigans develops into the attempted debilitization of the town, a threat to societal balance and a challenging of human dignity. While the application of substances that results in his invisibility induces his mental deterioration, it is obvious that his insanity is exacerbated by the increasing anxiety generated by his self-induced orphanic circumstances. In essence, Griffin causes the communal aspect of Iping, so effectively demonstrated in the earlier Whitsuntide celebrations, to disintegrate into fearful isolation. Indeed, eventually '[e]verywhere there is a sound of closing shutters and shoving bolts, and the only visible humanity is an occasional flitting eye under a raised eyebrow in the corner of a window pane'.[66] Finally, declaring 'The Terror', he attempts the establishment of a seclusion-based order of his own, a kind of broad imposition of his own orphanic state on to Iping in a way that attempts to effect the town's isolation, the unmaking of its unity, and an abstraction of its communal aspects in a way comparable to Hyde's dismantling of mock-familial ties and the disruptive atrocities of Helen Vaughn.

The Great God Pan: metaphysical severance and the aberrant orphan

Helen, the mysterious and profane entity of Machen's novella, like Hyde and Griffin, can be classified as a violative and sinistrous orphan whose ambivalence towards incorporation into society is accompanied by a fiendish programme of subversion and even death. Similar to Hyde and Griffin, Helen emerges from the Faustian endeavour to separate that which should remain intact; while Hyde is begat by Jekyll's attempt to disengage his virtuous and unrighteous personalities, and Griffin severs notions of visibility and physical presence, Helen is the by-product of the parting of the physical and the spiritual.

Reading Helen's orphanhood is largely complemented by a consideration of Machen's understanding of the physical and spiritual realms, both of which he saw not only as existing simultaneously, but as being intrinsically united.[67] An Anglican clergyman, he was theologically and morally repulsed by modernism's tendency to emphasize the material over the spiritual.[68] In his introduction to *The Great God Pan,* he writes that he 'was not even a small part, but no part at all' of the 1890s and its attendant concerns.[69] However, I believe this to be demonstrably false, as his vehement and consistent opposition to the advent of modernism and his very conscious activism against its propositions are obvious.[70] He came of age during a period that experimented with sexuality, the occult, spiritualism and inquiry into other non-conventional pursuits, a time that pitted scientism against humanism, the 'good mystic' against the 'evil materialist', and that addressed the disquieting notion of the uncontrollable body and the irrational beast within it.[71]

Machen's outlook was largely determined by his Anglo-Catholicism, which views man as sacramental, that is, possessing both spiritual and physical natures that function not separately, but in union with one another. It is important in understanding Machen to consider the theological system that encouraged Charles Kingsley, who was also a clergyman, to paint portraits of himself and his wife in the marital act while upon a cross. Far from the scandal such an artistic statement may initially seem to foment, it is actually theologically consistent with Church teaching, particularly in its understanding of the Incarnation and Christ's relationship with the Church: God's entering into the physical world as the fully God, fully man Jesus Christ exemplifies the union of the spiritual and corporeal realms, the standard for the sacramentality Machen would have recognized in humanity; furthermore, the self-giving union of man and woman in marriage, particularly within the context of their sexuality, is emblematic of Christ's union with His own bride, the Church, for whom He fully gives himself at the crucifixion.[72] Kingsley's depictions of himself and his wife, therefore, are merely graphic statements that demonstrate a clear Christian theological understanding of human sexuality, and that accentuate the equal importance of both physicality and spirituality. For Machen, the severance of the two phenomena, which he regarded as naturally coexisting and united, was done at great peril; thus, his marked disparagement over materialism's exclusive emphasis on the physical and its virtual dismissal of the spiritual. In regard to this segregation, he articulates in his 1922 work, *The Secret Glory*, that

> our great loss is that we separate what is one and make it two; and then, having done so, we make less the real into the more real, as if we thought the glass made to hold the wine more important than the wine it holds.[73]

Nash states that Machen 'seeks a reconciliation of natural and supernatural', and that the author attempts 'to construct a bridge connecting the opposing angry cliffs'.[74] But this image is a bit misleading; for Machen, the two are not necessarily contradictory but, rather, complementary. His position is not one that minimizes the physical; nor does it solely exalt the spiritual. Sacramentality necessitates the union of the supernal with a corporality that has been redeemed by God's entrance into human existence in the person of Jesus Christ, whose crucifixion, death and resurrection reconciles the fallen cosmos with God the Father. Rather than irreconcilable opposites, material and spiritual worlds are united realities operating synchronously, the physical representative of spiritual truth, the spiritual infusing purpose and meaning into the physical. Church teaching regards human sexuality as an illustration of this harmony. Therefore, Machen argues, when sexuality is dissociated from the context for which it was created, that is, then its physical and spiritual aspects are separated, things begin to go awry.

With these factors in mind, we may effectively approach Helen's orphanhood as a consequence of such a division, and a condition that has ramifications that exceed the mere questioning of class, identity or origin to which earlier manifestations of the orphan pertained. Her orphan state derives from the death of her mother, Mary, and the absence of her father, Pan.[75] While Mary, a human being and orphan herself, represents Helen's corporeal aspect, Pan, an unnatural half-human from another dimension, images the unearthly. Unlike the instances of other, typical orphans, whose parents' absence or death permits the potential for social exile, possible moral dilemmas, or questions of totality, Helen's lack of parental figures bears shocking supernatural consequences and results in aberration, for, while a physical being, the apathetic, exploitive, even evil Helen seems devoid of a soul and is, therefore, a purely physical creature.[76] This condition predisposes her to complicity in the unwholesome sexual activity with which the figure of Pan is associated and with which she brings her victims to ruin. With her sensuality disconnected from the sanctity so crucial to Machen in regard to sexuality, Helen is the embodiment of the deviant, depraved sexuality he saw as symptomatic of scientism, naturalism and other aspects of modernism whose inherent flaw was the loss of meaning due to dismissal of the spiritual. In *The Great God Pan*, the severance and absence of the orphan's parents represent the division of that which should inherently be united, while the orphan herself represents the malevolent consequence of such a rupture in the natural order.[77] The circumstances of Helen's orphanhood, the death of her mother and the absence of her father, and the severance of the physical and spiritual their nonexistence infers seem to determine Helen's particular method of anarchism. The division and disappearance of the parental units, in previous cases a precursor to orphanhood, here takes on metaphysical dimensions and yields an unnatural, demotic entity.

Like Hyde and Griffin, Helen seeks the ruin of her society. The harm she causes is twofold, in her method of wreaking havoc and in her choice of victims. For Machen, one of the most heinous acts against the natural order was deviant sexuality, that is, sexuality dislocated from the unifying and potentially procreative marital context for which it was created.[78] Helen's 'ineffable, inpalpable' atrocities with her doomed suitors are of such an abnormal sort that their practice encourages her victims to self-destruction. Though the text is never explicit concerning the specifics of these atrocities, that they are salacious seems apparent.[79] Hurley states they are 'clearly sexual in nature'; Joshi calls the book a 'frenzied expression of horror over illicit sex'; even the back cover of the Creation Classics edition labels it an 'incoherent nightmare of sex'.[80] Referring to Machen's works in general, J. Vernon Shea states they are 'full of repressed sexuality' and that they 'hint at sexual orgies of which Machen dared not write'.[81] Helen's dislocation of one of the primary aspects of marriage, itself the fundamental cornerstone of any society, was to Machen not merely a question of taste or a cultural problem, but an action the ramifications of which were not only spiritually wounding to the individual, but threatening to the balance of the universe.[82] Helen's perpetrations are not merely a matter of questionable taste, but bear crucial repercussions on several cosmological levels. Machen's cautionary exhortation against illicit sexual activity is an indictment of the spiritless materialism he saw as equally damaging.

Helen notably makes sport of Victorian professionals, men of high social standing, economic security and intellectual capacity, and presumably upstanding moral character. But her targeting this class of supposed role models of success, capability and assumed virtue, her seduction of them and her eventual driving them to suicide undermines Victorian society by challenging notions of the propriety and virtue implied by their station. The implications of such assaults are similar to those of Hyde's killing of Carew and Griffin's murder of Wicksteed, the repercussions of which extend into the fabric of society itself. Griffin's recommendation to Kemp that in order to initiate control of Iping they must execute several 'judicious slayings' operates on the same level as Hyde's killing and Helen's perversity. His is not the notion of random killings, but the clinical, deliberate assassination of socially esteemed and influential persons whose deaths would more greatly impact the social construction of the town.[83] But Helen not only brings about the death of these exemplars of Victorian society, she questions their very morality, drawing them into her perverse escapades and insinuating a latent proclivity to transgression within the society she seeks to corrupt.

Akin to the proceedings of *Dr Jekyll and M. Hyde* and *The Invisible Man*, *The Great God Pan* is primarily a narrative of disrupted domestic spaces. Again we are presented with an orphan figure whose intention is the act of impairing in some manner the normative functions of her surroundings through the disturbance of the architectural space most closely associated with the family.[84] Like the incidences of Stevenson's and Wells's novels, those of Machen's occur within or near houses. The narrative begins in Dr Raymond's home, site of the unholy operation whereby Mary is impregnated with Helen; Herbert, rendered destitute by his unfortunate marriage to Helen, sells 'the dear old house' of his upbringing, tellingly forfeiting the site of his previous position, presumed innocence, and familial connection.[85] 'Blank' is killed at the Herbert's doorstep; Mr Collier-Stuart, Herries and Lord Argentine hang themselves in their very bedrooms; Lord Swanleigh hangs himself on a peg in his dressing room; and Cranshaw commits suicide in his garden. Each incident occurs within intimate, personal areas traditionally associated with tranquility and safety. In addition, equally unsettling is Helen's ability easily to assimilate into society in order to provoke its decay from within. Austin speaks of her 'in the ordinary adventure of London society, talking and laughing, and sipping her coffee in a common-place drawing-room with common-place people'.[86] Unlike the more unnerving Hyde or the hostile Griffin, whose assaults on their communities are of a violent, hit-and-run variety, Helen is able subtly to ingratiate herself into the culture and instigate its demise within its very domestic centres. The ease with which she does so and with which she performs her misdeeds makes their perpetuation all the more suggestive of the community's vulnerability to seduction and ruin and, on a greater level, bears implications of fin-de-siècle Victorian England's vulnerability to the modernity to which they allude.

One of the primary aspects of the orphan is his or her eluding categorization. In earlier manifestations this evasion typically pertained to class association or questions of origin, alluding to middle-class anxieties concerning the upward mobility of the lower classes as well as their own potential economic decline. But the fin-de-siècle orphan's circumvention of classification often involves other troubling, even monstrous implications pertaining instead to moral and physical degeneration. The previous chapter's treatment of Renfield demonstrated the unhinged, unpredictable variances in personality and psychic constitution that proved so baffling to John Seward's clinical inquiries and that epitomized the orphanic condition. The nihilistic and destructive orphan types with which this present chapter is concerned, however, intensify concepts of exile, difference and dissociation by physically exhibiting their orphan conditions in disquieting and unnatural corporeal displays. Edward Hyde, for instance, of whom perceptions 'differed widely', furthers notions of orphans' peculiar undifferentiated character with an amorphous physical appearance specifics of which seem to vary according to the witness.[87] An enigma to which only inexact yet disturbing descriptions are attached, Hyde is said to convey 'an impression of deformity without any namable malformation'.[88] The irresolution that typifies the orphan is represented by irregularities of somatic representation.

Griffin's appearance is determined by a harlequinesque, even nightmarish assemblage of bandages, side-lighted spectacles, gloves, coat, hat, wig and mask in order to appear 'a muffled but acceptable figure'; by the narrative's end, when Griffin finally materializes, Wells's description is a disturbing piecemeal depiction of physical components disjointed from their normal context, with the appearance of 'clouded and opaque' appendages, 'a hazy grey sketch of a limb', the 'faint fogginess' of a body undergoing 'that strange change . . . like the spreading of a poison' and culminating in merely 'the dim outline of his drawn and battered features'.[89] Appropriately, we are never afforded a glimpse of Griffin in a 'normal' state. Even with the dispersion of his invisibility and his emergence into a visible condition, he remains a physical tableau of orphanhood's crises of disunity and irresolution.

Helen, too, a 'most wonderful and strange beauty', evokes a similar apprehension, presenting an indefinite physical appearance that provokes unease in the observer, something unsettling that cannot be articulated.[90] She effects a seeming foreignness that avoids specificity, a facet that in the middle-class reader would have been associated with the agitation of difference. Rumoured to be from South America and 'looking as if she came from another country', she is 'pale, clear olive, and her features were strongly marked, and of a somewhat foreign character'.[91] But her difference exceeds mere exoticism and is akin to the unnamable 'imprint of deformity and decay' that characterizes Hyde.[92] Echoing the vague responses of those who have encountered Jekyll's creation, Austin states that she 'would be called handsome . . . yet there is something about her face which I did not like'; witnesses at the police court label her 'at once the most beautiful woman and the most repulsive they had ever set eyes on'.[93] Even her name cannot be properly determined. Whether referred to as Helen Vaughn 'of earlier adventures', Mrs Herbert of Paul Street, or Mrs Beaumont of 'the house of flowers', like other orphan figures such as Renfield, Mowgli and Peter Pan, whom this book examines, Helen is known by a number of appellations underscoring notions of ambivalence attending orphanhood.[94]

Helen's bodily metamorphosis and dissolution at the novella's end are nearly the opposite of Griffin's gradual and hauntingly fragmentary reappearance, but it accomplishes a similar effect, namely a horrific manifestation of the orphanic condition. Her 'outward form changed' and her body 'began to melt and dissolve' and 'waver from sex to sex, dividing itself from itself, and then again reunited'; she becomes a 'form, shaped in dimness' and 'a horrible and unspeakable shape, neither man nor beast'.[95] In addition to her inferences of racial difference, these final transformations simultaneously image orphanic incertitude while addressing various other anxieties of the century's end. Her trans-species, trans-gender, trans-substance oscillation, a 'changing and melting . . . from woman to man, from beast to worse than beast' adumbrates orphanhood's irresolution while alluding to fin-de-siècle disconcertion in regard to sexual ambiguity and degeneration both moral and physical.[96]

Conclusion: the erasure of the rebel

By the completion of their narratives, orphan characters in earlier fiction typically accomplish a greater degree of self-awareness, identity and totality, essentially discerning an improved existence, a proper presence in society. The rebellious orphan types that have been the focus of this chapter, by contrast, actually seem incrementally to decrease in societal presence as their respective narratives progress. By the end of *Dr Jekyll and Mr Hyde*, Hyde is confined to the claustrophobic cabinet and is ultimately destroyed; indeed, with the exception of his evident need for what the London underworld may offer one of questionable moral predilections, Hyde's ultimate intention seems to be to isolate himself to the point of virtual societal absence. Unlike previous orphan figures that travail to acquire some level of selfhood defined by inclusion within a family or social system, Hyde, for all his indeterminable physical composition, is notably whole, being 'more express and single' than Jekyll, and 'pure evil' on his own accord.[97] In essence, he seems to need no one at all. Thus perhaps one of the most disquieting aspects of Hyde is his ability, unaided, to achieve the kind of sense of self that usually eludes the orphan without the stabilizing context of familial inclusion.

Griffin's adventures differ from Hyde's in that he contrives a literal disappearance, but one that does not affect his physical presence. It is the undeniable reality, however, that invisibility has no effect on his physical needs that proves the detriment of the orphanic state Griffin concocts for himself. That, in addition to the unsuccessful attempt to reconcile that state with a mock normality, a contrived 'presence', the mere appearance of the kind of identity which he finds cannot be effectively simulated, contributes to the madness that results in his beating and death.

Helen, meanwhile, appears on the surface not to suffer from the state of poverty and exclusion that typically plagues the orphan; in fact, she seems to have no difficulty at all inserting herself into society. The difference with Helen, however, is that her intention is not to become part of that culture to reconcile the deficiencies normally inherent in orphanhood. Rather, it is to achieve intimacy with its inhabitants in order to bring them to ruin. Interestingly, at the narrative's end, this figure, perhaps as 'express and single' or 'pure evil' as Hyde, loses any identity she may have claimed, literally disintegrating into nothingness.

In each of these cases of a defiant and destructive orphan figure there is the remarkable disregard for familial standards, an open hostility towards society, and the specific targeting of emblems of Victorian culture. Tellingly, each of these orphans is undeniably done away with by narrative's end. It is as though these agents of perversity and nonconformance cannot be suffered to go their own dark ways.[98] Each one is eventually engaged with a form of societal order against which he or she has contested. Hyde's destruction is brought about by Jekyll's moral revelations, the doctor's deferment to both the law embodied by Utterson and the Law that cannot abide Hyde's presence. Griffin is brought to justice by a community whose disunity he pursued but whose collective fear of him restores concord through the application of the law he challenged. When confronted with the inevitability of her having to answer to the establishment she has sought to undo, Helen opts for self-destruction. Thus, the rebellious orphan form acquires a kind of scapegoat status, resonating with the anxieties particular to the century's end, being arrested and restricted by and finally subjected to the order against which they have schemed, and ultimately being exorcised with the same kind of violence with which they waged war on the traditional world.

4
The Orphaning Island

'It's an island where I live. So far as I know it hasn't got a name.'

H. G. Wells, *The Island of Dr Moreau*

The island narrative of the fin de siècle reflects the same generational anxieties prevalent in other genres of the period. The manner in which the late Victorian age perceived itself as severed from the traditions of the past, witnessing the erosion of fundamental social and moral concepts and often reluctantly engaging with the implications of the modernity towards which it hastened, emerge in a number of ways, not the least of which is within the forms of unalleviated orphanhood depicted in the period's island fiction.

Offering a space as detached from normative paradigms, categories and identifiers as orphanhood itself, the island naturally relegates the castaway to an orphanic condition. But, while earlier narratives typically present castaways who are paragons of artifice, facility and versatility, who are at times even capable of converting the island to a 'civilized' space, and who essentially subordinate and even rectify the orphan state imposed upon them, late-century island tales offer notably fallible and inept figures unable to execute the same kind of recuperative dominion and mastery of that state and are frequently psychically crippled by it. Likewise, in late-century island literature the notion of the imperial subsuming of the island is cast into doubt. Narratives of the New Imperialism depicted the achievements of masculine colonists successfully establishing a British presence in continental areas like Africa and the India. Island literature of the same period, however, is fraught with incredulity and portrays the island as an impermanent site of habitation, an ultimately unobtainable place. Against the remoulding of the island accomplished by Robinson Crusoe or the Swiss Family Robinson are the abandoned island of *Treasure Island,* the burnt compound and forsaken Beast-folk enclave of *The Island of Dr Moreau* and the desolate and formidable Erraid of *Kidnapped.* And, while those earlier stout-hearted protagonists often serve to perpetuate patriarchal constructions of empire and family solidarity, fin-de-siècle island narratives are marked by irresolute, immoral or even monstrous father figures who do not relieve, but in fact sustain, a telling and disquieting orphanhood.

Separated from normative societal structures, often lacking the specificity of a name or ownership, and a potentially metamorphic space in the hands of those who do claim it, the island is the topographical orphan space par excellence. In this chapter I will examine how treatments of that space differ during the fin de siècle from those of earlier literary periods.[1] I will begin by discussing various perceptions of the island, which I regard as associated with its intrinsic orphan quality, namely, its severance from qualifying social constructs. Next, I will examine the orphaning condition the island effects on the adventurer, the castaway, the marooned, who, intentionally or otherwise, finds himself its inhabitant.[2] I will focus particularly on the island's necessitating characteristics of traditional notions of orphanhood, such as the severance from society, the loss of the distinctive qualities and accoutrements of 'civilization', and in general the deprivation of identifying essentials. Finally, in keeping with this book's simultaneous concern with family issues in relation to orphan forms, I will take a look at the interesting manner in which late-century island fiction often occasions father figures that are chaotic and fragmentary failures who serve to perpetuate orphanhood which they are incapable or unwilling to alleviate.

The island: an orphan space

I would like first to address some of the common perceptions of the island, as doing so will convey the difference that so characterizes this space from others and that contributes to its position as an orphanic entity. On the literal level, an island is a landmass separated from the mainland. Perceptions of the physicality of the island, particularly in contrast to the turmoil implied by the sea encompassing it, tend to render it as a geographical space of stability. The island, like the ship, is 'differentiated from the sea' and has been equated with symbolism of the mountain in that both express notions of 'stability, superiority, and refuge from prevailing mediocrity [associated with the sea]'.[3] On a more metaphysical level is the Hindu belief that the island is in opposition to the sea, an area 'where the forces of "immense logic" of the ocean are distilled'.[4] Contrasted with the chaos and inferiority of the sea, the island may serve as either a physical or psychological refuge from 'the menacing assault of the "sea" of the unconscious'.[5] Despite these implications of fixity, however, my focus will be on the island as a place not of stasis, but of immense potential change. The inhabitant of the island chances formidable alterations in the societal-self as well as his psychological state. These latent hazards emerge from the physical separation that characterizes the island and as such naturally effects notions of detachment, severance, independence and isolation.

The island proposes the notion of a 'closed world'.[6] Surely due to the implication of insularity conveyed by its physical detachment, the island is often associated with otherworldliness and the supernatural. It was, for instance, often associated in the mind of ancient man with the afterlife. The poetic way in which the ancients wrote of islands as 'golden clouds floating on an azure ocean' or 'precious stones set in a silver sea' underscores their mysterious and unearthly quality; in addition, they tended to refer to islands as 'fortunate' or 'blessed', so that to them most all islands were idealized into the Gathering-Place of Souls.[7] Numerous islands have been historically known for enchantment or magical attributes that distinguish them, such as the Irish Tir Na n'Og, where illness does not exist, or Hy-brazil, which is said to be visible only once every seven years; after receiving his mortal wound, King Arthur is said to have been ferried west to Avalon, the isle of the fairy fruit, to be healed; and the Irish of the Middle Ages accounted the voyages of Brendan and a group of monks to various mystical islands, such as the 'Island of the Silent Brotherhood', where God fed its inhabitants with white bread.[8] Other fabulous islands include the Islands of the Gorgons; Autilia, the Island of the Amazons; the Island of Perdita, or Lost Island; and Atlantis. Other mysterious islands include Inishbofin, which cannot be found again; islands that rise and sink at will or those inhabited by demons or sorcerers; and others like Bermuda, or the Isle of Devils, known for their particular association with shipwreck and disappearance.[9]

Others see in the island an image of post-lapsarian loss. In relation to its topographical features, the island alludes to paradisiac isles lost to man and to which he aspires to return through the medium of legends and folktales; furthermore, the sense of loss associated with the paradise of the Blessed Isle is connected with concepts of abandonment and failure regarded by modern existentialism as a fundamental characteristic of humanity.[10] Indeed, while the ancients regarded the island as a paradise, a topological heaven, a realm otherwise unattainable in this life, or as an enigmatic or ethereal place, more modern treatments, which this chapter will consider, portray the island as the locus of a personal, individual, physical and often psychological trauma and metamorphosis.

Perhaps in keeping with notions of the island as a place connected with mystery and, as I will examine below, with loss of identity, is the convention of the uncertainty of the island's location, so that it is not only physically separate from the more normative, and importantly identifying, mainland, but, like the classless and unidentifiable orphan, it is also characterized by ambiguity. Thus, for example, reference to Moreau's island as 'precisely nowhere'.[11] Indeed, Prendick's nephew Charles merely remarks that his uncle 'passed out of human knowledge about latitude 5 degrees S. and longitude 105 degrees E., and reappeared in the same part of the ocean after a space of eleven months'.[12] The island in *Treasure Island* is merely a location where treasure is hidden, the specificity of which remains unknown.[13] In introducing his narrative, Jim Hawkins states he will tell all 'but the bearings of the island'.[14] Peter Pan's Neverland is vaguely positioned '[s]econd to the right', but even birds 'carrying maps . . . could not have sighted it with these instructions'.[15] The exact location of the island in *Lord of the Flies* is indefinite, seeming to lie somewhere in the Indian or Pacific Ocean.[16]

Contingent on this notion of disjunction and physical distance from society, the island is also at times associated with flight, particularly in regard to the fulfilment of escape fantasies. The tropic island, for instance, can serve as 'a symbol of desire' deriving from its divergence from the 'normative, familiar island of Britain itself'.[17] Focusing on the island's potential for departure from conventionality, Weinbaum addresses what she labels the 'seduction' of visitors to tourist islands, which she states reflects needs that have emerged from the 'repressive control of sensuality' resulting from the depersonalization of industrial societies in the form of the manipulation of reproduction and the inhibition of sexual desires; she furthermore states that the tropics provide 'a non-mechanized and non-rationalized identity' that may be discerned within a 'primitive, matriarchal, pre-colonial, untouched haven and space'.[18] Her discussion underscores the concept of the island as a place either unencumbered or unregulated by the temperance of societal restrictions. As we shall see, earlier forms of the island fantasy genre present ambitious protagonists who are notably eager to encounter such propositions of adventure, possibility, even freedom, while later narratives instead present the island as a site of nervousness, chaos, and fear.

All of which is to say that the island is a place that has acquired various attributes that are reliant on its state of separation. Its capacity as a space set apart from the conformity of society and an area outside the customary boundaries of ordinance and moderation emphasize the island's ability to permit, perhaps even encourage, detachment from certain associations and mores of one's previous reality. It is within this state of disjunction and disorder that the island, often an indistinct, unnamed, imprecise *terra nullius*, is akin to the orphan condition, which is characterized by existence beyond social inclusion, identity and legitimacy.

I would be remiss not to acknowledge briefly the intermediary function of the sea, that expanse of nothingness and potential, the embodiment of chaos to the ancients and to modern man as well, that divorces the island from the mainland.[19] For it is the sea, Arnold's 'unplumb'd salt, estranging sea', which engenders the orphanic state of the island that so contrasts with the context of belonging and identity implied by the continent.[20] Nathalie Jaeck describes the sea as being 'away from domestic spheres and naturalist cities, a distinctive element of exoticism and deterritorialization', and states that it is characterized by 'infinity, multiplicity, indeterminacy, horizontality, "neutrality"'.[21] As the medium between the association and belonging of the mainland and the exile and anonymity of the island, the sea occasions a region between being and non-being, coherence and uncertainty, inclusion and orphanhood.[22]

The island narrative genre

I want to discuss the island narrative genre with three main intentions. First, I wish to show the consistent manner by which the island relegates the castaway to an orphanic condition, using examples from various texts to demonstrate how authors employ conventions associated with orphanhood to depict their castaways. Secondly, I want to demonstrate the notable tendency in the late nineteenth century to set up the castaway as a largely incompetent and often irreparably traumatized failure, and its attempt to de-romanticize the island narrative in general. Thirdly, I want to make particular note of the remarkable manner in which the island narrative appropriates early and middle nineteenth-century concerns with, as well as late nineteenth-century scepticism of, the family ideal.

The island narrative genre emerged from early fifteenth- and sixteenth-century fantasies, such as Renaissance travellers' tales, or utopian visions like Thomas Moore's *Utopia* (1516) and Shakespeare's *The Tempest* (1610–11). It developed into the realist island tales of the eighteenth century, such as Daniel Defoe's *Robinson Crusoe* (1719) and Jonathan Swift's *Gulliver's Travels* (1726).[23] The early and middle nineteenth century saw the genre addressing concerns of empire, jingoism and the significance of biological or provisional family structures. Such titles include Johann David Wyss's *Swiss Family Robinson* (1812), Captain Marryat's *Masterman Ready* (1841), R. M. Ballantyne's *The Coral Island* (1857) and Jules Verne's *Mysterious Island* (1874). Late nineteenth-century narratives, such as Robert Louis Stevenson's *Treasure Island* (1883), render the island a site of panic and disorder, or of theoretical evolutionary conflicts like those in H. G. Wells's *The Island of Dr Moreau* (1896).[24] And, although there are various genres of island and maritime literature, my primary focus is on what became known as the Robinsonade tradition, which derives its name from Defoe's eponymous protagonist, and its relation to the orphan condition.

Typically, the Robinsonade initiates with a person, usually a single male, although later a group or family, who is cast away, made to negotiate the hazards of island existence. One hallmark of such a narrative is the adventure interrupted by a period of island exile and a return to the place of origin.[25] The story involves the protagonist's severance from a typically unsatisfactory existence and his eventual return to an improved reality after a period of transition and discovery upon the island. *Robinson Crusoe*, for instance, employs the theme of conversion wherein its protagonist provides an allegory of the prodigal son who roams only to return reformed.[26] The changeableness intrinsic to the Robinsonade plot denotes and actually hinges upon the island's potential as a transformative space.

Orphan literature typically features the convention of the orphan's undergoing a period of suffering prior to his or her salvation through either familial or monetary means. The same notion interestingly applies to the orphanic castaway. Upon his island exile, the castaway initially endures a brief interstice of desperation over his predicament, which is followed by a period of retrieving what provisions are available to him from his shipwreck.[27] It is at this point that the castaway must endeavour to comprehend and manage his newly found condition. Within this narrative moment emerges the requisite need for the castaway to subdue any inclination to alarm that might ensue from his being separated from home and thrust into an alien environment.[28] Thus, the initial panic that often overtakes the castaway gives way to the resignation that he must confront this predicament. This time of reckoning is vital to an understanding of being cast away as an orphanic state, because not only is it within this period of island exile that authors often employ certain conventions that render their protagonists as orphans, but it is here, too, wherein the orphan state actually proves penitential or purgative. While earlier narratives depict the stint of island exile often as a *positive* step in the development of the castaway, however, the island narrative of the fin de siècle marks a remarkable divergence from this convention that often renders the castaway's orphan state as permanent and unreconciled.

Irredeemable psychological orphanhood

Inevitably, the castaway must elect either to succumb to the alternate existence proposed by the island, or to attempt to establish amongst the desolation and potential hostility of the island an imitation of the domestic space of which he is presently bereft.[29] One of the hindrances against the successful fabrication of a provisional sociological construction is the persistent potential for the castaway to be altered by the island, for he is essentially thrust into an isolated context without the defining elements of culture and society.[30] The castaway's condition requires him to exist, and subsist, on nature's terms, removed as he is from his normal, civilized context. An ever-present danger here is the degenerative and atavistic potential of what I have labelled an orphanic condition, a predicament consequent of disengagement from the cultural determinants that ally one to civilization. This is the same type of transformative detachment from societal criterion that resulted in the consideration of homeless orphan 'street Arabs' of Victorian industrial cities as lesser humans.

The great potential tragedy, therefore, is for the castaway to 'go native', that is, to abandon his former civilized manner and assume an identity so closely associated with the island that he becomes 'the Wildman'.[31] That is, he acquiesces to and adopts the orphanic state as an acceptable condition. We find such a character in the maroons Ayerton of *The Mysterious Island* and Ben Gunn of *Treasure Island*.[32] Ayerton is described as having '[s]haggy hair, untrimmed beard descending to the chest, the body almost naked except a rag round the waist', nails that have grown long, skin that is 'the color of mahogany' and feet that are 'hard as if made of horn'; 'such was this miserable creature who yet had a claim to be called a man'.[33] Gunn, marooned for some three years, appears upon Jim's discovery of him a tattered amalgam of elements scarcely indicative of the seaman he once was: he is clothed 'with tatters of old ship's canvas and old seacloth' that are held together by 'a system of the most various and incongruous fastenings, brass buttons, bits of stick, and loops of tarry gaskin' and he sports 'an old brass-buckled leather belt'.[34] His flesh and lips are discoloured by the sun. Jim states: 'Of all the beggar-men that I had seen or fancied, he was the chief for raggedness.'[35] Indeed, both maroons are depicted to some extent in a manner similar to that used to describe the typical orphan waif.

By the end of the nineteenth century, however, there emerges a notable addition to the notion of the physical degeneration inherent in 'going native' in the form of such irreparable psychological damage as to haunt and alienate irretrievably the castaway even upon the return to civilization. There is, in these late nineteenth-century narratives, an internalizing of the island-imposed orphan condition so that its effect is perpetuated even upon the castaway's return home, where there proves the incapacity of reckoning with the shocking implications of the island experience. Stevenson's depiction of Gunn serves by contrast to underscore the psychic injury done to young Jim; despite his appearance of having 'gone native', the somewhat dazed Gunn is not irreparably damaged. By the narrative's end, though somewhat irresponsible having run through his thousand-pound share of the treasure in some nineteen days, he is nevertheless given a lodge to keep, regarded as a good fellow and ultimately is assimilated back into the society from which he came. He represents the redeemable castaway who successfully returns to civilization no worse for wear. Verne's Ayerton, too, is an example of one who, despite a descent into wildness that is possibly even coupled with an inherent criminality, is nevertheless successfully incorporated back into the world of men.[36]

In contrast to the basically reformed Ben Gunn, Jim proves haunted by his island experience. One critic states that by the narrative's end, Jim's 'achieved self is restored to society and the individual to the fold'.[37] However, I would argue that, although Jim is safely returned to civilization, his experience remains with him in an unshakable way. Jim states that nothing could compel him to return to 'that accursed island', and that 'the worst dreams that ever I have' are related to the haunting, repetitive and remindful voice of Silver's parrot.[38] His experience has been one of thoughtless violence, selfish cruelty, insurgency, dissention, abandonment and the threat of human failure that cannot be effaced and that recurs through the narrator's nightmares.[39] Though not debilitated, Jim is marred by his experience so that he cannot enjoy the financial rewards it bestows upon him and vows never to go on such a journey again. The effect of the island experience has insinuated itself into the lad's mind, corrupting him in a way unseen in earlier island narratives.

The Island of Dr Moreau similarly presents a character whose island experience permanently disrupts his ability to rejoin humanity. Prendick is a typical castaway, thrust into orphanic status by his circumstances. He is bereft of belonging and any identifying context: he endeavours to assimilate into Moreau's camp, only to realize that the inhumanity of the experiments taking place there are perhaps less tolerable than the proto-societal configuration contrived by the Beast-folk. Ultimately he is incapable of incorporating into either structure. His sense of morality elicits disgust in Moreau's encampment, while his intelligence and discernment effect an insurmountable psychological difference that prevents his complete immersion into the Beast-folk's ravine society. Upon the realization that he has no safe haven, 'that over all this island there was now no safe place where I could be alone and secure to rest or sleep', Prendick resolves to attempt assimilation into the tenuous social construction of the Beast-folk's territory.[40] For a period of some ten months, he undergoes what Ruddick calls 'a process of reduction', a kind of degenerative quality, so that he physically matches his environment.[41]

He regards 'some strange changes' that he undergoes: 'My clothes hung about me as yellow rags through whose rents showed the tanned skin'; his hair grows long and matted, and his eyes 'have a strange brightness, a swift alertness of movement'.[42] Like the piecemeal accoutrements characterizing Ben Gunn, such traits as skin becoming burnt by the sun, hair growing to unacceptable lengths, clothes becoming tattered or even being replaced by goatskin are typical conventions depicting the physical transformation of 'going native'.

The Wildman of earlier island narratives simply acquires a savage, uncivilized nature; he abandons, for the duration of his stint on the island, at least, the decorum and propriety of the civilized. The island-imposed degenerative condition in fin-de-siècle literature, however, is not revealed in an inability to appear civilized. Realizing the inevitable degeneration of the Beast-folk with whom he has taken his necessary refuge, for instance, Prendick eventually returns to the ruins of Moreau's enclosure, forging from its wreckage a crude pastiche of its former lodgings favoured for its relative safety, demonstrating a desire for something more human and familiar. Despite this appeal to a more 'civilized' habitation, upon being rescued, he finds himself in an irreparable state of physical and psychic exile. He determines to travel alone, 'not desiring very greatly to see men again' and 'with no desire to return to mankind'.[43] Even upon his own admission that his suspicions are most likely attributable to paranoia, he nonetheless exacts a self-imposed exile 'near the broad free land', 'withdrawn from the confusion of multitudes and cities'.[44] Denied assimilation on the island, Prendick is now devoid of even the intention of inclusion into society, 'shrink[ing] from them, from their curious glances, their inquiries and their assistance, and long[ing] to be away from them and alone'.[45] The orphanic condition into which Prendick was thrust on Moreau's island engenders a similar state that not only is no longer situational, but which is even desired.

Prendick, and Jim Hawkins to some extent, are changed by their experiences to such a degree that they can no longer believe in a civilization beneath which they perceive a kind of lurking, chaotic horror. They are regarded as peculiar or demented by the society with which they no longer feel a sense of solidarity. As the crew of the brig rescues him, Prendick must protect himself 'from the suspicion of insanity' and discern 'that solitude and danger had made me mad'.[46] The new awareness and defamiliarization of the forever-changed in such cases proves to isolate them from other men, who are incapable of perceiving reality in the same way. Prendick states that none of his fellow men possess 'the calm authority of a reasonable soul'.[47] Indeed, the degeneration of late-century island exile manifests itself in the ungovernable questioning of what civilization is and seems to be, an unnerving inquiry that prevents the resituated castaway from properly rejoining the world of the civilized. Indeed, the horrors of the new paradigm follow the fin-de-siècle castaway home. In effect, late-century island narratives present the perpetuation, on an intellectual and psychic plane, of the orphanic state of island exile that, while not rebellious or threatening as in the case of Hyde, Griffin or Helen, is similarly antisocial, derelict and orphaning.

There are of course examples from pre-fin-de-siècle maritime fiction of protagonists whose return home is troubled by the implications of their experiences, but there are notable differences that distinguish Prendick and his similars from their literary predecessors. Gulliver, for instance, though similarly shipwrecked, is actually accepted by the Lilliputians, afforded his own domestic space and even made a member of the court, and thus assimilates into the social structures of Lilliput. In Brobdingnad, he is cared for by the farmer and the farmer's daughter, as well as brought by the queen into her court. Marooned on his third adventure, he is saved by the Laputans and accepted into their society. In all three incidences, Gulliver experiences a level of inclusion that Prendick, for example, cannot in either Moreau's compound, the Beast-folk's enclave, or, ultimately, the world of man.

Gulliver's altered view of humanity at first may seem quite similar to the disillusionment and malcontent that colors both Prendick and Marlowe's final assertions. But Gulliver's disenchantment ensues from different circumstances. The fin-de-siècle castaway's crisis is the result of a perpetuated orphanic state characterized by violence, abandonment, or betrayal, an engagement with the potential descent of which man is capable and, while Gulliver does suffer from the same kind of inability properly to resituate into society, particularly insofar as a dim view of humanity in general, his diminished regard for mankind comes from his having encountered not only more developed and intelligent, but amiable, creatures, not the least of which are what he considers the more advanced, superior Houyhnhnmns. To Gulliver, these ennobled horses indicate the potential for refinement and improvement, a model to which to aspire and against which men back home may be contrasted. For Prendick and others like him, though, there is merely degeneration, devolution, a dismal treatment of Darwinian anxieties that would not have affected Swift's thought. Gulliver's overall experience of acceptance and enlightenment with various exotic social conditions and the glimpse into developmental possibilities they permit are the occasion for his post-return discontent, while the fin-de-siècle castaway's disappointment results from witnessing the decline and fall of an irredeemable mankind and their perpetuation of orphanic exile.

Capability and impotence in reckoning the orphan state

Island exile ultimately violates the stability of the protagonist's normal circumstances, the reality to which he is generally accustomed.[48] Assuming the castaway does not submit to the temptation to 'go native', this disturbance of equilibrium forces him into reparative and restorative action. The orphanic state presented in the Robinsonade is typically so dire and potentially life-threatening that it necessitates the acquisition of a discipline requisite for survival, as well as the application of ingenuity and capability that combats such a state.[49] The period of island exile is often characterized by the employment of skills and competence meant to reckon with the deficiency of shelter and food that correlates with the poverty and disparity frequently associated with orphanhood. There is a notable trend in island literature of characters whose capacity to combat the wants of the orphanic condition must be put to use.[50] Such literature praises the 'warrior-explorer-engineer-administrator-imperial paladin'.[51] This figure is notable for his courage and self-reliance, an appearance of discipline, serenity and even cheerfulness in the face of difficulty and even threats to his life.[52] In fact, one of the most noteworthy conventions of the earlier Robinsonade is the castaway as ideal Renaissance man who surmounts all odds against him through adaptability and ingenuity. The island thus serves as 'an educative impetus', a testing ground for the individual's abilities.[53] Rousseau notably used *Robinson Crusoe* as the centerpiece of his vision of education in *Emile* (1762) as an example that 'provides the most felicitous treatise on natural education', the greatest aspect of which, for him, was that it demonstrated one man's mastery of several disciplines.[54]

There is, too, an aspect of imperialism inherent in the castaway's subjugation of the island and his successful imposing a kind of imitative rendition of his homeland's conditions onto the exotic space. Following the aforementioned period wherein the castaway endures a brief spell of despair is one of monitoring and adjustment which frequently includes the assessment of the island. These 'rituals of possession' afford the castaway a notion of control.[55] This has been labeled the 'monarch-of-all-I-survey' moment, whereby the castaway first determines that he is indeed on an island, and then proceeds to establish dominion over the space.[56] In *Lord of the Flies*, the effect of a dislodged boulder crashing into the jungle below 'like a bomb' instills a sense of superiority in the young castaways that prompts

Ralph's subsequent claims, 'This belongs to us' and 'All ours'. This assertion of power, this endeavour to impose some type of order upon what would be not only alien, and alienating, but potentially chaotic, is the beginning of the castaway's trial to overcome his or her orphan condition. Such is the orienting consequence of the survey, or the making of the map, to name the unnamed, to classify that which is otherwise undetermined, to categorize the indefinite.

The surveying of the land, or the making of the map, is predicated on the notion of exploration and contributes to the achievement of the 'monarch' moment. It is necessary for the castaway to discern the parameters of his exile, to know the extent of his orphanhood upon the island. In order for the orphan to reconcile his condition, the journey of discovery requisite of all orphans must be undertaken. This convention is one that is present from the earliest orphan fiction, a pilgrimage of self-knowledge which in island literature simply acquires the context of a tropical setting. The production of an imitation of the island space in the form of a map permits that assertion of self over the island space and thus serves as the beginning of the process of managing the orphanic condition that the island imparts. The imposition of order that the survey and the map necessitate correlates to the orphan's ascertainment of identity. By contrast, the map that already exists actually serves as an initiating device of island literature that compels characters to 'rediscover' the area it represents. The whole impetus for *Treasure Island*, for instance, is the map with the 'X' that indicates the presence of treasure. The fascinating aspect of this is the orphaning effect the extant map has on those who pursue its intimations. They must abandon home and civilization, as in the case of Squire Trelawney and Dr Livesey, who detach themselves from the defining and identifying prominence of their social status in order to go on the quest for fortune.

Mastery of the island furthermore includes the endeavour to recreate a civilized space by the fabrication of a provisional domestic structure, such as an encampment, hut or treehouse, which serves to some degree as 'home'. This act, rather the opposite of acquiescing to the degenerative impulses of island existence exhibited by the Wildman's 'going native', serves to reconcile the castaway's orphan state by imposing a conditional context within which the orphanic condition may be allayed, if not rectified. The eponymous unit of *The Swiss Family Robinson*, for instance, constructs a tree house complete with three protective walls, hammocks and bedding, wherein upon its completion, the narrating father states, 'for the first time we stood all together in our new home. I drew up the ladder and, with a greater sense of security than I had enjoyed since we landed on the island, offered up our evening prayer and retired for the night.'[57] There are of course implications in the word 'security', not the least of which is the notion of the domestic space's being threatened by forces beyond it; on a larger, perhaps nationalistic level, the fortress-like home provides an ordered microcosm contrasting with the chaos and potential violence of the native space, a space 'in need' of subjugation. Attending this is the crucial role of belonging to the family, of perpetuating that solidarity to defray the vulnerability of orphanhood. By the novel's end, the island has yielded to the Robinsons' renovation, and has been christened New Switzerland, 'good, happy, and free!'[58] Crusoe, likewise, is successful in the establishing of a home-like environment, what he refers to as 'my Country-House, and my Sea-Coast House'.[59] Crusoe states that he 'barricado'd my self round with Chests and Boards that I had bought on Shore', and that he 'was gotten home to my little Tent, where I lay with all my wealth about me very secure'.[60] Crusoe's surrounding himself with material items from the shipwreck underscores the natural impulse in the castaway to avoid the orphanic condition imposed by the island.[61] Contrasting with this sense of accomplishment and capability is the frequent presentation in island literature of the fin de siècle of castaways who are unable successfully to contend with the orphan state in which they find themselves, as well as their frequent presentation of failed endeavours to impose the order of 'civilization' onto the island.

Attending examples of achievement in earlier island literature is a robust sense of exploration typical of texts bearing an underlying notion of indoctrination of imperial paradigms. In *The Coral Island*, for instance, Ralph Rover, upon being shipwrecked, states, 'my heart expanded more and more with an exulting gladness, the like of which I had never felt before'.[62] And, despite threats of shark attack, natives and pirates, Ralph compares his island experiences to 'a delightful dream' and claims he spent the 'happiest months [of] my life on that Coral Island'.[63] However, whereas the typical hero of the desert island romance feels an inner compulsion to go to sea, the late nineteenth-century protagonist is burdened by a sense of dread, as that demonstrated by Jim Hawkins, who shudders with horror at the prospect. Stevenson provides an example of an author who implements the conventions of the Robinsonade only for them 'to be parodied, deflated, or subversively deformed'.[64] Unlike the sense of adventure that characterizes earlier maritime fiction, Jim is fraught with unease, 'uneasy and alarmed', 'in mortal fear', 'utterly terrified'.[65] He is furthermore denied the surveying experience about which he fantasized and which is typically allowed the visitor to the island, and is therefore denied the notion of supremacy that such an experience affords.[66] While the typical Robinsonade plot tends to elaborate on the various tasks that the castaway must perform successfully in order to improve his state, *Treasure Island* seems merely what Henry James called 'a record of queer chances' whereby Jim seems merely lucky rather than necessarily talented or capable.[67] Earlier island literature also shows the protagonist rewarded for his hard work and courage. Stevenson, however, digresses from this tendency, consistently undercutting the fatherless boy's moments of naïve boastfulness by psychically scarring him for life, and, as I will discuss below, constantly relegating him to the subservient role under imposing and insufficient father figures.

One of the outstanding facets of the orphan condition is an overwhelming lack of identifying with one's environment. For instance, Jo the street sweeper, of Dickens's *Bleak House* (1852–3), seems to belong nowhere, and is constantly shuffled from one place to the next; George E. Sergent's *Roland Leigh: The Story of a Street Arab* (1857) tells the tale of a London boy so ragged that he is even denied entrance into the church; and the characteristic is not limited to lower-class orphans, as Mary, the orphan protagonist of Francis Hodgson Burnett's *The Secret Garden* (1911), is bereft of belonging first in her own loveless home, then in her uncle's lifeless mansion. This is another facet that connects island and orphan narratives. Islands provide authors with an environment in which they may examine not only various modes of belonging and exile, but also the crises of identity that emerge once the castaway is deprived of his usual context.

In *Kidnapped*, 'a novel about the testing of identity', David displays an inability to relate to the landscape of Erraid, the seeming island upon which he finds himself stranded.[68] While island narratives are typically structured around severance from home, a period of island exile and, finally, reclamation of the self, David fails to accomplish that resubstantiation within the island context. Unable to contend with island exile in the way Crusoe, Robinson pater, Masterman Ready, or Cyrus Harding can, David is a notably incapable protagonist who, the orphan condition thrust upon him, is not the emblem of surety and domination of his literary forebears.[69] Whereas previous incarnations of the castaway frequently benefited from their island experiences through individuation and management, David's island experience proves to initiate the loss of his sense of self. The more David, 'cast upon a little barren isle, and cut off on every side by the salt seas', senses his physical detachment from the mainland, the less he seems attached to his notion of self.[70] Somewhat oddly, upon its publication, *Kidnapped* was recognized as an heir to Defoe's novel, 'a kind of miniature *Robinson Crusoe*'.[71] But David's reference at this juncture to other castaways, contrasting his state with those whose predicaments he feels were not as desperate as his, seems to emphasize the difference between him and more efficient characters of previous island narratives: 'In all the books I have read of people being cast away, they had either their pockets full of tools, or a chest of things would be thrown upon the beach along with them, as if on purpose.'[72] Unlike the very able Crusoe, once he is stranded in an alien place with which he is at pains to relate, and forced to confront the discomfort of isolation and self-reliance, David is the antithesis of the versatile castaway, and is absolutely victimized by the orphanic state.

Furthermore, in the case of *Kidnapped*'s David, the castaway condition may serve to underscore an already extant orphanhood. While David is a literal orphan, his situation is notably inverted from that of the typical orphan's. As 'the rightful heir of an estate', he is already aware to some degree of his lineage and his claim to an inheritance, and must endeavour not so much to claim it as to *reclaim* it.[73] His predicament on Erraid, 'now starving on an isle at the extreme end of the wild Highlands', serves as a literalization of an orphan state accentuated by unjust estrangement from the financial security and domestic stability offered by the House of Shaws.[74] A metaphorical condition of being cut off from these identifying elements, David's island exile is notably depicted in terms reminiscent of orphan conventions. Stevenson employs tropes of orphanhood one might associate with a typical Dickensian type orphan: David describes 'my wet clothes and weariness, and my belly that now began to ache with hunger'; he is 'distressed with thirst'; denied shelter, he speaks of 'hoping to find a house where I might warm myself' and, although he discovers the semblance of a domestic space, it is merely 'a little hut of a house like a pig's hut . . . but the turf roof of it had fallen entirely in; so that the hut was of no use to me, and gave me less shelter than my rocks'.[75] As though further to entrench notions of his being separated from his rightful inheritance, David is cut off from the domestic sites he can discern in Iona, and marks the chimney smoke over the Ross 'as if from a homestead'; orphanlike, he portrays himself as 'wet and cold and had my head half turned with loneliness'.[76]

Similarly, *The Island of Dr Moreau*'s Prendick remains throughout overwhelmed, uncertain of himself in his island exile. Upon first encountering the island, he states that 'it was too hot to think elaborately', describes himself as 'greatly disturbed', filled with 'vague dread' and 'rigid with fear', 'tormented', and states that he 'completely lost my head with fear'.[77] Likewise, as opposed to the aforementioned creative, constructive castaways, in a moment of haste and abandon, Prendick is notably the one who overturns a lamp and causes the fire that claims the one 'civilized' place on Moreau's island. In contrast to Ballantyne's heroic depiction of the orphanic castaway as an emblem of imperial capacity, courage and even joyful inquiry, Stevenson and Wells's treatments represent a de-romanticizing of such concepts, with an emphasis instead on the desperation, isolation and terror intrinsic to late nineteenth-century island narratives.

Tenuous domestic constructions

Divergence in the fin de siècle from certain conventions typical of earlier island narratives reveals a concern with the issue of family ideals consistent with that which characterizes genre fiction of the period. I have noted, for instance, the correlation of Stoker's persistent portrayals of family units in peril with his stress on the plight of the figure without a family. I have also discussed the specific targeting of family and family-like structures by insurgent orphans and in chapter 5 I will address the perception of the empire as a potential surrogate family construction for the orphans of colonization.

As is often the case with orphan narratives of the fin de siècle, the stability of domestic spaces proves tenuous at best. This is underscored, for example, in Montgomery's inquiry about the home from which he is ostracized and for which he clearly yearns, and his suggested connections with the familiarity of his and Prendick's shared interests. The terse alcoholic, 'an outcast from civilization, instead of being a happy man enjoying all the pleasures of London' and to whom Prendick refers as 'unfitted for human kindred', alludes to the study of biology at university and speaks of natural history; he inquires about Tottenham Court Road, Gower Street and Caplatzi. Within the room given to Prendick are artifacts of 'civilization', such as 'a convenient deck-chair before the window', as well as 'an array of old books' including 'surgical works and editions of the Latin and Greek classics'.[78] But, despite these allusions to the world of men, Moreau's compound, the only structure on the island that seems connected with civilization, is more of a fortress of secrecy and perversion than a domestic space. It is more like a prison for Prendick, the 'uninvited guest', whose window is notably 'defended by an iron bar' that is 'firmly fixed'.[79] The gate to the entrance is 'framed in iron and locked' and Moreau characteristically persists in an 'elaborate locking up of the place'.[80] Within the aberrant semblance of humanity of the Beast-folk is a latent compulsion to formulate a kind of social construction. At the height of their human-likeness, they assemble 'some rough shelter', as though to form their own domestic space in which to live and even marry.[81] Although it is plunged in darkness and plagued with an odor 'like that of a monkey's cage ill-cleaned', this meagre configuration is referred to by the ape-man as 'home'.[82] Amid this rudimentary fabrication, Prendick finds 'some rough vessels of lava and wood' and 'a rough stool'.[83] These crude accoutrements vaguely suggest domesticity, an attempt on the part of the exiled Beast-folk, in their partial humanity, for assimilation and inclusion, to rectify the orphan condition imposed upon them. These allusions to specific links to the civilized world temporarily infuse untenable notions of inclusion and belonging into the island's orphaning context of violence, isolation and non-communication, notions which are swiftly and easily eliminated.

Similarly, *Treasure Island* and *Kidnapped* are tales of the disruption of domestic spaces both actual and provisional, which must be defended or lost to anarchic outside forces. Both texts begin with the death of the protagonist's father and a severance from the familiarity and comfort of home. In *Treasure Island* Bones's arrival disturbs the peace of the Admiral Benbow and its clientele; Black Dog battles Bones within the place's very walls; and Pew and his entourage break into the inn, reducing it to 'a state of smash', bringing the family business to ruin.[84] The island stockade serves as a tenuously bastioned locus of habitation, with slight provisions and even the flying of colours to purport the perhaps false assurance of civilization; it is under constant threat of invasion by the chaotic forces of the pirates and ultimately falls into the hands of Silver and his men. Even the *Hispaniola* becomes a mock domestic space that serves as a point of contention between the warring parties. *Kidnapped* is a narrative of the usurpation by a family member of the House of Shaws, which, like the Admiral Benbow, is reduced to 'a kind of ruin' and which resembles 'the wing of a house that had never been finished'.[85] It is also a tale of an orphan's exile from his rightful home, an exile underscored later by David's brief island experience.

Failed fathers and forsaken orphans

During the nineteenth century, the island fantasy genre continued to depict the figure of a commanding white male holding sway over the island. Rather than stranding him in isolation, however, it exhibited him as accompanied by, if not a literal family, as with the Robinsons, then by a group of other castaways for whom he serves as tutor, instructor and overall father figure. Island narratives such as *Masterman Ready*, Kingston's *Peter the Whaler* (1851), *The Coral Island* and *The Mysterious Island* display protagonists who effectively impose upon a potentially chaotic and anarchic context the systematizing hierarchy of a normative family structure by authoritatively stepping up to serve the need of leadership and guidance.[86] There is within *The Swiss Family Robinson*, for example, a remarkable hierarchy based on the synergistic relationship of the family with the father at the helm, while the proficient commands of *The Mysterious Island*'s Harding provide those dependent upon his expertise with unfailing guidance.

With the fin de siècle, however, that authoritative, knowledgeable and virtuous father figure is challenged. Late nineteenth-century island literature subverts previous notions of this figure's honour and reliability, portraying him as physically deformed, intellectually perverse, or morally uncertain. This incredulity is notably coincident with the diminishing concept within maritime literature in general, of the gentleman sailor as a believable character, and emerging doubts about the morality of the imperial mission that figure embodied. As early as the 1850s, the responsible and capable hero becomes something of an exception, so that there emerge characters like Kingsley's unstable and ineffective Amyas, of *Westward Ho!* (1855). By this time the sea-story form itself seems somewhat obsolete and by the end of the century seems doomed as a genre.[87] The doubts associated with the gentleman sailor ultimately manifest themselves in the fin-de-siècle image of the failed father figure who proves incapable or unwilling to fulfill his obligatory role. This depiction seems both to belie the questioning of authoritative archetypes as credible or believable as well as to demonstrate the potential detriment such failures bear on the stability of the civilization represented by the microcosm of the island. While Crusoe and the father of Robinson family establish dominance over their respective spaces, to the extent that they either plan to return or never even leave, by the end of the nineteenth century, the island has degenerated into an amoral territory, a site of malleable ethics that can be manipulated according to one's circumstances. As I will examine below, this moral vacuum largely exists due to the corrupt actions of profligate father figures who have displaced the unrealistic and outmoded, but perhaps sorely missed, gentleman sailor.

The island narrative posits these father figures against potential sons who inevitably suffer from their neglect or betrayal. Contrasting with the failed father figure opposing him, the orphan figure often demonstrates a moral superiority similar to that of earlier incarnations of orphan figures. Both *Treasure Island* and *Kidnapped* offer protagonists who are groomed by men who are to some degree exiled from society and, while characters like Jim and David are somewhat stable, their dubious older role models are notably less so, and furthermore are less civilized than the societies from which they are ostracized; thus the orphans seem somewhat conventional compared with their eccentric and even dangerous elders.[88] The frantic and volatile Alan, for instance, provides a remarkable contrast to the younger David, who stands as more resolute, more mature.[89] Indeed, amongst the characters with whom he comes into contact, David seems stable in his normalcy. The orphan protagonist actually proves more civilized and morally secure than the majority of those around him, such as the unreliable and volatile Alan, the conniving and dangerous Uncle Ebenezer, or the deceitful and thievish Long John Silver. Even the half-man M'ling, of *The Island of Dr Moreau*, appears superior to the corrupt and neglectful Moreau and the erratic and inconstant Montgomery. However, while the convention of the suffering and morally superior orphan remains intact throughout these narratives, the reconciliation afforded to earlier presentations of the orphan state does not.

Moreau, of course, is the terrible father figure of the island that bears his name.[90] Akin to the autonomous and impulsive

Victor Frankenstein, and equally as careless and irresponsible, Moreau executes 'aimless investigations' into the making of innumerable creations for which he feels little emotional attachment. Unencumbered by the ethical implications of his research, he is able absolutely to objectify his creations. He kills his first production, to which he refers as a 'monster', claiming that it proved useless and left him 'discontented'.[91] Indeed, any connection he has with his creatures dwindles as their inevitable degeneration ensues. 'They only sicken me with a sense of failure', he claims; 'I take no interest in them.'[92] Prendick's consideration of them relegates them to the status of orphans abandoned by an insensitive father. He reluctantly considers 'the pain and trouble that came to these poor victims after they had passed from Moreau's hands', and remarks that 'the Things were thrown out to live a year or so, to struggle and blunder and suffer, and at last to die painfully'.[93]

Moreau's malevolence is not only in his denial of what he makes, but in the very occasion of his undertaking. His actions are not for the benefit of the medical or scientific community, nor are they altruistic or even aesthetically beautiful; instead, they are perversions of the creative process, merely 'to find out the extreme limit of plasticity in a living shape'.[94] His is the appropriation of the notion of prolificacy put to the service of licence and indulgence, a kind of masturbatory application of knowledge to which Prendick refers as 'a strange wickedness'.[95] Even Moreau's physical composition is of an intimidating, unwelcoming nature and not as a potentially nurturing father. Prendick states that he is 'powerfully built' and of a 'pugnacious resolution' and able to lift the castaway 'as though I was a little child'.[96]

Montgomery's irresolute relationship with M'Ling positions him in a father role as well, but one which he is ultimately unable to fulfill. Prendick notes M'Ling's 'strange tenderness and devotion' concerning Montgomery, and notes that 'it loved nothing so much as to be near him'.[97] But Montgomery's regard for the Beast-man varies wildly. Stating aboard the schooner in M'Ling's defence that 'that man of mine is not to be ill-treated', he initially appears to have a genuine concern for the creature; Prendick states that 'he would notice it, pat it, call it half-mocking, half-jocular names, and so make it caper with extraordinary delight'.[98] This kind of protective demeanour, however, changes with shocking rapidity to behaviour more akin to an abusive father, for 'sometimes he would ill-treat it, especially after he had been at the whiskey, kicking it, beating it, pelting it with stones or lighted fuses'.[99] What emerges as 'a sneaking kindness' and 'a vicious sympathy' for the Beast-folk, a fatherly regard in general, degenerates ultimately into Montgomery's fatal introduction of alcohol into their fragile society, resulting not only in their descent into violence and his own death, but the death, too, of the faithful and tragic orphan figure, M'Ling.[100]

M'ling is perhaps the most remarkable of Moreau's beings, as he typifies the evasion of class identification and the incapacity for complete inclusion that are the hallmarks of the traditional orphan. A 'complex trophy' of Moreau's enterprise, M'ling occupies a space between the 'civilization' of the humans and the faunal nature of the Beast-folk.[101] Dressed in dark-blue serge, capable of speech and able to perform domestic tasks, he serves the capacity of servant, as well as a kind of companion for Montgomery. He even displays a loyalty to the humans in a way that poignantly delineates him from those who might challenge Moreau's status quo when he adopts a leadership role in pursuit of the Leopard-man, who has broken the Law.[102] He also attempts to offer some form of surrogate leadership, once Montgomery gives way to drink, in a way that portrays him as a superior being, his 'quick starts' and 'sharp eyes' contrasting with the drunkard's 'stumbling footsteps' and 'dull eyes'.[103] However, M'ling is somewhat reminiscent of the orphan Rosanna Spearman, of Collins's *The Moonstone*, who, despite her former occupation as thief is permitted to work in the Verinder household. One of the novel's narrators, Gabriel Betteredge, states of Rosanna that there 'was just a dash of something that wasn't like a housemaid, and that *was* like a lady'; Rosanna, too, is marked by deformity, having 'the misfortune of having one shoulder bigger than the other'.[104] While Rosanna's educational aspirations and inclinations to propriety separate her from the other servants of the house, the questionable nature of her origins and her disfigurement prevent her incorporation into a higher class. Similarly, M'ling, the 'singularly deformed' and 'misshapen man' characterized by 'a crooked back, a hairy neck, and a head sunk between his shoulders' is too distorted to be regarded as fully human.[105] Prendick notes that his 'facial part projected, forming something dimly suggestive of a muzzle, and a huge half-open mouth showed as big white teeth as I had ever seen in a human mouth'.[106] M'ling is notably ostracized on the schooner, and even struck by the captain, who refers to him as an 'ugly devil'.[107] Begat by an unloving and manipulative creator, ultimately deprived of the fallible father figure of Montgomery, denied complete acceptance into any social structure and eventually killed by his similars, M'ling stands as the denotative orphan character of Wells's novel, embodying in every way conventions of isolation and deficiency associated with orphanhood.

Moreau's other creations epitomize notions of orphanhood as well. The mass of orphaned beings which he has ejected from the suggested domesticity of his enclosure are scarcely classifiable. Like family-less waifs of the city streets, they elude categorization, are denied inclusion into what semblance of society Moreau's concocted space connotes and insinuate humanity tinged with something less than human. Unlike Rosanna, whose orphan state is perpetuated by class difference, that of M'ling and the Beast-folks is not only contingent on difference of species, but too possesses the aspect of paternal abandonment typical of these late-century island narratives. Prendick's descriptions of them permit the indeterminacy of their physical appearance to literalize their orphanic condition; they are inexact, depicting the Beast-folk as horrid amalgams, ever-shifting, unstable and irretrievably incomplete. This 'amazingly ugly gang' of 'grotesque-looking' and 'unaccountable' creatures with 'elfin faces' are 'distorted in some odd way' and bear 'indefinable queerness'; they are 'grotesque, dim figures' with 'clumsy backs' and 'misshapen heads half-hidden by their shoulder blades', 'crouching and gesticulating monstrosities' in 'knotted black struggle' and that 'melt into a vague patch'.[108] As David Balfour's island exile proves a metaphor for his actual orphan state, so too does the undifferentiated and irresolute physicality of the Beast-folk serve as a typification of the orphan condition that marks them all. Unlike David, however, M'Ling and the other Beast-folk, and Jim Hawkins as well, are never afforded the kind of denouement David experiences.[109] In fact, while earlier portrayals of orphanhood generally end in family inclusion or the identity conveyed through the acquisition of fortune, the late-century island narrative frequently leaves the orphan condition notably unresolved.

One of the ways these narratives refuse reconciliation is in the denial of a beneficial father figure for the orphan protagonist. *Treasure Island* begins with the undercutting and then dismissal of Jim's father, of whom we are never even afforded a glimpse. Importantly, Jim's ailing sire is depicted as weak and ineffectual, evidently refusing to confront Bones about his debts, and Stevenson swiftly disposes of the father soon after. This is crucial as it generates the emptying of the paternal space that could potentially be filled by a number of prospects. Following the ruin of his home and the death of his father, Jim is cast into this orphan role. Dislocated (with the temporary exception of his mother) from familial responsibility, he subsequently encounters a number of possible but inadequate surrogate father figures.

I have noted previously the convention in orphan narratives of the excision of the parents, the removal of their 'limiting' dominion, in order to permit the orphan's quest for identity. Peck notes that maritime fiction tends to present young men in search of a 'replacement father', one who eventually turns out to be 'a much truer father' than the boy's biological one.[110] In late-century island literature, however, the surrogate father is morally questionable, unreliable, even potentially harmful. Furthermore, he is typically adventurous, unconventional, perhaps swarthy. And, yet, he is often disturbingly charming, unsettlingly endearing, so that the young boy is somewhat seduced into circumstances in which he may not normally find himself. The rather anxious Jim is somewhat conscripted into his adventure by the males around him: Bones initiates a strain of male figures who include an unwitting or unwilling Jim into their plans, telling the boy to keep his eye open for the one legged man; 'You'll make a famous cabin-boy, Hawkins', the squire tells him without his input; and Jim becomes Gunn's envoy.[111] Like Davy Balfour, who is kidnapped onto the *Covenant* by pirates and forced to work in their world, Jim exhibits a certain hesitant fascination with a pirate world teeming with potential father surrogates. Both Jim and Davy, however, eventually find pirate life unrewarding and ultimately disenchanting, largely due to the failures of potential father figures. The island narrative of the fin de siècle exploits the orphaned protagonist's vulnerability in a manner that relegates him not to a state of adoption or inclusion, but one of further exile and abandonment. Jim's fascination with Silver, for instance, exhibiting the fatherless lad's inclination toward a strong male replacement, merely foregrounds the eventual disappointment Silver will perpetrate and Jim's ultimate predicament of disillusionment and unreconciled orphanhood that characterizes such narratives.

Stevenson is emblematic throughout *Treasure Island* of this tendency on the part of authors of late-century island narratives of consistently undercutting potential father figures.[112] Indeed, each of the men who appear initially capable of serving as possible surrogate parental roles is either of a morally uncertain disposition or is physically weakened or otherwise disabled.[113] This moral ambiguity is manifested in the obsession on the part of the novel's adults not with the welfare of the orphaned boy, but with financial gain. Bones's very life is threatened because of his knowledge of the treasure. Trelawney talks of 'money to eat, to roll in, to play duck and drake with ever after'.[114] Livesey takes the dead Pew's oilskin packet.[115] Gunn, while appearing somewhat addled and bewildered, is nevertheless focused on the treasure (and cheese). While the pirates expectedly demonstrate a dangerous and unsocial manner, one notes the rapidity with which Trelawney and Livesey forsake the defining social standing of their professions and abandon their civilized identities in emulation of the pirates in pursuit of the treasure. One of the most disturbing aspects of the novel is the ease with which the English gentlemen are motivated by a similar avarice, the same desire for material wealth and self-interest that compels the 'gentlemen of fortune'.[116] Particularly unsettling is the manner in which the 'dead-shot' Trelawney is 'cool as steel' when asked by the captain to kill Israel Hands.[117]

The novel repeatedly displays Stevenson's penchant for disfiguring adult males.[118] Bones is crossed with scars and suffers from apoplexy. Black Dog is missing two fingers. Pew is not only blind, but 'hunched, as if with age or weakness' and appears 'positively deformed'.[119] Gunn is not deformed, but is presented as a tattered semblance of the sailor he was previously. Long John Silver is missing a leg. These maimed and ailing figures are scarcely believable as actual persons; indeed, they are hyperbolic portraits whose dubious, far-fetched distinction effectively underscores their insufficiency as parental substitutes. Silver, of course, is the exceptional case for several reasons. First, more than any other male of the novel, he is foremost the one who is 'unwearedly kind' to Jim.[120] Heimmediately assumes the role of educator, informing the boy about 'the scene about ships and such' and proceeds with

> telling me about the different ships that we passed by, their rig, tonnage, and nationality, explaining the work that was going

> forward – how one was discharging, another taking in cargo, and a third making ready for sea – and every now and then telling me some little anecdote of ships or seamen or repeating a nautical phrase till I had learned it perfectly.[121]

Silver's instructional role encourages a relationship to develop between him and Jim, so that the pirate assumes a parental influence that relegates Jim to the vulnerable role of surrogate son. While the other pirates intrude into Jim's personal space, causing him anxiety and fear, Silver notably instills in the boy a certain reassurance that results in trust and admiration. This combination of tutelage, flattery and even guardianship is to Jim not only an opportunity to acquire a fatherly confidant, but also a kind of affirming component of his tenuous fantasies of adventure; they are, however, actually associated with Silver's betrayal of Jim's notions of adoption, attempted modes of indoctrination Silver employs to lure Jim into his duplicitous and mercenary way of life.

Silver is a crucial character insofar as the idea of father figures in that he ultimately betrays this sense of assurance and confidence with which he initially beguiles the young, fatherless Jim. There is a notable shift around the mid-Victorian period within maritime literature towards concern with more interior elements that threatened to upset society, enemies capable of infiltrating the culture to destabilize it from within.[122] By the century's end, this enemy acquires the guise of the unreliable and even threatening father. Silver is such a character, having the ability to assimilate into a group and provoke its collapse. The potential father figure here, rather than serve a constructive, parental role, instead initiates the perversion of the group's very members. Silver is particularly unsettling in that he not only desires monetary wealth, but he intends to use it to introduce himself into society, considering even the plausibility of one day obtaining a position in Parliament, employing a shrewdness and intellect on par with that of the doctor and the squire. This emphasis not on exterior but interior threats seems an indictment of the failed father, with a caveat in regard to the damage such a figure might wreak upon the stability and unity of the family structure. As is evident in Machen, Stoker, Wells and other authors, there emerged the growing anxiety of the family unit as vulnerable not only to forces beyond it, but to perils within its very fabric. Silver is the embodiment of such a threat. He is set apart from other weakened or unworthy father figures in that not only does his physical disability not actually hinder him, but in that he is the single male who intentionally ingratiates himself into Jim's world and acquires the boy's trust, making his subsequent treason even more despicable. Silver's emotional withdrawal from Jim is compounded by his slipping away at the end of the narrative, whereby he abandons the boy at a point where he could have reconciled with him through repentant moral behaviour. Instead, he certifies his inability to sustain his complimentary façade and the unfulfilled implications of his proposed tutelage.

Silver embodies this treasonous mien in his Gothic fragmentariness and malleability. Indeed, rather than retaining a consistent personality, he is an amalgam of possible persons, as inchoate characteristically as he is physically, alternating between various dispositions as circumstances prescribe. Initially displaying a kind regard and even protectiveness for Jim, Silver eventually exhibits selfishness and cruelty. Jim first describes him as a 'clean and pleasant-tempered landlord', but later as 'paler and more stern'.[123] As though to add further insult, despite this irresolution, Silver is also married and, therefore, associated with the kind of domestic stability implicit in marriage and the kind of inclusion and belonging of which Jim is partially bereft.

Various possible male influences encounter David Balfour of Stevenson's *Kidnapped* as well, but they are all characterized by uncertainty or a kind of latent villainy. The first scene of the book introduces David's loss of home and family, followed by betrayal by a murderous next of kin.[124] Hoseason proves a rather inconsistent figure, constantly presenting himself as a collision of numerous personalities determined by the present need. Stevenson depicts him as 'rough, fierce, unscrupulous, and brutal'; he also describes him as being 'two men', and states that he 'left the better one behind as soon as he set foot aboard the vessel'.[125] Like Silver, Hoseason seems to occupy more than one category at a time. David's uncle, Ebenezer, 'a mean, stooping, narrow-shouldered, clay-faced creature', not only appropriates David's inheritance, but attempts to kill him and devises his abduction.[126] Alan Breck, although somewhere around twice David's age and appearing a potential father figure to the orphan, is psychologically tenuous at best; he is irresolute and fickle, somewhat irritable and irresponsible. Only when the English are pursuing the two does Breck seem in some small manner to assume a kind of fatherly role for the orphaned David; however, this is of little avail, as ultimately Breck becomes a burdensome liability with which David must contend.

The convention of the failed father of course is not limited to any single genre, but the island narrative of the fin de siècle serves as a literalization of the abandonment and deprivation of the orphan state that the unavailing parental figure perpetuates and is incapable of reconciling.[127] But, while the father figure as reliable, capable patriarch declined in late-century island literature into a fearful and possibly threatening menace, further entrenching notions of the island as a treacherous, forsaken and evasive orphaning space, as I will discuss in the following chapter, adventure narratives of the New Imperialism tended to exalt the father figure in the form of the British colonizer, a figure worthy of emulation by the subject races, and furthermore depicted the British Empire in notably familial terms that relegated the colonized to the status of orphan in need of the Queen Mother.

5
Orphans of Empire

'. . . that which had been adrift so long had reached the shore at last'.

John Seton Merriman, *Flotsam: The Story of a Life*

In this chapter I wish to discuss the manner in which the masculine adventure narrative of the New Imperialism, that is, late nineteenth-century literature concerned with ventures and campaigns taking place within the context of colonized space, engaged orphanhood in ways that produced and substantiated imperial ideologies concerning racial disparity. Narratives of empire tend to depict orphans of British stock in a way that differs noticeably from portrayals of native orphans. Due to the supposed, and systematically promulgated, superiority of his lineage, the British orphan of imperial literature is less susceptible to the hazards typically associated with the orphan state such as the desperate quests for assimilation and identity contingent on economic factors and demonstrated in realist and domestic fiction of the same period. The native, non-British orphan, however, proves remarkably vulnerable to crises of inclusion and selfhood, particularly in regard to the dilemma presented in clinging to his own threatened heritage and culture, or acquiescing to the British notions of civilization being introduced to, or even imposed upon, his homeland. I will begin by establishing that the notion of British supremacy was, indeed, asserted through the educational system and magazine and other literary publications, and that the British orphan, whose sense of self proved more intact than that of his foreign peers, was utilized to further such propagandistic concepts. I proceed with contrasting several orphan figures from the writings of H. Rider Haggard in an effort to demonstrate this remarkable variance. Next, I will discuss Rudyard Kipling's Kim as a native-born orphan who is ultimately moulded into the Briton of coherence and service requisite of his lineage. Then I read Kipling's orphan Mowgli's allegorical role as trans-species hybrid that provides an emblem of imperialism, and whose capabilities and intelligence are employed to benefit the empire. Finally, I examine Henry Seton Merriman's *Flotsam: The Story of a Life* (1896), which depicts the misfortune and ruin that attend the British orphan who disregards or abuses the advantages of inclusion in the empire.

The orphan and the British sense of self

The British presented themselves during the nineteenth century as the most effective governing race in human history, with 'both the right and obligation to rule'.[1] Indeed, 'the race which knows no rest or fear' seemed endowed with a synthesis of competence and morality exceeding that of any other commensurate race or culture.[2] Chamberlain, for instance, referring to England's acceptance of a protectorate over Uganda, claimed that the Anglo-Saxon race was characterized by 'that spirit . . . of adventure and enterprise . . . which has made us peculiarly fit to carry out the working of colonization'; Haggard believed 'in the divine right of a great civilizing people – that is, in their divine mission'.[3] The English public school system, inspired by an educational initiative begun in the 1840s by Dr Thomas Arnold of Rugby, merged Christian ideals of self-sacrifice and an obligation to service with the group mentality of participation in team sports. Kipling referred to the divine providence that had established that 'a clean-run youth of the British middle class shall in the matter of backbone, brains and bowels surpass all other youths'.[4] The British officer who emerged from this system 'commanded by force of character' and embodied an 'innate self-confidence' that suggested British predominance.[5] Numerous critics such as Edward Said, Gayatri Chakravorty Spivak, Patrick Brantlinger and Suvendrini Perera discuss nineteenth-century fiction's complicity with the production and perpetration of racially biased ideologies.[6] Indeed, publications such as *Boy's Own Paper*, *Chums*, *Pluck*, *Union Jack* and *Young England*, whose primary readership was young males, infused adventure narratives with concepts of political duty that proved preparatory for imperial enterprise. G. A. Henty conveyed that sense of camaraderie, conformity and unanimity with his tendency to refer to his audience as 'My dear lads'.

As Daniel Brown has remarked, orientalism was an unconscious symptom of Englishness, 'lurking under the surface of a variety of discourses'.[7] But one of the most overtly propagandistic genres was imperial romance. Martin Green has observed, 'Adventure . . . is the energizing myth of empire'.[8] Writers like Henty, Haggard and others actually helped fashion imperial ideology.[9] Haggard's *King Solomon's Mines*, for instance, provided Britain's Foreign Office with 'the archaic language' it deemed appropriate for dealing with the Matabele monarch, Lobengula.[10] Leonard Woolf, a government official in Ceylon, remarked that the whites there were 'astonishingly like characters in a Kipling story'.[11]

One of Said's major theories is that the West projects onto the East aspects about itself which it finds discomforting, and various Victorian authors provided numerous literary and historical accounts that created and perpetuated imperial ideologies of racial difference.[12] In Henty's *At the Point of the Bayonet: A Tale of the Mahratta War* (1901), the natives around Bombay are noted to be 'wild and lawless', as opposed to the English, who 'made up for inferiority in numbers by speed, activity and dash'.[13] In Kipling's 'Letting in the Jungle', Mowgli's parental figures, Messua and her husband, flee the violence of their village to appeal to the British in Kanhiwara, who 'govern all the land'.[14] In Kipling, even animals trained by the British defer to an ordered hierarchy counter to the chaotic tendencies of those that are 'savage', the undisciplined beasts a seeming analogy for the Indian peoples governed by the empire.[15] Kipling's Indian native often defines his identity through superstitious practices, psychic or paranormal experiences, or an obsession with artistic inspiration; furthermore, he demonstrates a fatalistic sense of doom, and his pathological state is prone to instability and hysteria. The British Kim, by contrast, bears an intrinsic, self-assurance that characterizes his Anglo-Irish lineage. In Haggard's *King Solomon's Mines*, Sir Henry's 'tone of quiet confidence' contrasts with the frantic, mob mentality of the natives; Ignosi requests that the British remain to instruct the natives as to how to build 'white men's houses'; the Portuguese Sivestre proves incapable of finding the diamonds and bequeaths the map to the more proficient and accomplished Briton, Quatermain; and the non-European Ventvogel is unable to endure the abusive climates of the journey and perishes in the same location where Sivestre met his death.

In his outlining of Said's discussion of various negative stereotypes about the East, John McLeod comments that the East was typically portrayed as feminine, submissive, degenerative and immoral.[16] In his discussion of Henty's work, Jeffrey Richards notes the consistent failure of Africans to establish even the rudimentary elements of a 'civilized' culture, their proclivity to civil instability, their non-Christian religious customs, the crudity of their economic systems and, perhaps most importantly in regard to imperial pursuits, their essential need to be cultivated and subjugated by a 'superior' race.[17] Two eyewitness descriptions of Nigeria, published in the 1890s, speak of 'vile, native customs' of 'wild, lawless people', refer to the country as a 'kingdom of darkness' and contrast the neatness and cleanness of the missionary settlement in Bonny with the 'grossness and depravity' of the natives.[18]

Said and other postcolonial critics have attempted to articulate the manner by which the colonizing West formulated a reality of convenience by which it was able to impose interpretations, definitions and other limiting or negating concepts onto the colonized subject in order better to manage its imperial acquisitions. One example of this was the introduction into the seeming anarchy of the native space of language of a familial nature, with essentialist inclinations linguistically to regard the native in general as a sort of puerile dependent in need of the parental type of instruction and leadership only the British could provide.[19] The native was seen as incapable of self-sufficiency, too erratic for self-governing, a childlike being requiring the supervision of the more accomplished and wiser Mother England.[20] There were, therefore, references to Victoria as 'the Queen Mother' and instances of African natives calling her *ma-baap*, or 'mother-father'. Imperial literature further entrenched this familial discourse by often rendering natives as dislocated from their own lineage. One of the aspects of the East which Said and McLeod locate is its sense of 'timelessness', or the lack of a sense of itself historically prior to the West's 'discovery' and subsequent mapping and documentation of a given area.[21] In Haggard's *King Solomon's Mines*, for example, the natives of Kukuanaland have no knowledge of who created their roads or writings, or who forged their royal armour, only the vague idea that it came 'from our forefathers'.[22] Although the native peoples have their own culture, once it is appropriated and redefined by the colonizer as inferior, disordered or otherwise inadequate, a notion of the native's need for inclusion into the more structured and normative empire is able to develop. Within this vacuum of identity, this severance from a cultural unity, the native is relegated by the empire to an orphanic indeterminacy which permits colonization by the more assured and resolute British.

It should be noted that imperial narratives present remarkable familial complications for Britons as well, but these prove less problematic than they do in the case of natives and are ultimately surmounted. There is an absence of the customary family model, which seems to belie fin-de-siècle cultural anxieties concerning the disintegration of the ideal family. In *King Solomon's Mines*, Quatermain is a widower and Sir Henry is unmarried; in *She*, Holly, Leo and Job are unmarried and Vincey 'has absolutely no relatives living'.[23] In Kipling's 'In the Rukh', Grisborne is unmarried and virtually cut off from society. These imperial narratives are also notably populated by males. Their overall focus is the masculine pursuit of exploration, acquisition and colonization, leaving very little in the way of romantic situations.[24] In narratives in which the stable nuclear family is no longer a viable objective for the amelioration of the orphan state, union with the British Empire surrogates for that resolve, particularly in relation to the formation of what Nicholas Daly calls 'the male family'.[25] This is a social construction including various men, possibly of different categorical distinctions, but always shepherded by a prominent leader of British stock who marshals and directs the others.[26] This patriarchal authority reasserts notions of imperial supremacy that the British orphan often embodies. Given the lack of traditional family structures here, the notion of familial belonging is displaced, with the group leader emerging as a father figure who manifests British superiority, so that deference to and emulation of him insinuates inclusion into the larger, theoretically more legitimate, family of the empire. Indeed, there is a prevalent sense of union among British characters in general that escapes the often quarrelling and fragmentary indigenous peoples, so that the national commonality among the British bears a familial quality.[27] Hence we find multiple examples in Kipling of native characters endeavouring to assimilate into the empire, through imitation, marriage or adoption of the colonizer's culture. Given the dialogue of invalidation and negating critique of those outside the imperial 'family', inclusion into the empire connoted belonging to, and identification with, a larger, national family structure capable of reconciling what could be considered a kind of metaphoric orphanhood of cultural dimensions.

By way of example, Kipling's orphan mongoose Rikki-Tikki-Tavi, washed by flood 'out of the burrow where he lived with his mother and father', is one of Kipling's allegories of empire.[28] Because he is indigenous to India, Rikki-Tikki represents the native but, just as importantly, his orphan condition emblematizes that indeterminate space wherein the native finds himself at the crux of divergent cultural imperatives. Dislocation from previous identifiers such as home and family relegates Rikki-Tikki to the realm of the hybrid, that formative status whereby the colonizer may recast and impress the native into conformity and service.[29] Ultimately the colonized indigene must choose either rebellion or acquiescence.[30] The former is done at the native's peril. This option is figured by Nag and Nagaina, indigenous cobras endeavouring to infiltrate and dismantle the Englishman's domestic settlement. Their lack of compliance, that is, refusal to relinquish what was previously and rightly their space to the intrusion of the English family, results in their death and the annihilation of their offspring. The latter, exercised by Rikki-Tikki, affords not only his assimilation into the English enclave, but the procurement and utilization of his abilities for its protection and preservation.

The few occasions Rikki-Tikki mentions his mongoose family actually serve to establish that his severance from them has precipitated an improved condition, thus implying the benefits of British colonization for the native. He states, for instance, that he could discern more about the English people's house on his own 'than all my family could find out in all their lives'.[31] Similarly, having killed Karait the snake, Rikki-Tikki considers consuming it in its entirety from the tail, 'after the custom of his family at dinner', but realizes that the perpetuation of this custom would endanger him and possibly slow his reactions.[32] He therefore alters this inherited convention 'for the honor of his [human] family'.[33] What qualities Rikki-Tikki retains, such as 'the peculiar rocking, swaying motion' he learned from his family, or his mother's instruction as to how to conduct oneself in the presence of a white man, are notably applied to the advantage of the English.[34] The orphaned Rikki-Tikki, then, illustrates the submissive other whose facilities and initiative are redirected to the benefit of the colonizer, who abides the prerogatives of the imperial enterprise, and whose orphanic state finds reconciliation within the context of colonization.

Despite this dialogue of British superiority, there are conflicting notions as to late nineteenth-century perceptions of the perdurability of British colonial enterprise. Allen J. Greenberger, for example, places what he calls Britain's 'Era of Confidence' from 1880–1910, with the 'Era of Doubt' from 1910–35.[35] Therefore, the texts discussed in this chapter would seem to emerge from a period of British surety at its peak, and a time when British readers might see literary depictions of themselves as intrinsic bearers of authority and the colonized as inherently subordinate. Robert Dixon, however, locates anxieties attending imperialism of the late nineteenth century and resultant endeavours to rationalize the notion of empire. He cites the resurgence of romantic adventure literature that emerged around 1870 as seeking to reconcile problematic aspects of empire and to reassert espousal of diminishing imperial ideals.[36] Steven Arata refers to Kipling as representative of 'that gallery of crumbling certainties' which other writers had either discarded or disavowed, and Ian Baucom regards England as a place that had lost its command of its own identity.[37] Some intellectuals of the time were of the opinion that writers of imperial literature were no more likely to affect public opinion than Gothic literature was likely to inspire belief in the supernatural.[38] While such anxieties seemingly were not as pervasive in earlier decades of the century, some critics regard the fin de siècle as being vexed with apprehensions and misgivings concerning Britain's civilizing mission, proficiency and racial and moral integrity.[39] Read this way, the resurgence of the masculine adventure of this period may be viewed as reactionary to internal as well as external elements, such as the feminism, degeneration and emasculation of the male that impugned the concept of the patriarchal society upon which much of the empire was built. Brantlinger, therefore, observes the 'elegiac' quality in late Victorian and Edwardian fiction, a lament over 'the loss of adventure, heroism [and] true nobility'.[40] If Dixon, Brantlinger and others are correct in their perception of a crisis in imperialism around the fin de siècle, the disparity between depictions of orphans in imperial literature would seem to serve the function of propaganda reasserting imperial ideologies. For in late-century imperial narratives the conception of British supremacy and native mediocrity is perpetuated in the presentation of orphans.

The cynosure of this literary revival of imperial adventure was the cult of the male, with the primary attributes of Anglo-Saxon masculinity being a substantial combination of 'patriotism, physical toughness, skill at team games, a sense of fairness, self-discipline, selflessness, bravery and daring'.[41] And it is in regard to this conception of the British hero, the 'brave, forceful, daring, honest, active, and masculine' figure, wherein we discern the distinction between colonial literature's depictions of orphans in ways that validated paradigms of inequality crucial to the empire's success.[42] For example, despite being an orphan, Harry Wylam, of Merriman's *Flotsam: The Study of a Life*, exhibits the remarkable leadership qualities inherent to his race. Regardless of his native appearance, Kipling's Anglo-Irish orphan Kim is rendered as commanding over his indigenous playmates. A number of Henty's protagonists are orphaned early on in their respective narratives, in some manner dislocated from the context of family inclusion and propelled into challenging predicaments, only to surmount their circumstances precisely due to their being British. Frank Hargate, for example, of *By Sheer Pluck* (1884), is poverty-ridden upon the death of his widowed mother, but the quality of his education in addition to his having been reared by a father who was a British army officer endows him with a demeanour of distinction. British lineage prevails even when it is unknown, as with the case of Henty's orphan Harry Lindsay, of *At the Point of the Bayonet* (1902); although Harry is initially unaware of his bloodline, he proves stronger and more capable than his non-British acquaintances and develops an 'unquestioned leadership' over them, proving willing 'to take responsibilities on his shoulders and to be so full of resource'.[43] In the case of the British orphan, the manner in which orphanhood had been typically attended by the trauma of exile and an absence of totality is virtually negated by the familial affectation of the empire, while the native counterpart, due to his supposed genealogical insufficiencies, suffers a sense of displacement, a debilitating lack of psychic cohesion and an ultimate deferment to and reliance upon the cultural model and provisional family dynamic proposed by the British Empire.

Divergent orphan forms in *King Solomon's Mines* and *She*

In numerous ways Haggard's *King Solomon's Mines* inculcates the paradigm of the British Empire as a construction with nuances of familial inclusion, existence beyond which is fraught with peril. The British adventurer Allan Quatermain is immediately established as a parental figure. A widower, Quatermain is notably willing to endanger himself in order to provide for his beloved son, Harry, for whom the narrative is written. In addition, Quatermain is depicted as a representative of imperial pursuits. Insofar as accomplishment he is a paragon of the imperial standard, having led the life of a proficient hunter and explorer who has evaded death even beyond the normal statistical averages for one in his trade.

Therefore, despite his frequently self-critical tone, whereby he refers to himself as 'timid' and even 'a coward', Quatermain is nevertheless situated as a paternal emblem of empire on whose expertise and judgment others consistently rely.

Haggard likewise underscores the import of affiliation with the empire by demonstrating the repercussions of the failure to fulfill familial obligations. The negligence of Sir Henry's father to prepare a will properly not only endangers his sons financially, it precipitates the rift that severs the siblings' relationship. George, Sir Henry's brother and only living relative, abandons his homeland, adopts the name Neville and in all manners disengages himself from his family. George's denial of association with Sir Henry, and by extension of his affiliation with the larger family of the empire, notably results in George's disablement and virtual captivity in the unstable and dangerous context of the native space. With the relinquishment of his British lineage, then, he acquires, at his own peril, an orphanic condition.

In addition to the motif of the consequence of fidelity to kinship, Haggard contrasts Sir Henry's devotion to his prodigal brother with the betrayal and violence of the novel's Africans. As opposed to Sir Henry's maintaining that 'blood is thicker than water', Twala, the wicked twin of Ignosi's father, Imotu, murders his brother, denies Ignosi his rightful throne, and forces Ignosi and his mother's subsequent flight from their home and Ignosi's eventual orphanic wandering.[44] This betrayal casts Ignosi from his krall; 'I am of the Zulu people, yet not of them'.[45] Upon him is thrust the onus of orphanhood, with its absence of belonging and identity, his goal becoming merely 'to see his own people and his father's house before he died'.[46] This of course contrasts with George's self-created orphanhood, with the crucial difference being Sir Henry's salvific fealty to the family of which Ignosi is bereft.

Throughout the entire novel, Ignosi, despite his royal lineage, is depicted as ultimately inferior to, as well as reliant upon, the British father figure, Quatermain. It is indicated that whatever attributes permit Ignosi some modicum of distinction from other kaffirs is attributable to his having left the Zulus 'to see the white man's ways' and having wandered 'where white people live, and . . . having learned the wisdom of the white people'.[47] It is Quatermain who removes the diamonds from Twala's headless body and proclaims Ignosi 'lawful King of the Kukuanas'.[48] Even upon reclamation of his throne, at which point he 'could exercise the almost unbounded rights of sovereignty', Ignosi is virtually incapable of action without Quatermain's counsel.[49] Having referred on numerous occasions to Quatermain as 'my father', Ignosi requests that the Englishman assist him, 'and let me, who am but a child in wisdom beside thee, hearken to thy words'.[50] It is also clear that Twala would have sacrificed Ignosi after Gagool singled him out during the witch hunt were it not for the interference of the British on his behalf. During the last stand of the Greys, Ignosi stands, evidently calm but remarkably inactive, until Quatermain compels him to partake physically in a battle the victory of which Ignosi credits to Quatermain's planning. Furthermore, Ignosi states that the restoration of his kingship was contingent upon the 'three white hands' of the British, and at the great 'indaba' council the British are greeted with a royal salute and receive the ceremonial respect equal to that of the king.

The glaring distinction between British and native orphan figures is evinced by the familial nuances of George's self-imposed orphanic condition and Ignosi's, which has been forced upon him. Ignosi's predicament has been effected by a treasonous and murderous relative who compromises notions of loyalty and reliance intrinsic to the concept of family, necessitating dependence upon representatives of empire for the re-stabilization of his own political system. The orphaned figure in this case emblematizes native 'need' of a directorial imperial entity. In sharp relief to Ignosi's plight, George's, though initiated by familial strife, is ultimately alleviated precisely due to Sir Henry's unfailing fraternal loyalty, verifying that alliance with the British Empire proves sufficient to reconcile the orphanic condition in a manner that the violent and perfidious aborigine cannot. The mode of orphanhood in *King Solomon's Mines*, then, is utilized to reassert imperial conceptions of racial disparity.

In addition to the reconciled George's orphanic state, we may contrast Ignosi's with the orphanhood of the Englishmen Ludwig Horace Holly and Leo Vincey, of Haggard's *She*. Holly, despite having 'neither father, nor mother, nor brother', does not suffer due to his lack of kin.[51] Admittedly 'misanthropic and sullen', he states that he 'brooded and worked alone, and had no friends' and, furthermore, prefers to isolate himself from the outside world and 'cut myself off from those opportunities which with most men results in the formation of relations more or less intimate'.[52] This trait may be attributable to the eccentricities attending his academic disposition, or to the fact that Holly is, in his own words, 'set apart by Nature to live alone', afflicted as he is with 'the stamp of abnormal ugliness'.[53] It seems it is either his intellectual idiosyncrasies or his physical features and not his orphanhood that determine the extent of his perceived ostracism. In spite of his claims of seclusion, he is gifted with both 'iron and abnormal strength and considerable intellectual powers' for which he is admired by his acquaintances.[54] Furthermore, despite his proclamations of insularity, Holly is a respected Cambridge don, an incorporated part of a decidedly English social structure and, moreover, a member of the broader family of the British Empire. Indeed, he suitably figures the self-confidence typically absent in the orphan by demonstrating the superiority intrinsic to his race when he refuses to bow to Ayesha, a member of another, ancient race. Despite an admission of fear, he asserts his lineage with a 'most dignified stride', noting that deference to her would present a 'patent acknowledgment of inferiority' unbecoming to an Englishman.[55] It is actually this projection of his Englishness that ingratiates Holly to Ayesha; she even comes to enjoy his company, admiring the autonomy of his 'thinking brain' and preferring him to the obsequious, and notably native, servants who surround her. Despite his and Leo's sexual weakness for Ayesha, and the submission this entails, her intention to overthrow Queen Victoria is abhorrent to them; their vital connection with, and allegiance to, the extended family of empire that negates the implications of orphanhood remains intact.

Leo is an orphan as well, his mother having died in childbirth and his father, Vincey, blaming Leo for her death, having virtually abandoned him. His negligent father, however, arranges for Holly's adoption of Leo, a further example of the synergistic interdependence of the larger British family one does not find in the case of Ignosi, for instance; thus Holly's statement: 'Few sons have been loved as I love Leo, and few fathers know the deep and continuous affection that Leo bears to me.'[56] The empire takes care of its own. Despite being motherless and having been forsaken by his father, then, Leo proves the consummate Englishman, 'one of the most English-looking men' Holly has ever seen, and is characterized by a 'proud and vigorous air'.[57] He is endowed with the confidence of the colonizer, claiming in reference to targeting a waterbuck, 'I could not miss it if I tried' and is similarly efficient, being the first to have his weapon in hand when the lions approach him and his companions.[58] When attacked, Leo possesses that determined pluck often attributed to the British, his eyes expressing 'a curious light' and his face 'set like stone'.[59] Although Holly states that Leo is 'brilliant and keen-witted, but not a scholar', the latter is notably educated and worldly, as is evinced by his ability to speak Arabic.[60] And, despite the inadequacy of the family structure from which he emerged, Leo 'always takes a cheerful view of things', and even after receiving near fatal wounds is 'cheerful as a cricket'.[61] Indeed, upheld and nurtured by Holly, his 'more than father', but more importantly fraternally united with the British Empire, Leo endures none of the irresolution and exile typical of orphanhood.[62] Such an association with the empire becomes the only recourse for the remedying of the orphan state for those orphans who, unlike the man of clear British lineage, are either displaced Britons or natives whose hierarchical standing allegorizes imperial conceptions of power and subjugation, as demonstrated by Kipling's Kim and Mowgli.[63]

Kipling's Gothic orphans

Perena argues that Victorian fiction registered an increasing unease about the colonial subject and notions of 'engulfment, feminization and violence' associated with the colonies.[64] Brantlinger notes the manner in which Victorian novels in general present the racially different as 'either comic stereotypes or figures of monstrosity meant to repel rather than evoke sympathy'.[65] Much of Kipling's earlier work often punctuates this abnormal, even grotesque, aspect of a kind of Gothic India, what K. Bhaskava Rao calls 'a tortured vision' of the country.[66] 'The Mark of the Beast', for instance, features an Anglo-Indian under the curse of a Hindu leper priest, while 'The Strange Ride of Morrowbie Jukes' offers a cow-eating Hindu and a pit of imprisoned Hindu outcasts. Both 'The Dream of Duncan Parrenness' and 'At the End of the Passage' involve disturbing doppelgängers. Doubts about the reality of past events that plague the narrator of 'The Gate of a Hundred Shadows' grow worse as the tale progresses. *Naulahka* includes the dead city of Gunnaur and the various ill inhabitants of the decrepit Rhatore State Dispensory. Other tales, such as 'My Own True Ghost Story', 'The Phantom Rickshaw' and 'The Tomb of His Ancestors', feature such stock Gothic elements as haunted spaces, graveyards, opium dens and various images of engulfment. This treatment of India established a sensationalized backdrop of arcane theologies, participation in the extra-normal and the outright bizarre and unexplainable that contrasted with the order, rationality and ideologies of British imperial achievements, and thus served to underscore the notion of India's 'need' for colonization.

Kipling's later fiction concerning India, such as *The Jungle Books* and *Kim*, seem much less concerned with such Gothic elements as intimations of the occult, disquieting plots and notions of terror, and more with a celebratory observation of the intoxicating cultural panorama of Kipling's memory. Kim's India, for example, is a vast place of potential, a fantastic realm of the possible exploration of various contradictory states of being.[67] It is, furthermore, an India less fraught with conflict between colonizer and colonized.[68] The English are seen in *The Jungle Books* as establishers of order and a court of appeal rather than an imposing and unwelcome cultural juggernaut. The actual site of opposition in these later works, then, is Mowgli and Kim's interior abstractions. Kipling repositions the locus of conflict endemic to imperial narratives to the psychological landscape of the orphan. I argue, therefore, that, while *The Jungle Books* and *Kim* are not overtly focused on terror or the unusual, Kipling's preoccupation with the Gothic persists through to his final novel within his exploration of the internal disjunction of the orphans Mowgli and Kim. Concern with the fearful is displaced and redirected onto psychic development whereby Kipling dislodges the trope of Indian oddity and imposes it onto the orphans who assume the burden of protean incertitude.

The focus becomes the orphans' indeterminacy, the imbalance of their self-perception, the quasi-Gothic uncertainty of an identity in question. Kipling renders Mowgli and Kim as ambivalent enough that both may acquire when requisite a number of potential identities along their respective quests for cohesion and validation. Indeed, both boys cross various social categories, Kim vacillating from one race to the other, Mowlgi transgressing the boundaries between species. Immersion into haunted spaces, encounters with troubling doubles and the implications of ruined cities are refashioned into explorations into the developing psychology of orphans who are partially admitted and partially excluded, who seem a certain classification one moment, another the next.

Kim's and Mowgli's ambiguity poses both threat and promise to the concept of imperialism. Mowgli at once epitomizes the potential for degeneration and racial slippage while embodying a kind of imperial domination and racial superiority over his 'brothers'. In spite of his Anglo-Irish heritage, Kim is in appearance scarcely distinguishable from his native counterparts and, therefore, seeming to have been diminished on the racial level. At the same time his Britishness and his intimacy with the Indian culture endow him with a facility that, like Mowgli's, once applied in the right manner, has the capacity to lead to the rectification of the orphan state. There is throughout the work of Kipling a lachrymose yearning – either nostalgia for a lost home or the search for a new one – which is paramount to the narratives of the orphans Mowgli and Kim. Both are part of their respective cultures to some degree, yet they are outsiders as well, so that neither absolutely occupies a community; both are rendered as incapable of absolute assimilation, 'comfortable to different degrees, but at home nowhere'.[69] Kim, Mowgli, and Rikki-Tikki for that matter, each are ancillary members of provisional family structures that are in constant danger of being lost to them. Rikki-Tikki's placement remains for a time undetermined, between the order and comfort of the Englishman's home and the tenuous nature and potential violence of the garden. Mowgli and Kim are disengaged from the indentifying referents of their families and are beyond class or even race; and yet they are mutable enough at least partially to insinuate themselves into a given social structure while simultaneously having at their disposal the attribute of supremacy. Thus the two orphans execute a kind of imperial fantasy of assimilation without the relinquishment of authority. Despite their respective immersions into a variety of communities, both perpetuate a kind of 'psychological distance' from their environments which grants them a modicum of control over their otherwise overall tenuous existences, a sense of dominion rarely at the disposal of the orphan.[70] This standing proves a two-edged sword, however; the indeterminacy of their particular racial designation permits them a range of command over others, but that same lack of distinction necessitates disconnection that entails a certain level of exile. The reconciliation of Mowgli's and Kim's orphan states, similar in some ways to that of Rikki-Tikki, may only be brought about by their being recast into the mould of an entity for which their particular appetencies may be employable and admission into which might be absolute. For Kipling, that entity was the British Empire. Just as the aberrations of Kipling's earlier Indian narratives suggest the supremacy of British rationality and order, Mowgli and Kim's predicament of fracture may only be remedied by British superintendence.

Kim and the Europeanizing of the orphan

Kim is remarkable for his hybrid qualities, denoted by the kit he carries which includes an English revolver, medicine box, compass, an Indian robe, amulet and a begging gourd. This mingling of elements includes an intimate acquaintance with Indian society and the authoritative disposition of the British. He is 'burned black as any native' and 'spoke the vernacular by preference' and yet 'Kim was white – a poor white of the very poorest'.[71] He is British, but more or less reared by a half-caste woman of dubious reputation. He prefers Indian clothing, but simultaneously appeals when he prefers to the eminence and capabilities endemic to his race. He is, for example, able to resist mesmerism by the recitation of the multiplication tables, his employment of the rationality of mathematics defraying the influence of eastern mysticism. And despite his orphan status, lack of caste and lack of education, Kim accomplishes more developmentally than any of his native counterparts.[72] His similarity to the Other is unsettling, while his Anglo-Irishness and its attending superiority contrast with the subjugated natives. This disturbance, however, is reconciled by Kim's assumption into the context of imperial power.

Although his indefinite racial affiliation might appear a cause for confusion, throughout his earlier years in Lahore Kim avoids the kind of psychic trauma and debilitating uncertainty typical of orphan figures; in fact, his orphanhood permits his enthusiastic mutability and adaptability. Unlike that of the usual orphan, the consequences of Kim's lack of family are less a crippling hindrance and more an enabling occasion that allows the autonomy he enjoys. Although he is not entirely assumed into a community, Kim never seems lost or deprived.[73] While orphans generally desire to attain the signifiers that denote a clearly defined place of inclusion and acceptance in society, Kim's absence of the potential constraints imposed by parents or the possible inhibitions of class affiliation endow him with the opportunity to 'improvise his identity'.[74] Like Stoker's Renfield, who vacillates from one imitative personality to another as his circumstances demand, Kim exploits his malleability to his benefit. His simulation, however, is less a result of the desperate pursuit of inclusion into a family or some other identifying social construct that animates Renfield and more a kind of sport, a preparatory dalliance for the Great Game into which he will eventually find himself. This imitative tendency serves as a variant of Bhabha's conception of mimicry in that Kim is a member of the colonizing race who assumes the customs and dress of the colonized, an ability that permits his control of the native space and which is eventually put into the service of the empire.[75]

Indeed, Kim evades the overall distress that frequently defines the orphan and instead revels in the license of caste-lessness. This kind of parentless and limitless fantasy cannot be perpetuated, however. In the case of both Mowgli and Kim, the maturation of the orphan necessitates a choice of father, a selection of caste, family and an entity to serve. Once he leaves his native city, therefore, Kim must engage the eventual question, 'Who is Kim?'[76] In the case of both orphans, the social construct to which they ultimately defer and into which they are assimilated is the British Empire.

Kim is on a quest that differs in some respects to that of the typical orphan, but it is nevertheless a quest for identity. In contrast to the lama's endeavour at the complete annihilation of identity and the loss of self requisite to the salvation he seeks, Kim's is eventually a journey towards reclaiming and acquiring his British lineage. As Kim matures and he increasingly assumes the selfhood of his true heritage, and his British identity becomes more evident, his ability to shape-shift and imitate will decrease. As John McBratney states, Kim will be 'less the laminar who delights in self-transformation for its own sake and more the Briton who wears disguises to work'.[77] The indication is that Kim's hybridity will diminish, to be displaced by a demeanour more indicative of his affiliation with the empire.

The lama's quest is an eastern one for detachment; Kim's is a western quest for selfhood and the realization of his true identity. Kim's parents have both died, his mother from cholera, his father from drink and opium, but the novel presents a narrative varying from the traditional nineteenth-century theme of the search for a father figure in its presentation of numerous potential paternal figures representing various aspects of a notably diverse culture.[78] Mahbub Ali associates with the English but retains his Muslim customs; Hurree Chunder Mookerjee attempts to mimic British manners and speech; Mr Bennett and Father Victor attempt to bring Kim into their respective churches. Although he is able to discern his lineage through the Red Bull on a Green Field symbol, Kim locates a temporary surrogate father in the lama, a more spiritual alternative to Kim's failed, biological father. But this seeming acquiescence to eastern parentage is complicated by the predominantly western disposition inherent in Kim. He is aware of his potential to be a sahib, and knows that one day he 'will command natives'.[79] His admiration, respect and even love for the lama, including the enactment of formalities requisite of a *chela*, do not deter Kim's eventual trajectory, which is the phenomenal world.[80] Kim is, for example, more occupied with the lama's physical safety than with the spiritual sate to which the guru aspires, and Kim ultimately adheres to the allure of familial placement within the empire, and not with the lama who pursues the renunciation of belonging. For Kim, the lama's journey is on 'too narrow a path to walk without straying'.[81] Indeed, Kim ultimately proves more loyal to his British heritage than to the Indian culture within which he has grown. In doing so, he selects to emulate the attributes of his British potential father figures that are most beneficial to his participation in the Great Game and thus in service to the British Empire; he has Strickland's knowledge of the indigenous population, Lurgan's familiarity with the area's languages and Creighton's insight into the Indian perspective. The numerous patriarchal characters that help to mould him and guide him to the realization of his true self and his calling remarkably increasingly represent a British influence, and Kim's recasting is actually a recognition of and fulfilment of his lineage.

Mowgli and the allegory of empire

Mowgli's journey is a series of events that reaffirm his orphan state, beginning with abandonment by and separation from his biological parents, continuing with his subsequent adoption by a surrogate family of wolves into which he may be only partially incorporated, temporary expulsion from the jungle and subsequent banishment from the village of men, and culminating in his eventual virtual severance from the animal world. And, like numerous other orphans discussed in this study, this 'outcaste – a *mlech*' is known by numerous appellations that testify to the indeterminacy of his identity. His wolf-mother's name for him is 'the frog', due to his hairlessness but appropriate as well given his amphibious adaptive capabilities. At various times he is known as 'Man-cub', 'Wolf's Brat', 'sorcerer's child', 'jungle-demon', 'Devil-child', 'Godling of the Woods', 'Faunus' and, if not truly Messua's son, then so near in appearance to him that she calls him 'Nathoo'. The curiosity that is Mowgli is perhaps summed up in the question of the Father of Cobras, 'Whose cattle are *ye*?' and Grisborne's inquiry, 'I wonder what in the world he is'.[82]

Mowgli can operate to varying degrees in both jungle and village, but cannot seem to belong wholly to either. At one point, the jungle is 'shut' to him; at another, he claims he 'never wished to see, or hear, or smell man again'.[83] Philip Mason compares Mowgli to Crusoe and Prospero, 'alone on his island'.[84] While his wolf brothers provide a provisional home, Mowgli's animal enemies instigate his exile from the jungle and, although Messua offers maternal comfort, the men's mistrust results in his banishment from the village. As Shere Khan points out, Mowgli is 'neither man nor cub'.[85] The boy seems for the most part more complacent among his animal friends, and 'he would have called himself wolf if he had been able to speak in any human tongue'.[86] Later he states: 'I am not a man', 'I am a wolf' and 'It is no will of mine that I am a man'; he insists: 'I *am* of the Jungle' and 'The jungle is my house'; and furthermore he asks: 'What have I to do with Man?'[87] Indeed, he seems unaffected overall by his orphan state until the crisis of identity that emerges in the final story of *The Jungle Books*, 'The Spring Running', where the orphan convention of ostracism is firmly asserted as the jungle in the time of the New Talk grows alien to Mowlgi; 'There is no one here', he states; 'The night noises of the marsh went on, but never a bird or beast spoke to him, and the new feeling of misery grew'.[88] Mowgli's familiarization with the natural world, upon which the management of his orphanhood has been contingent, begins to fail him; the jungle becomes as forbidding and unwelcoming to him as the Isle of Erraid is to the castaway David Balfour. The consoling context which has previously permitted Mowgli to evade the hazards of orphanhood dissipates, generating the ever-increasing need for the secondary context he will discern in the British Empire.

As early as 'Mowgli's Song', however, some indication of inner turmoil is evident as Mowgli states 'I am two Mowglis' and his two natures 'fight together in me as the snakes fight in the spring'.[89] The undifferentiated state of orphanhood takes on new dimensions with Mowgli's interior struggles as to his identity. Upon his being exiled from the village, his interior struggle emerges in oppositional emotional reactions; although he 'looked up at the stars and felt happy', his heart is 'very light' and 'heavy with things that I do not understand.[90] And there are moments where the uncertainty of Mowgli's identity begets some anxiety, where he endeavours to comply with his natural human tendencies, such as his penchant to 'go down the hillside into the cultivated lands by night, and look very curiously at the villagers in their huts'.[91] He furthermore demonstrates an intrinsic ability to construct, 'mak[ing] little play-huts of fallen branches without thinking of how he came to do it', evoking the Bandar-log's request for his instruction as to 'how to weave sticks and canes together as a protection against rain and cold'.[92] When Messua pronounces a word to him, he 'would imitate it almost perfectly'.[93] It is after his time among men that Mowgli bears the knife around his neck that endows him with a threatening eminence over the animals, and only he can feed and control the Red Flower from which all animals cower. In attempting to second guess the actions of the men in 'The King's Ankus', he states 'I now remember that I was once a man', and makes such proclamations as: 'Well, if I am a man, a man I must become'.[94] Becoming a man, for Mowgli, equates to relinquishing his former place within the animal world, and thus acquiescing to the true, human self that may only find totality within imperial space.

However, the natural attraction to and curiosity about the human community is complicated by several factors that endanger his assimilation and contribute to the perpetuation of Mowgli's orphanic exile. Bagheera, for one, interposes a mistrust of men Mowgli carries with him even as he enters the village. In his youth, Mowgli's response to the world of men is largely of an incredulous nature, as demonstrated by his challenging of the men's tales of 'ghosts and goblins' as 'cobwebs and moontalk'.[95] And, yet, testament to the ambivalence of his self-perception may be noted in Mowgli's insistence upon singeing Shere Khan's whiskers while skinning the tiger in imitation of the native hunters who do the same to prevent a tiger's ghost from haunting them. There is with Mowgli a consistent implication that he is not currently what he should be, that he has either devolved from one state or is in the process of developing into another. In either circumstance, the interstitial state of the orphan is evident in Mowgli's uncertainty of self.

As a human being, clearly superior in ability and intellect to and capable of matching the physical attributes of many of the jungle animals, Mowgli seems on one level an emblem of imperial authority. He is 'Master of the Jungle',[96] a commanding figure whom most consider a friend but whom all revere with some timidity. As a symbol of Empire, he has infiltrated an area originally not his own and assumed an authoritative position.[97] As Lisa Makman notes, Mowgli 'combats disorder symbolically by ensuring that the animals abide by their own law'.[98] On occasion, Mowgli affirms his imperative standing, for instance in his use of half-mocking names like 'Flat-head' for the serpent Kaa, his derision of the dholes as Chikai, his scoffing at Hathi's mythical accounts, and his calling his wolf-brothers '*sags* [dogs], as a man should'.[99]

Eliot L. Gilbert reads Mowgli's tale as a *bildungsroman* wherein the boy severs from the 'deadly "safety" of his father's house' and furthermore rediscovers 'his father in himself'.[100] But any insight into Mowgli's father, supposedly Messua's husband, in 'Letting in the Jungle', offers a portrait of a petulant and self-concerned feebling; Mowgli may be many things, but fearful and querulous are not among them. In fact, in his commanding, authoritative capacity, Mowgli emulates an imperial father-figure like Quatermain, and exacts a certitude generally not afforded to orphans; thus, on quite another level, Mowgli embodies the native whose aptitude and talents, like those of Kim and Rikki-Tikki, are employed for the service of the Empire. And this is crucial to Mowgli's development, for it is only in the chronologically final Mowlgi story, 'In the Rukh', that his orphan state is finally reconciled through admission into and subjection to the British Empire.

In 'In the Rukh', Kipling offers an older Mowgli who has assented to the authority of the Empire and, like Kim, has located a father, a caste, and has become an active, contributing component of the hierarchical imperial system to which the younger Mowgli's arrangement merely alluded. We are introduced immediately to the systematization of imperialism, 'the wheels of public service'[101] being the focus of the narrative's opening. It is to the service of that institution that the perplexing Mowgli's rapport with the *rukh* is directly apportioned. Grisborne determines Mowgli to be 'that ideal ranger and forest-guard for whom he and the Department were always looking'; Muller insists Mowgli 'take service under me, who am the Government in the matter of Woods and Forests'.[102] And Mowgli is remarkably deferential to the authority of the Empire in a way that he never was to the animals of the jungle, referring from the moment of their introduction to Grisborne as 'Sahib', and offering to carry the Forest Officer's gun and to protect his valuables. In addition, this former 'Master of the Jungle' states, 'The Sahib is in charge of this *rukh*' and 'It is the Sahib's *rukh*'.[103] It is clear that the imperious boy of *The Jungle Books* who was raised by wolves has developed into a man desiring interaction with other human beings, telling Grisborne, 'There is no man to talk to out there in the *rukh*'[104] and marrying Abdul Gafur's daughter. Mowgli's maturation is evident too in his scoffing at the idea of singeing the slain tiger's whiskers and proclaiming that he is 'no lousy *shikarri*'.[105] This distancing from native superstition also indicates Mowgli's endeavor to designate himself as of a more rational, more British, disposition.

These exchanges and Mowgli's clear submission to authorial imperial figures not only provide the orphan with pay and a pension, but inclusion into a social structure more appropriate to his maturity and which will supplant his waning position as 'Master of the Jungle'. Toward the story's end, the scene with Mowgli and Abdul Gafur's daughter demonstrates the transition he is undergoing from amphibious being of the jungle to married employee of the Empire. The crown of flowers he wears is a token of the fragility of his position as Master of the Jungle, for although his four wolf brothers dance to his flute-playing, the enclosed, Edenic clearing where the scene occurs indicates the eroding limits of his relationship with the jungle and seems a tenuous imitation of his former days. Mowgli's 'brothers', with whom he has spent the majority of his life, have actually served as father-types for his development: from Kaa he acquires wisdom; from Bagheera, hunting skill; from Baloo, knowledge of the law; and from Akela, the concept of leadership. But these lesser father-figures are ultimately replaced by their imperial counterparts. Mowgli's incorporation into the Empire also provides the orphan, a being 'without a village', 'a man without caste, and for that matter of that without a father',[106] with two father figures in Grisborne and Muller. Ultimately, Mowgli's orphan state, like that of Kim, is remedied by reception into and subordination to the British Empire.

Merriman's Reckless Orphan

Contrasting with these narratives of eventual assimilation and the acquisition of totality within the context of the Empire is Henry Seton Merriman's *Flotsam: The Story of a Life*. The novel is remarkable for its analysis of 'the enterprise of ignorance and a characteristic heedlessness of consequence' and 'dashing recklessness' of its orphan protagonist,[107] Harry Wylam, and the repercussions of his squandering and refusal of the advantages of inclusion within the Empire. This 'brilliant yacht tossed hither and thither on every wave of life'[108] exhibits the incertitude typical of the orphan, claiming at turns to aspire to being a sailor, a red-coat and a soldier. And Harry's tragic flaws, a penchant for greed and aspiration to social status at the expense of honor and ethicality, would seem to hark back to the convention of the orphan's vulnerability to vice and immorality without what Merriman calls the 'wise discipline' of 'parental pride which handicaps many childish virtues'.[109] That his disposition, 'a fiery nature', is said to 'easily have been inherited',[110] speaks to the potential perils of the orphan's indefinite derivation. Marqueray, furthermore, states that Harry is 'easily led'.[111] Harry's first guardian, Lamond, proves a treasonous and deceitful character, though Harry's age during his time in Lamond's care hardly seems to implicate his guardian as a negative influence at that point in the orphan's life. It actually appears that Harry seems intrinsically flawed. As Oliver Edwards observes, Harry's tragedy 'was born with him; it was in his character'.[112] Harry's Major warns him that it is 'Yourself' that Harry should fear, and Harry is referred to as 'his own most inveterate enemy'.[113]

Indeed, despite the fact that he inherits a fortune, is put into the custody of the wealthy Gresham, is permitted into a provisional family complete with a potential spouse in the virtuous Miriam, and even becomes married – all traditional remedies for orphanhood – Harry nevertheless, through selfish choices and imprudent decisions, perpetuates his own orphan state. Moreover, he seems incapable of acknowledging his own fault, 'convinced that his misfortunes were wholly the outcome of an evil fate that seemed to dog his footsteps'; he curses 'his ill-fortune' and claims that he is 'possessed of a devil'.[114] As though to demonstrate the ramifications of refuting communion with the Empire, as well as to underscore the importance of the family structure that is a microcosm of that Empire, Merriman subverts the conventions associated with orphan narratives, positioning Harry early on in circumstances that typically conclude orphan narratives, only to have the orphan in every instance unmake his potential redemption.

Harry's tragedy begins with an unnecessary assertion of his racial superiority. The first impression of him is as 'a waif of tender years, cast upon the great world',[115] beating his ayah with the leg of a rocking horse.[116] Though he initially knows nothing of his lineage, 'the hereditary character shows itself early', so that 'all the insolence of the dominant race'[117] emerges even in Harry's youth. But whatever racially-innate command he possesses, Harry's 'irrepressible energy' exceeds acceptable assertions of authority, so that 'the masterfulness of the dominant race' that has enabled the Empire's success is ruinously exerted without distinction or prejudice.[118] When this proclivity to control is suppressed, Harry makes the first of several tragic choices, which is to abandon the incorporation, wealth and promise of the Gresham household to become a sailor. And while the occupation of sailor still places Harry under the auspices of the Empire, the important fact is that the orphan has elected to abandon a loving, functional domestic space for a trade characterized by separation and transience.

At a moment when many orphan narratives would conclude, with the protagonist's acquisition of a fortune to allay the symptoms of orphanhood, Harry's rebuke of potential reparation of his orphan state ironically continues with the reception of his inheritance and his celebration thereof. Challenging the drunken Montague to a duel to defend Miriam's name, Harry not only disregards the authority of his foster father, but also imperils his relationship with Miriam, simultaneously jeopardizing familial and possible marital associations. This recklessness furthermore leads to Harry's expulsion not only from his regiment, but from England itself. Due to his imprudence, then, the orphan has severed himself from four potentially restorative contexts and ensured his own exile.

Despite his evident contrition in the form of an apologetic letter to Gresham and in addition to receiving Miriam's pledge of fidelity, Harry persists in displaying a predilection for impetuosity that follows him to India. There, exhibiting 'a very keen taste for enjoyment' and 'a nature given more to the enjoyment of the present than to thoughts of the future',[119] he threatens his inheritance with a weakness for gambling, a vice that entails numerous damaging ramifications. This irresponsible misuse of one of the elements that typically remedy the orphan state engenders the financial desperation that leads to Harry's assistance in the destruction and pillaging of an Indian temple, his share of which he also squanders. The orphan seems offered yet again the feasibility of acquiring the belonging and totality of familial and marital union by the notion of eventual marriage to Lamond's opportunistic daughter, Maria. His tendency for self-destruction, however, is hardly helped by the failed father figure, the 'snake-like'[120] Lamond, whose interest in Harry has always been financial. Lamond's betrayal is somewhat countered by Marqueray, a man 'of quiet observance',[121] who suggests Harry retrieve his daughter from Maria and return to England, an option with implications of fatherhood and marriage. Harry's observance of Marqueray's advice and the securing of his daughter's care under Miriam would seem to suggest his arrival at a point of conversion. However, his choice not to remain in England yet again proves the orphan's undoing. His fateful decision to abandon once more the promise of home terminates in his subsequent illness and death. Merriman's moral of the dangers to which the orphan exposes himself upon rejecting affiliation with the larger family of empire comes to its tragic fruition: the orphan, consistently provided opportunities for assimilation and wholeness, has denied familial structures, refused the responsibilities of inheritance and wasted the promise of fatherhood and a happy marriage, the consequence of which is ultimately the death of the unreconciled orphan.

6

Orphans in Haunted Arcadia

'It wants its mother.'

Francis Hodgson Burnett, *The Secret Garden*

This chapter segues into children's fantasy of the Edwardian period, focusing on J. M. Barrie's *Peter Pan* (1911)[1] and Francis Hodgson Burnett's *A Little Princess* (1905) and *The Secret Garden* (1911), which depict orphans employing their creative capacity to formulate alternate realms which are characterized by provisional domestic constructs contrasting with the familyless reality from which the orphans emerge. In addition, the chapter examines how these imitative constructs ultimately prove untenable and incapable of adequately replacing the actual family ideal; it also discusses the orphan's assumption of a tenuous autonomy that is particularly influenced by various types of absent, spectral mother figures.

I use the term 'children's fantasy' somewhat hesitantly. As Jacqueline Rose points out in her *The Case of Peter Pan or the Impossibility of Children's Fiction*, the term is a somewhat problematic one. Rose's argument concerning the 'impossibility' of the genre lies in the notion that children's fiction operates largely to keep the 'problem' of sexuality 'at bay', and is more for adults than the children it purports to address; her claim is that the genre 'gives us the child, but it does not *speak* to the child', and that *Peter Pan*, for example, 'has never, in any easy way, been a book for children'.[2] The idea that children's fiction really pertains to the adult is compatible with my own regard of Edwardian 'children's' fantasy less as entertainment or education for young readers and more as an articulation of 'adult' anxieties emerging from the crises of abandonment, exile and identity so ubiquitous in the fin-de-siècle.

While fantasy has been a typical escapist feature of children's literature, with the advent of the Edwardian period, the fantastic territory literalizes the anxieties begat by the unavailing realities of the modernity toward which the Edwardians progressed. Within the creative act of forging a novel space of inclusion and self-confidence a representation of the Edwardian garden party, an insular pretense that recalled some idyllic past that once may or may not have existed, but certainly could not last.[3] Furthermore, the employment of the ghostly, influential mother figure belies an appeal on the part of the Edwardian world to the stability and reassurance of tradition symbolized in the Good Mother. Following a period in which genre fiction had questioned the family ideal and had portrayed the father-figure largely as an unreliable, somehow disabled or even a threatening liability to the orphan, the mother-figure persisted as an influential, self-sacrificing and salvific role model by which the orphan was inspired and through whom is to some extent able to reconcile his or her orphan condition.

Peter Pan's Neverland is necessitated by the abandonment his mother enacts. The land serves as a surrogate reality which permits Peter's perpetual youth, but it is motherless and incomplete. Peter's avowed denial of his need for the mother who shut him out is belied by his desire for the provisional motherhood provided by Wendy. While Peter's mother effects the need for Neverland and Wendy's mimetic role, both are threatened by the maternal specter of Mrs Darling, whose unfailing nurturance and faith ultimately endanger the imitative family structure Peter has devised by proving a superior reality and a constant distraction to Wendy. Therefore it is both Peter's mother and Mrs Darling who initially engender but eventually threaten what Neverland represents. Just as

Peter negotiates his orphanhood with his imaginative capability, Sara Crewe, of *A Little Princess*, displays the imagination of an extraordinarily creative child, an ability that initially endears her to the other girls in Miss Minchin's seminary, but ultimately serves as the primary coping mechanism for Sara to deal with the death of her only family relation and the servant status cast upon her. Though certainly bound to her absent father in a deep emotional manner, it is arguably the ideal of Sara's mother, who died during childbirth, that instills in Sara the maternal spirit that compels her to nurture the simple Ermengarde, befriend the lonely servant Becky and become the 'young adopted mother'[4] to the motherless Lottie. Similarly, the emotionally disturbed orphans Mary Lennox and Colin Craven, of *The Secret Garden*, both afflicted by a lack of parental affirmation, establish their own alternative space within the novel's eponymous area. There the two emulate Dickon, the cock-sure foil to Mary and Colin's uncertainty and the product of the perpetual auspices of Dickon's Mrs Darling-like mother. Mrs Sowerby's influence from afar permeates the entire novel, attended by the magical spirit of Colin's dead mother, Lilias. Both mother figures induce the metaphoric transformation of the garden as well as influence Mary's own transition from disagreeable horror to selfless mother-figure for Colin. All three of these texts, products of the end of the long nineteenth century, indicate the trajectory of orphan literature in the twentieth century, with its emphasis not on the orphan's reconciliation with his or her past, but rather on an attempt to recreate the self within a new and different construct. This endeavor, however, is frequently attended by mother figures whose power influences and even determines the orphan's success or failure.

The Mother Figure

When Mary Louisa Molesworth writes in *The Palace in the Garden*, 'A lady – a woman in the family makes all so different',[5] she underscores a notion that had steadily progressed as the nineteenth century advanced, that of middle-class domestic ideology's reverence for the home and the mother. In the century's later decades, with one of the main tenets of domestic ideology being the separation of work and home, and children being the center of the home, child-rearing responsibilities shifted from activities overseen by the father to ones that centred around the mother.[6] The mother was not only the bearer and rearer of children, but 'the guardian of the hearth' and the warden of the home's sanctity, and the emphasis on the need for women to remain home stressed 'the centrality of the stable home and family in Victorian culture'.[7] The preoccupation with the world of the mother, the notion of the home and a reverence for the protection and inclusion that the mother provided had emerged by the mid-Victorian period,[8] and whereas by the end of the century the New Woman had challenged notions associated with traditional female roles, Edwardian children's fiction demonstrates a return to the cult of the mother, an emphasis on her importance and influence. The mother came to be regarded as being the daughter's 'primary protector' who directed her moral and spiritual maturation, was the exemplar by which the daughter established and preserved the values associated with the family, empowered the daughter with the capacity to endure adversity and conquer despair, and was the role model by which a daughter learned to be sympathetic to and understand others.[9] Even the memory of a good mother could provide empowerment and a reason to endure hardship,[10] thus Barbara Thaden's theory that women writers, such as Gaskell and Oliphant, who were also mothers, demonstrated the persistence of the good mother's influence beyond maternal death through memories that effect the orphan even into childhood; in *Mary Barton*, for instance, the mother formulates a 'dream world' to which Mary may escape and from which she emerges strengthened; this as opposed to childless authors like the Brontës, who tend to create independent heroines who succeed despite being motherless.[11]

The mother, then, served a vital function in Victorian fiction, which makes it all the more striking that mothers in genre fiction of the period are notably done away with in some way early in the narrative.[12] In the event that the mother is present, she is somehow rendered ineffectual, at times even more in need of maternal nurturing than the daughter, and therefore must be removed in order not to hinder the orphan's progress. Various critics have noted the absence of the mother as a necessary narrative device which permits and even encourages the orphan's development beyond the confines of a maternal influence that might otherwise prevent the requisite disturbance of narrative equilibrium to initiate the story.[13] Others note that maternal absence is a pivotal element of Freudian and Lacanian notions of individuation.[14] The mother's non-presence sanctions the establishment of the self apart from the influencing identity of the mother, detachment from the order, protection and moral surety conveyed by the mother necessitating a sense of self-reliance for the orphan. Parental death allows for the orphan protagonist a greater range of potential error and narrative complication, an agency attended as much by the potential for failure as for progress. Peter Pan, Sara Crewe and Mary Lennox exhibit this type of agency. Peter is abandoned to form his own fantastic realm of eternal, if not necessarily joyous, youth; Sara must either persevere to overcome her orphanhood, or submit to its crushing implications; and the parentless Mary is left to aimlessly wander the labyrinthine but ultimately fecund grounds of Misselthwaite.

It should be noted that maternal influence is not always perceived in a positive light. Some critics see it as limiting the child's development.[15] In other cases, if the dead or otherwise absent mother tends to be a virtuous authority, the living mother or surrogate mother-figure is not. Substitute mother-figures who are in some way sympathetic to the orphan tend to be hampered by physical handicaps, illness or some similarly debilitating quality. The Terrible Mother, meanwhile, is egocentric and sadistic, and may even prove a source of despair or even mortal danger for the orphan.[16] Mrs Jellyby of Dickens's *Bleak House* serves as a typical Terrible Mother type, at odds with the ideal Victorian mother, who, rather than serve as the center around which an ordered and functioning ideal Victorian home focuses, instead generates a chaotic maelstrom of contrived concern on the periphery of which the shambles of her domestic space fall as they may.[17]

Having noted these conventions typical of Victorian fiction, I would like to discuss the manner in which both Barrie and Burnett tend to challenge them. Mary's neglectful mother, for example, subverts these stereotypical treatments. Though Mary's biological mother, Mrs Lennox lacks any of the nurturing instinct typical of the mother who dies early in the narrative. In fact, when both Mary's parents die, her psychological damage has been exacted to the extent that the effect of their deaths is virtually negligible. So removed from her mother is Mary that when contemplating a positive maternal image, she can do so only through the 'mediating' notion of her dead Aunt Lilias,[18] an experience that is possibly the first instance of Lilias's supernatural influence. Burnett's inversion of mother-related conventions is evident as well in the nurturing influence of the near-mythical Mrs Sowerby, whose non-physical impression, through sent gifts and advice quoted by her children, assists Mary in overcoming the trauma and neuroses of her earlier years by providing an invitation of inclusion and belonging. In contrast to the aforementioned convention of the still-influential dead mother, both Barrie's Mrs Darling and Burnett's Mrs Sowerby are living and vibrant, and though temporarily physically distant, are models whose vital, positive effects mark a development in the presentation of the living mother.[19]

Mrs Darling, despite being absent for the majority of *Peter Pan* and serving more as an idea or inspiration, offers for Wendy the emblem of the Good Mother whom, to the lost boys' benefit, she emulates, but to Peter's dismay, ever threatens to draw Wendy back to England. Barrie's depiction of Mrs Darling, for example, 'tidying up her children's minds' and relegating 'the naughtiness and evil passions' of the day to the bottom of their minds while placing 'prettier thoughts' on top, demonstrates both her nurturing nature and the moral stability and reliable support she offers.[20] In contrast with the chaotic mind of the child, which is 'not only confused, but keeps going round all the time' and where 'nothing will stand still',[21] Mrs Darling's constant monitoring and restructuring is the kind of corrective and determinant of which the orphan is bereft, and which establishes her as an emblem of paradigms of moral, familial and religious traditions from which the late-Victorian and Edwardian periods drifted. Likewise, her sentimental regard for Peter shows her innate motherly instinct; despite her maturity, she is capable of recalling him from her own childhood, and 'something in the right-hand corner of her mouth'[22] prevents her from calling him names. Further demonstration of her selflessness emerges when the narrator explains that, were he to deviate from the story of the children to see how she is faring, Mrs Darling would reply, '[W]hat do I matter? Do go back and keep an eye on the children', and furthermore that she 'would never forgive us'[23] in the event that the children's beds were not properly aired prior to their return. Her insistence that the window 'must always be left open for them, always, always'[24] provides a poignant contrast with Peter's mother, who chose instead to close the window behind him and ensure his orphanic condition.

Though as notably absent from the majority of the narrative as Mrs Darling, Mrs Sowerby – of *The Secret Garden* – provides the maternal model which Mary has been denied and which she will ultimately aspire to emulate. Burnett renders Mrs Sowerby as an abiding, influential and perpetually affecting mother comparable to Mrs Darling, despite the former being as notably absent from the central action of the story as the latter. The 'comfortable wonderful mother creature' and 'kind clever woman' with a 'comfortable rosy face' and who understands the children 'as Dickon understands his "creatures"' is a perfect emblem of the Good Mother.[25] As someone who 'always knows what a body needs',[26] for instance, she sends doughcakes for the children to eat, charges Martha with cheering Mary up, and initiates Mary's exercise regimen by recommending the girl skip rope. She is a source of maternal wisdom as well, stating that one should 'keep out o' doors as much as you could, even when it rains a bit, so as tha' wrap up warm' and, underscoring the joy inherent in her maternal capacity, 'believes as half a hour's good laugh every mornin 'ud cure a chap as was makin' ready for typhus fever'.[27] Such is her influence that even the initially incredulous Colin regards her 'with a kind of bewildered adoration' and declares that he wishes she were his mother.[28] Accordingly, she is perceived by the otherwise secretive children to be 'safe for sure', and allowed to 'come into the secret'[29] of the garden.

Particularly when compared to these mother-figures who challenge traditional depictions of the living mother as typically malevolent, Colin's deceased mother, Lilias, seems more a conventional Good Mother type who has died but whose positive force persists after death. However, rather than merely exist in memory, Lilias transcends the boundaries of mortality first through the 'Magic' that pervades the garden and colludes with Mrs Sowerby's influence to compel Mary to revive the forsaken space, and ultimately through the more overtly supernatural medium of her auditory petition of Craven to return to the garden. Her nurturing spirit is manifested in her love of the garden. Ben Weatherstaff regards her love of roses as comparable to a love of children, and even claims, 'I've seen her bend over an' kiss 'em'.[30] The Magic with which she is associated, and which is also evident in Dickon,[31] permeates the space, assists in moving Mary from introversion to selflessness, and, according to Colin, compels Mrs Sowerby to 'think of ways to do things – nice things. She is a Magic person'.[32] This magical quality is as profound for Mary as Mrs Sowerby's physical offerings; Lilias is on a supernatural level what Mrs Sowerby and Mrs Darling are on the physical plane. Dickon remarks that Lilias's spirit is 'about Misselthwaite' looking after Colin, 'same as all mothers do when they're took out o' th' world. They have to come back tha' sees'.[33] He also credits her spectral presence with the restorative work that has occurred in the garden, stating, 'Happen she's been in the garden an' happen it was her set us to work, an' told us to bring him [Colin] here'.[34]

The portrayal of Lilias is distinctive as well in regard to Colin's reaction to this positive Good Mother. Although he selfishly guards his image of her and claims that 'she is mine and I don't want everyone to see her',[35] he conceals her portrait so she is unable to look at him, claims that he hates her for dying, and blames her death for his own illness and his father's perceived hatred. This kind of indignation for a deceased Good Mother is a novel approach to the maternal figure and posits Colin as emblematic of the bitterness attending the generational anxiety of the fin-de-siècle and Edwardian era. In contrast to Mary, who recognizes the value of maternal affection and her own need of it, the self-diagnosed invalid, refusing the potential of a healthful future, resents the deceased representative of belonging and affirmation in a nihilistic, self-interested pose of degeneration and disintegration. It is as though Burnett were juxtaposing the two available alternatives of the turn of the century, either an appeal to the stability and inclusion of the tradition embodied in Mrs Sowerby, or the corruptive and unproductive descent into the umbrage and animosity embodied in Colin's self-implosion.

Lilias's ethereal maternal presence eventually triumphs. When Colin's healing initiates, he attributes it to his mother, 'a sort of Magic person'.[36] Mary suggests that Colin is 'her ghost made into a boy', to such an extent that Mrs Sowerby claims he is 'so like thy mother th' made my heart jump'.[37] Once this connection between Colin and his mother is recognized, the notion permits Lilias to affect both father and son. Perceiving himself not as an imminently doomed and crippled version of his father, but instead as the reincarnation of his loving and lively mother, Colin is inspired to tell Craven about the Magic, that it might 'make him more cheerful'.[38] Though initially self-obsessed, through Lilias's magical coercion, both orphans are able to reconcile their injured conditions; Mary does so by selflessly assuming the guise of maternal nurturer, and Colin does so through recognition of his mother and sympathy for his father.

The Failed Father

I would be remiss not to briefly address the father figures of these texts, as their depiction actually serves to uphold the merit and significance of the mother. Chapter 4 discussed the convention in fin-de-siècle island fiction of challenging the authority, physical competence and moral certitude of the patriarch; *Peter Pan* and *The Secret Garden* employ a similar questioning of the father, the former of a functional Victorian nuclear family, the latter of a fragmented and dysfunctional household. In both texts, the father exhibits to a certain degree an ineptness that contrasts with and emphasizes the virtue and capability of the Good Mother.

Barrie's narrative portrays Mrs Darling and Wendy as virtuous, reliable and selfless mother-figures, but his depiction of Mr Darling is less flattering. While Mrs Darling, for instance, is patient and understanding with her children's play, Mr Darling insists on putting a stop to their fantasy and speaks of the notion of Peter Pan as nonsense.[39] Mrs Darling is noted as being proud of her daughter, 'prejudiced in Wendy's favour',[40] while the lie attached to Mr Darling's failed endeavor to fool the children into taking their medicine is a betrayal that marks the moment Wendy begins to grow up. Indeed, Mr Darling is seen as a humorless disappointment to his incredulous offspring and whose authority is undermined by his wife's patronizing request that the children 'be especially nice to father', who complains childishly, 'Nobody coddles me!'[41] Regarded as a 'cipher in his own house',[42] Mr Darling is a well-meaning but clumsy authority, for example, arriving at different totals each time he adds numbers. Even when 'the strength of the character of the man'[43] is exhibited during his self-imposed penance in Nana's doghouse, Mr Darling's purgation is nearly nullified by his simultaneous assumption of a childlike demeanor clamoring for Mrs Darling's attention. Overall, Mr Darling functions as a present, if humorous, paternal element of the Victorian family, though one that belies faults in the patriarchal figure and which ultimately complements, and compliments, the mother.

In sharp relief to Mr Darling's comical but nevertheless paradigm-affirming fatherhood, the emotionally detached and psychologically traumatized widower, Archibald Craven, actually contributes to the orphanic condition that in various ways incapacitates and absolutely defines his son, Colin. Like Stevenson's marred pirates, Craven, a man 'with a crooked back who shut himself up also',[44] bears a physical manifestation of his internal state. So distraught over the death of his wife, Lilias, for which he blames Colin, Craven virtually refuses to acknowledge, let alone nurture, his son. He is ordinarily absent from Misselthwaite, preferring instead to wander Norway, Switzerland and northern Italy, having at one point 'forgotten and deserted his home and his duties'.[45] Rather than be physically present for his ailing son, Craven merely supplies Colin with books with pictures of gardens, various games and 'a beautiful writing-case with a gold monogram on it and a gold pen and inkstand'.[46] But such opulent gifts are incapable of compensating for Craven's lack of affection and affirmation, and cannot heal the wounds of orphanhood inflicted upon Colin. Any interaction he has in close proximity to Colin is as a disinterested witness to his son's deterioration. He 'wondered vaguely' about Colin, questions 'what he should feel' when observing the boy lying in bed before him, and ultimately 'shrank from it'.[47] The potential consequences of the father's regard are demonstrated in Colin's reaction to this paternal rejection; the effect is a hypochondria that involves an overwhelming sense of early death and paranoia that he will develop the same hunchback that marks his father. Furthermore, one of Colin's 'darkest miseries' is the self-loathing that accompanies 'being a sick weak-backed boy whose father was afraid to look at him'.[48] In essence, the son inherits and perpetuates the failures of the father.

Sara's father, Captain Crewe, of *A Little Princess*, presents a more complicated rendition of the turn of the century father. The widower does what he can to love, affirm, and emotionally and materially provide for his daughter. He does not inflict upon Sara the laughable foibles of Mr Darling, or the inattentive self-absorption of Craven. Rather, Burnett follows suit with the challenging of the father figure by having Crewe physically removed from the narrative almost immediately and eventually having him killed by fever and financial worries. Like the predicament generated by the death of the Good Mother, Crewe's death forces Sara to either collapse, like Lottie, into the misery of orphanhood, or to persevere in notable imitation of her soldier father and the inspiration of her deceased mother. Interestingly, Crewe possesses qualities such as affection, humor, nurturing and patience that are typically attributed to the mother, so that Sara's taking on of a mother role is as much in imitation of Captain Crewe as it is of the mother she never knew. Read this way, the novel subverts Crewe's masculinity by endowing him with characteristics usually associated with the feminine and maternal, subtly emphasizing with effect equal to that of Mr Darling and Craven, the eminence of the mother-figure.

The Malleable Motherless Child

While the removal of the mother serves as an obvious, effective convention to instigate a narrative, and while some critics, particularly of a feminist nature, read maternal influence as a hindrance, I want to focus on the detrimental aspects of the mother-figure's absence, the toll such a deficiency of maternal affirmation wreaks upon the orphan, and the manner in which this damage may be reconciled. While maternal absence may imply a certain range of freedom for the orphan, it involves the lack of parental love as well. The lack of a good mother or sufficient mother substitute has not only come to be perceived as an 'insurmountable obstacle to happiness' but also a detrimental factor in 'normal cognitive and emotional development'.[49] John Bowlby's studies of war orphans determined the ruinous effects of maternal absence on their social and intellectual maturation.[50] Those separated from their biological parents are notably 'developmentally at risk' and bear with them 'a sense of loss'.[51] Thus we see the use of the term 'Peter Pan Syndrome' to refer to a male who does not mature properly. Considering various orphans in *Peter Pan, A Little Princess* and *The Secret Garden*, I would like to examine the orphanic qualities of these characters, particularly as they contribute to the orphan's endeavor to compensate for the maternal absence that defines them.

Chapter 2 discussed the way in which the inconsistent and fragmentary Renfield was prone to imitate the more socially and psychologically stable persons in his proximity out of the orphanic compulsion towards integration into a social structure. *Peter Pan, A Little Princess* and *The Secret Garden* depict orphans whose constitutions are similarly malleable and who express a certain proclivity to the mimicry of characters who do not suffer from the abandonment, exclusion and lack of self-certainty that characterizes orphanhood. Though perhaps capable of pluck and intrepidity, these orphans are nonetheless marked by that persistent ache that typically accompanies those beyond the confines of family; likewise, there seems a deliberate detachment from the reality of their past in preference to an unknown future, but a detachment that is informed and inspired by mother figures, either living or dead, whose influence is ever-present. It is within this paradigm that emerges the orphan's imitative nature in a desperate attempt toward assimilation and identity.

The Gothic Fairy

One focus of this book has been the malleability, incertitude and undifferentiated nature intrinsic to orphanhood, referred to frequently as its 'Gothic' nature – that is, its changeableness, mutability, and refusal of normative and identifying categories. Barrie's Gothic fairy, Peter Pan, may initially convey a stable nature and the confidence it generates, with his unflinching spirit and irreverent demeanor. U.C. Knoepflmacher states that by the turn of the century, 'Peter Pan can remain untainted by the City of Experience, sheltered and immune on his island of never-growing boys'.[52] However, I read Neverland as inherently flawed, and its architect, above all of the book's characters, as bearing wounds that fantasy may momentarily stave off, but can never heal. Beneath that façade of assurance is merely an injured youth compensating for the pain which his mother's abandonment has inflicted upon him. Patrick Baybrooke notes a 'certain wistfulness' about Peter that is 'akin to melancholy', and a sense of 'striving against the inevitable' attending Peter's actions.[53] Indeed, Peter is largely characterized by being forsaken. His mother abandons and replaces him, and though he takes the Darling children on a fantastic adventure, he is eventually abandoned by them as well. Peter's initial pose of spunk and apathy is neutralized by both his visitation to the Darling's nursery window to hear the end of the Cinderella story and by his invitation to Wendy to be a mother to him and the lost boys. The indignation he bears toward the mother who closed the window behind him does not negate the fact that Peter needs and wants a mother as much as do his obsequious gang of orphans.

Peter's existence is, then, riddled with contradiction. He denies wanting a mother and jeers the role mother's play.[54]

His claims about his mother, for instance that her mouth contains more 'thimbles' than Mrs Darling's, seem mere speculation, for '[o]f course, he knew nothing about his mother; but sometimes bragged about her'.[55] Humphrey Carpenter states that the novel is 'partly satirical, a deliberate exaggeration and mockery of such things as parental affection';[56] however, I read the novel more as a solemn caveat against the loss of the parent. We must recall that Peter is present at the Darling's window to hear the conclusion of Mrs Darling's bed-time story because, he pitifully claims, none of them knows any stories, and that he contrives in a 'frightfully cunning'[57] manner to persuade Wendy to parent him and the lost boys. He promises her their respect and lists numerous ways she might confirm her vocation, such as darning socks, making pockets and tucking the boys in. Furthermore we see Peter's hatred for Wendy's story praising the doting and demonstrative Mrs Darling, the figure who threatens to recall Wendy back to the reality of Number 14; the same vengeful nature is evident in Peter's quickened breathing at one point because, as lore has it, an adult dies each time a child breathes; a vindictive Peter skips around the room and plays his pipes claiming that Wendy's departure from Neverland would not affect him; and though he nearly weeps when she leaves, he masks his sadness with a 'haughty laugh'.[58]

If the Victorian child was an emblem of innocence and purity, the Edwardian child was one of hedonism.[59] Peter could be seen to a certain extent as the Edwardian playboy looking for a good time, representative of Pater's directive to 'burn always with this hard, gem-like flame'.[60] As such, he seems merely an emblem of self-indulgent license and jubilant disobedience. Alison Lurie states that with Peter, 'the emphasis was no longer on loss and pain and deception, but on pleasure and discovery'.[61] The primary impetus of the novel, however, is Peter's mother closing the window and effecting his orphanhood; the perpetuate childhood that serves as context for Peter's nonchalance is the result not of discerning some secret to eternal youth, but of parental abandonment. Quite in contrast to the proclamation that he is 'youth' and 'joy',[62] Peter retains his childlike state not merely in order to play, but to avoid what he perceives the most treacherous and hurtful condition of adulthood. When Wendy points out when invited to be the boys' mother that she is only a little girl, Peter replies that they merely require 'a nice motherly person'.[63] But his response is characteristically evasive, for when he belies his still-lingering need for a mother, it is a little girl, and not a woman, whom he conscripts to accommodate the role.

An argument has been made that when Peter comes to retrieve his shadow and hear the end of 'Cinderella', he 'is not the seducer, but the seduced', and furthermore that it is Wendy's claim to know lots of stories that convinces Peter to stay.[64] This may be true to a certain degree, but I would state it in a way that does not deprive Peter of the agency he exacts in approaching the Darling household in the first place. It is important to understand Peter's motivation, to ever acknowledge is complicity in acquiring Wendy's services; if he is 'seduced' it is because his orphan state renders him vulnerable to figures like Mrs Darling and Wendy who might have the capacity to rectify his problem. Too, the narrator notes the devious nature of the plan, underscoring the idea that Peter's primary goal is to compensate for the mother who shut him out.

Perhaps the first indication of Peter's instability is the evidence of leaves that remain at Wendy's window. His adornment of skeleton leaves has been read as an indication that Peter is 'a ghost child – a boy who does not belong in the waking human world'.[65] There is also the peculiar loss of his shadow, the refusal of which to 'join like drops of water'[66] with him leaves Peter bewildered. When Wendy learns Peter's name, she asks, 'Is that all?',[67] further entrenching the notion that Peter is incomplete. When battling with Captain Hook, Peter claims, 'I'm youth, I'm joy . . . I'm a little bird that has broken out of the egg', at which point, we are told, Hook realizes that Peter 'did not know in the least who or what he was'.[68] And here is the crux of Peter's condition, the inevitable effect of his mother's desertion; he cannot identify himself.[69] We see the same notion of uncertainty betray itself in a manner that more reveals its attendant anxiety when Peter inquires somewhat nervously about the validity of his and Wendy's mock parental roles, 'It is only make believe, isn't it, that I am the father?'[70] Subsequently, altering the dynamics of their supposed relationship, and relegating himself to a more appropriate and less demanding role, Peter assures Wendy that his thoughts about her are those 'of a devoted son'.[71] Abandoning the possibility of fulfilling a parental, and therefore responsible and mature role, Peter insures instead that he is merely son to Wendy's motherhood.

Throughout the novel Peter exhibits the kind of imitative tendency inherent in the orphan; he is consistently mimicking others and even acquiring various pretentious appellations. When he returns Tiger Lily safely to the redskins, he is named The Great White Father, a name which emboldens him to make such proclamations as 'Peter Pan has spoken', which 'meant that they must now shut up'.[72] Wendy refers to Peter as the father of the lost boys, who in turn call him 'father'.[73] Upon Hook's death Peter assumes the name 'Captain Pan', whereupon he dons the characteristics of his nemesis, including clenching in his teeth Hook's cigar-holder, bending his forefinger in the shape of a hook, and having Wendy contrive an outfit made from 'Hook's wickedest garments'.[74] When asked by the lost boys to dance, he states in imitation of an old man, 'Me! My old bones would rattle![75] Peter is 'an adept' at imitating the redskins, effectively mimics Hook's voice to confuse Smee, is capable of convincingly echoing the ticking of the crocodile's clock 'so wild beasts should believe he was a crocodile', is compared with a snake, and disguises himself in Wendy's cloak 'so that he should pass for her'.[76] We must keep in mind as well that Peter's entire ensemble is a composite of borrowed fairy elements, from his being clad in skeleton leaves to his use of pixie dust.[77] His first exchange with Wendy, for instance, where 'he rose and bowed to her beautifully', involves his imitation of the 'grand manner'[78] of etiquette learned from fairy ceremonies. So considerable are the occasions of his imitative tendencies that I believe it arguable that any time Peter accomplishes anything, it is in the process of emulating someone or something else.

Peter is notably irreverent even to reality, an attribute I argue derives from his need to establish an alternative reality to stand in the stead of that which has effected his orphanic condition. Neverland exists because Peter requires it, and the validity of its diverse elements and aspects are largely contingent upon his acceptance or refusal. As the novel's narrator explains, while the other boys know what make-believe is, to Peter 'make-believe and true were exactly the same thing'.[79] His whim determines, for instance, that an imaginary feast 'was so real to him that during a meal of it you could see him getting rounder'.[80] Wendy is never quite sure whether or not Peter's adventures are true, and only 'when you went out and found the body'[81] they are confirmed. It is this need in Peter to determine Neverland's actuality that becomes challenged by Mrs Darling's interference by threatening his proposed order.

This weakness in Neverland's design contributes to Peter's exacting a particular distance from the events around him, as though not to position himself in any kind of emotionally invested, and therefore vulnerable, stance. In fact, other than the issue of his mother resurfacing in various ways and the episode where he attempts to bring about Tinkerbell's recovery, Peter is largely an indifferent observer of the formulated reality he has constructed. Though physically active in and among the goings on, he seems emotionally detached, perhaps due to the psychological wounds inflicted upon him by his orphanhood. Thus, for example, his tendency to change sides during a battle, or his continuing to imitate the sound of the crocodile's clock '[w]ithout giving thought to what might be the feelings of a fellow-creature thus abruptly deprived of its closest companion'.[82] We are told as well that Peter 'had no sense of time', that he 'had seen many tragedies, but he had forgotten them all', that though he often met unfairness, 'he always forgot it', and that he even eventually forgets who Hook and Tinkerbell even were.[83] Tragically, it is this emotional severance from events that actually perpetuates Peter's isolation from social or family structures. Forever an embittered outside witness, the orphaned Peter is so emotionally damaged that that, as he looks through the window upon the reunion of the children with their parents, we are told that this is 'the one joy from which he must for ever be barred'.[84]

'O Man Unfathomable'

It is perhaps easy to overlook the fact that the fearful and dread Captain Hook is also an orphan, and that in addition to, in fact determining, his role as mature terror to Peter's immature nonchalance, is Hook's own quest for a mother to resolve a near debilitating orphan state. Hook is emblematic of the fin-de-siècle psyche, appealing to some reliable and stable 'parental' entity to compensate for his lack of identity and purpose. Like Peter, Hook, whose real name is not Hook,[85] bears numerous and contradictory traits typical of the malleable and fragmentary orphan. His physical appearance literalizes this inner turmoil: he is described as 'cadaverous and blackavized' and yet has eyes 'the blue of the forget-me-not' and 'soft as the periwinkle'; a handsome countenance is lent 'a singularly threatening expression' by his curly black hair; he notably smokes two cigars simultaneously, while his hand and hook similarly represent the dichotomy warring within him.[86]

His emotional reactions belie this intrinsic instability. He is known at times to speak 'darkly' and to have a 'dark nature', is known as 'ever a dark and solitary enigma', and is capable of preparing a poisoned cake for the lost boys and a lethal concoction for Peter.[87] And yet Hook heaves a heavy sigh, presumably due to 'the soft beauty of the evening' that elicits 'a quiver in his voice'.[88] This 'man of indomitable courage' is mortified by the sight of his own blood and 'fell in a little heap' at the sight of the crocodile.[89] Though Hook 'alone seemed to be a match'[90] for Peter and the lost boys, he is hesitant before descending into the tree leading to Peter's home. When confronting his own men, Hook notes in himself a tinge of fear, and 'his proud spirit broke', at which point he whispers to himself, 'Don't desert me, bully'.[91] Upon realizing Peter has survived his attempted poisoning, Hook's 'fierce heart broke'[92] and he fails twice to speak. Following a momentary lapse into fear at Peter's threshold, because of his anger, '[i]n a moment Hook was himself again'.[93] The same Hook who contemplates murdering Smee due to the latter's display of bad form becomes 'as impotent as he was damp', but just as suddenly, upon seeing his crew's drunkenness, 'all traces of human weakness' leave him.[94] A moment after childishly referring to the pirate Cecco as a 'doodle-do', Hook threatens the pirate Starkey with his hook, 'the red spark . . . in his eye'.[95] Frustrated at the notion of mutiny, a befuddled Hook is then inspired with the concept of submitting the children to the supposed 'terror' in the cabin, at which point 'his face lit up again'.[96]

There is a 'touch of the feminine' about Hook, and we are told he is 'not wholly unheroic' and 'not wholly evil' but actually 'loved flowers . . . and sweet music, and is a capable harpsichord player.[97] More than once on summer evenings Smee 'had touched the fount of Hook's tears and made it flow'.[98] Upon showing Smee the Neverbird as an example of what a mother is, Hook's voice breaks 'as if for a moment he recalled innocent days when – but he brushed away this weakness with his hook'.[99] And perhaps most tellingly in regard to Hook's emotional vulnerability steeped in his desire to be a mothered son and part of a domestic scenario, the idyllic scene of Peter sleeping in his bed 'shook him profoundly'.[100] Indeed there is as much evidence about Hook pertaining to the effeminate Edwardian dandy as to the fearful, masculine pose for which Hook is perhaps more famous.

Although a pirate by trade, Hook maintains the contradictory decorum of an educated man of a higher class, and within this aspect lies his only realistic recourse concerning the potential alleviation of his orphan state. Though a character that could have emerged from an island narrative, he is notable for his educated demeanor, his proper speech, his good form and apparel that 'apes the dandified'.[101] Hook, who is said to never be more sinister than when he is most polite, 'retained the passion for good form'.[102] One moment of the novel that deserves comment is that in which Peter, knowing that it would be unfair to stab Hook, who, at the moment is on a lower level of rock than he, extends a hand to the pirate to assist him up to an equal footing. That Hook takes advantage of this gesture by biting Peter's hand seems a loss of his manners that simply attests to the instability that affects Hook. The fact that he shows bad form haunts Hook for the rest of the novel.

Once a student at Eton, 'something of the grand seigneur still clung to [Hook]' and the school's traditions 'still clung to him like garments'.[103] For instance, he treats Wendy 'with ironical politeness'[104] and actually escorts her to the site where the captured lost boys are gagged. The 'elegance of his diction' distinguishes him from the rest of his crew, so that he 'never felt more alone than when surrounded by his dogs'.[105] Importantly, the ideal Hook associates with his education, his former inclusion within the school's social structure, further emphasizes both the fact that he is no longer a part of that structure, as well as the notion that he, 'aloof from his followers in spirit as well as in substance', is set apart from his pirate comrades who are 'so socially inferior to him'.[106]

The sense of loss Hook perceives in regard to the belonging he once felt is belied in the 'profound melancholy'[107] that characterizes him, as well as in his obsessive preoccupation with the sense of form acquired there. It is images of his youth at Eton that possess Hook at the moment of his death; and yet his 'content'[108] submission to the crocodile is gained due to

Hook's having cited Peter for having bad form, an act that links Hook in one final reconciling gesture that in small measure rectifies Hook's orphan condition. If, as 'one of a different caste from his crew',[109] he cannot assimilate into the class of pirates, nor construct a kind of provisional family with Wendy as his mother, he may yet retain the qualities of what appears to be the one social construction of which he has ever been a part.

'I Don't Think I Know Exactly *What* I Am'

Despite the stability of her disposition, Sara Crewe exhibits the modifiability associated with the orphan's compulsion to emulate others, a capacity which proves a benefit for her once her father dies. Unlike other orphan figures, however, Sara, who is known for her story-telling abilities, tends toward the imitation of imagined beings in a manner that displaces the misery of her situation. She claims that 'because I am a fairy nothing can hurt me or make me uncomfortable';[110] she often refers to herself, in emulation of her father, as a suffering soldier, such as when she refers to her relegation to the attic as 'a long and weary march' and she has 'a quaint sense of being a hostess'[111] of the attic when attending to her secretive visitors. She claims that when telling a story, 'I feel as if I were all the people in the story—one after the other'.[112] She is also known by various titles, such as 'The Princess', 'the little *un*-fairy princess', 'the-little-girl-who-is-not-a-beggar', 'little missus', 'Mamma Sara', and 'Missee Sahib'; and though 'she looked exactly like poor children she had seen', her voice is 'so unlike an ordinary street child's voice' and her manner is that 'of a well-bred little person'.[113] Even her last name, Crewe, implying the collective noun, bears notions of multiplicity.

This sense of creative versatility is surrogated by notions of inner division and a crisis of identity when the newly orphaned Sara mounts the stairs to take up her new station as servant in the attic. She feels as though she is abandoning 'the world in which that other child, who no longer seemed herself, had lived', feels as if she has become 'quite a different creature', and states to Ermengarde, 'I *am* different'.[114] Indeed the loss of Sara's father, the only family she has, results in a temporary loss of self. Not only does Sara respond to Ermengarde's inquiry as to how Sara is with, 'I don't know', but she loses the composure, the 'cold steadiness', that has distinguished her by snapping at Ermengarde.[115] Knowing only that 'I am not a princess any more', she explains to Mr Carrisford, 'I don't think I know exactly *what* I am'.[116] Having learned of her father's death, relegated to the status of a servant and made to live in the attic, Sara seems divorced from herself, to the extent that 'she scarcely knew that she had a body at all'.[117] Being cast into the orphan condition not only deprives Sara of the material comforts and familial affirmation to which she has become accustomed, it too abstracts her identity, the implications of which are that, dislodged from the family structure, the orphan is bereft of the sense of self.

'A Sort of Robin Without Beak or Feathers'

Below I will discuss the stability that characterizes Wendy Darling due to her inclusion within a functioning family structure and the manner in which the surety of that belonging enables her to imitate the mother figure without succumbing to the seductive allure of delusion. Just as a consideration of Wendy's invariability contrasts with my examination of Peter and Hook as erratic orphans, I think it useful to take a look at Dickon – from *The Secret Garden* – as a similar character in order to appreciate the malleable constitution of that novel's orphans, Mary and Colin. For Dickon is as protean as any orphan, but for remarkably different reasons.

Similar to the variegated spectacle that is Captain Hook, Dickon's appearance seems a decrial of his numerous competencies. Physically he is as undifferentiated as any orphan of the late nineteenth century. He is described as 'a funny looking boy about twelve' with a 'poppy-cheeked face' and 'a rough rusty-red head'; he 'has a big mouth' and his nose 'does turn up'.[118] His 'patched clothes'[119] seem emblematic of his multi-faceted capacity. Indeed, Dickon at times seems an amalgam of various elements of the Yorkshire moor from whence he comes. He is 'as tough as a white-thorn knobstick', there is 'a clean fresh scent of heather and grass and leaves about him, almost as if he were made of them', and his eyes are 'like a bit of the sky'.[120] He claims to be able to imitate grass, trees, and bushes; his nose 'fair quivers like a rabbit's' and he states that at times he thinks 'p'raps I'm a bird, or a fox, or a rabbit, or a squirrel, or even a beetle, an' I don't know it'.[121] He is 'strong as a moor pony', is regarded as a 'sort of robin without beak or feathers' and his movements 'also were robin'.[122] Dickon, of course, bears a likeness to Pan; the reputed 'animal charmer' beguiles rabbits and pheasants 'as the natives charm snakes in India', and Mary wonders at one point if 'was he only a wood fairy?'[123] This association with Pan further entrenches the notion of Dickon's intrinsic connection with the regenerative and curative facets of nature. Importantly, Dickon's correlation to these divers particulars is not the result of a deficit of self-awareness or questions of identity; rather, it is due to the fact that he is absolutely aware of who he is and is therefore confidently capable of communing with the world he inhabits. For Dickon, his comparisons to other forms are not imitation; they are intimacy.

Like Wendy, Dickon is the product of a stable family environment that nurtures his physical, mental and emotional health and fosters his curiosity, creativity and natural abilities. This equally endows him with the ability to assume various roles without being pretentious or contrived. Indeed, his upbringing makes him, like Wendy, discriminating and sensitive. For instance, although he speaks broad Yorkshire when he is interested in something, there are occasions when 'he tried to modify his dialect so that Mary could better understand'.[124] But this alteration of himself is not born of a desire to conform or assimilate, as with the case of both Mary and Colin, who acquire the Yorkshire speech in order to be more like Dickon. Rather, Dickon, who would 'be at home in Buckingham Palace or at the bottom of a coal mine',[125] changes himself in order to help Mary feel more included. One of Dickon's particularly remarkable aspects is the parental, arguably feminine, model he provides for Mary to emulate. To a half drowned orphan fox cub and on several occasions several motherless lambs, Dickon serves as nurturing savior, compelling Dr Craven to state, 'Dickon's a lad I'd trust with a new-born child'.[126] This paternal, even maternal, capacity provides for Mary a role to imitate which, in addition to Lilias's spiritual presence and Mrs Sowerby's attention, precipitates the mother-figure she will provide for Colin. Being part of a family, and allied with the identifying and harmonizing affects associated with it, permits Dickon a kind of worldliness and well-roundedness the adaptive capabilities of which are not the frantic quest of the orphan in search of a qualifying model. Instead, unlike Mary and Colin, who must mimic Dickon's personality, accent and nurturing abilities, Dickon evokes the same wholeness, self-certainty and confidence that Wendy commands, and which typically eludes the orphan.

'She Forgets Herself'

Mary's orphan condition is rather atypical in that it includes neither the lack of material possessions nor ignorance of genealogical affiliation that generally attends orphanhood. Instead, it is marked by a notable deficiency of affection. On a culturally symbolic level, she is emblematic of the Edwardian garden-party culture insomuch that the material wealth that surrounds her does nothing to allay the tedium of a spiritually and philosophically barren existence.[127] Furthermore, the emotional chasm between Mary and the majority of adults with whom she comes into contact and yet who refuse to offer her any type of affection or affirmation is analogous to that effected by the paradigmatic shift from the traditional world to the modern one that produced the generational anxiety exhibited in turn of the century authors. For instance, not only do Mary's parents not want a girl, but she is also immediately placed in the care of an Ayah, who is ordered to 'keep the child out of sight as much as possible'; even when her mother and father are alive, Mary 'had never seemed to belong to anyone'; and she is told that her uncle is not going to 'trouble himself about you'.[128] Exemplary of a generation unsure of itself on numerous levels, and somewhat similar to Renfield, Mary is often referred to merely by nick-names that indicate a lack of definition; at the clergyman's, for example, she is called 'Mistress Mary Quite Contrary', and Mrs Medlock cements Mary's dehumanization by calling her 'a plain little piece of goods'.[129]

Mary exhibits, then, an understandable tendency to insinuate the personality of a more stable entity into the place of her own, and she finds this in Dickon for reasons addressed above. She even begins to physically take on attributes similar to his; her hair 'was as tumbled as Dickon's and her cheeks were almost as poppy red as his'.[130] Just as Dickon, who seems at times formed out of the moorland that is his world and who is at numerous times compared to different animals, Mary experiences the impulse, like the thrush, robins and skylark who 'could not possibly help it' to 'flute and sing aloud herself'.[131] Another of the notable manners by which she alters herself is her acquisition of Dickon's speech. 'She wished she could talk as he did'; when asking a question, she attempts to do so 'in Yorkshire because that was his language'.[132] And indeed she rapidly secures the Yorkshire accent that characterizes Dickon and the entire Sowerby family. She notably refers to the garden as 'wick' and tells Colin that the wind's 'wutherin'' had kept her awake the night she discovers his room; when hurrying Colin, she quotes Dickon verbatim, 'An' tha' munnot lose no time about it'.[133] Significantly, upon speaking Yorkshire in one instance, 'she forgot herself'.[134]

That Dickon 'had taught Mary to use all her tools'[135] pertains to processes beyond the function of gardening; ultimately, Mary learns the actions associated with Dickon that are notably maternal, especially nurturing and selflessness, which seem intrinsic to and resulting from his inclusion in his family.

'I Am A Real Boy'

In Colin we find the literalization of Mary's initial emotional paralysis. Prone to tantrums and 'whining fit[s]', detached, imperious, incapable of discerning the needs or feelings of others, Colin 'was probably like herself', while Mary 'was no more used to considering other people than Colin was'.[136] The two serve as mirror images of the other, though whereas Mary's orphanic predicament debilitates her emotionally, Colin's psychological damage finds its outlet in imagined somatic maladies. He believes himself to be physically deteriorating, including paranoia about his imminent early demise and fears of acquiring the hunchback his father bears. Hampered by the emotional desolation of his orphanic state, Colin is 'like this always, ill and having to lie down'.[137] Attending his neuroses, this debilitation renders Colin an absolute contrast to the lively and vibrant Dickon. Claiming to 'hate fresh air' and reluctant to venture beyond the confines of his imagined death-bed, Colin has 'lived on a sort of desert island all his life'; rather than a lived reality, the boy engages an imitation of experience, preferring to read and look at 'pictures in splendid books', meager substitutes for the attention his absent father denies him.[138] Interestingly, and perhaps underscoring the notion of the inclusion that benefits Dickon is Burnett's telling remark that Colin had 'no one to compare himself with'.[139] In sharp relief to the confidence and stability endowed to Dickon by the surety of the Sowerby family is the frailty, rage, and perceived bodily degeneration wrought by maternal death and paternal abandonment of Colin's experience.

Like Mary, Colin finds in Dickon a substantial, notably maternal, ideal whom he quickly learns to emulate in the initial steps of his journey toward psychological restoration and physical reparation that will culminate in the conversion of his orphanic state. As such, he falls into the category of the 'faux-orphan/ faux "cripple"' stories wherein a seemingly orphaned or disabled child is restored to health by the natural environment and is able to become complete and integrated.[140] Having achieved her status as mother-figure, Mary encourages Colin to pattern himself after Dickon, by 'only repeating what Dickon had told her'.[141] For instance, she recommends that Colin breathe in the moorland's fresh air, emphasizing that doing so, Dickon 'says he feels it in his veins' and that it strengthens him and makes him feel 'as if he could live forever and ever'.[142] Soon after, Colin's imitation of Dickon is as unmistakable as the implications of Mary's assumption of the Yorkshire dialect; he states, 'I am breathing long breaths of fresh air. It makes you strong'.[143] Colin, too, endeavors 'with dreamy carefulness' to ape Dickon's speech, to the extent that Mary remarks to him, 'Tha'rt shapin' first-rate – that tha' art'.[144]

Eventually, Colin is capable of viewing his existence as a realm of possibilities rather than a condition of incapacity and disillusionment. In a cascade of life-affirming proclamations, the former invalid, through his mimicry of Dickon, expresses a newly attained sense of self; he proclaims that he is 'going to live to be a man' and that he will be 'as strong as Dickon'.[145] And indeed, the resolution of the symptoms of his orphanic state is attended by actual physical changes so that Mary notes he looks 'like an entirely different boy'.[146] Similar to the Dickon-like rosy plumpness Mary's cheeks acquire, Colin's countenance is 'fillin' out and doesn't look so sharp an' the waxy color is goin'', and his appearance alters so that he looks as though 'he were made of flesh instead of ivory and wax'.[147] Mary even notes that Colin "'ooked quite beautiful', and once Colin is able to stand, Dickon remarks, 'He's as straight as I am'.[148]

Ultimately, Colin is even referred to in similar terms as the Pan-like Dickon, having assumed the identity of 'a strange boy spirit'.[149] Finally, he proclaims, 'I am a real boy',[150] meaning that he is no longer hindered by the constraints of his orphanic condition. Once hampered by his father's fear and neglect and the perceptions of illness and sense of self they engendered, toward the novel's end, Colin speaks 'so like a healthy boy'.[151] So profound, in fact, is Colin's transformation that amidst his attainment of the sort of wholeness and fulfillment denied the orphan until the decisive and reparative moment of revelation, that Colin, who expresses 'the fascination of actually making a sort of speech like a grown-up person', proclaims, 'I am going to be scientific'.[152] The same orphan figure first referred to simply as 'the Someone' becomes 'a laughable, lovable, healthy young human thing' who assumes such affirming appellations such as 'the Athlete, the Lecturer, the Scientific Discoverer'.[153] By modeling after the coherence and assurance of Dickon, who himself conveys so many maternal attributes, the orphanic Colin becomes 'a real boy'.

Imitating the Mother

I have previously discussed the emphasis in orphan narratives of the perpetuation of the stable, functioning, ideal family to provide for the orphan a social structure into which he or she aspires to be assimilated. There are instances, however, where the family structure is either temporarily displaced or irretrievably lost, in which case the orphan may provide the directive and nurturing capacity not for herself, but for other orphans around her. While the absence of the mother is a useful convention often inaugurating the condition of orphanhood and permitting and necessitating a broader if tenuous agency for the orphan, there exists a tendency in Edwardian children's fiction for the orphan not only to assume an authoritative and notably maternal role, but to do so under the guidance of the perpetual ideal of an existing but absent mother figure, or of the exhortative spirit of a deceased mother. Though the assumption of the motherly role endows the orphan with some sense of autonomy and control over lamentable conditions, the inceptive contribution of the maternal ideal or inspiring ghost belies a residual desire for the stability and tradition of a largely abandoned past associated with the mother figure. In the Edwardian advancement into the modernism that characterized the twentieth century resided a still powerful, if subtle or even unconscious, appeal to the past embodied in the figure of the Good Mother.

We see therefore the compulsion of figures like the seemingly uninterested and noncompliant Peter Pan to persuade Wendy to adopt him and the lost boys, or the motherless Sara Crewe's fascination with the Large Family, which includes 'a stout, rosy mother and a stout, rosy father, and a stout, rosy grandmother'[154] and is the epitome of all of which Sara has been dispossessed. Sara also demonstrates the incentive to attend to the less fortunate around her. Furthermore, we see the psychologically damaged and emotionally stunted Mary Lennox's notion to revive Lilias's abandoned garden and her similar eventual assumption of selfless mother figure for Colin. In addition, the egomaniacal Colin's own admission to the necessity of the healing capacities of his deceased mother's garden, as well as the effect of the realization of his physiological connection with his mother eventuate his ability to sympathize with and forgive his detached and broken father. For Edwardian children's fiction, the mother figure proves an enduring symbol of an ideal of which the orphan is bereft to some extent but a paragon the orphan cannot efface.

Wendy, Sara and Mary are each extracted from the context of their homes. Wendy is persuaded to leave the Darling household with Peter to experience Neverland; the motherless Sara is first left by her father at boarding school, then removed from even that social construction once her father dies; and the unwanted Mary is sent to forlorn Misselthwaite upon her loveless parents' death. Despite this, each acquires in her own manner a maternal nature, the facility to step outside of her own needs to mother others. Wendy is by no means an orphan, as her mother and father continue to fret about her, lament her absence, and love her enduringly; however, upon deciding to forsake her home, she is made potentially vulnerable to the perils characteristic of orphanhood. Her assumption of mother role for Peter and the lost boys is easily accomplished, as the memory of her own mother remains with her and reminds her of the activities in which the Good Mother engages. Sara, however, begins life without a mother, though she perceives that her mother visits her from heaven to perpetuate the guardianship and tutelage she would have performed had she lived; this, along with her undaunted imagination and appreciation for her father even after his death, permits Sara's own imitation of maternal affection. Finally, Mary's development into a mother figure is more incremental, a slowly emerging result of Mrs Sowerby's attentiveness and example, and of Lilias's metaphysical prevalence. All three girls ultimately serve as provisional mother figures for other children, neglecting the implications of their own orphanic predicaments, and constructing mock domestic spaces that imitate family compositions.

Wendy Darling, 'the comforter',[155] is immediately depicted as sensible and rational beyond her years. She is 'the kind that likes to grow up' and 'liked everything just so';[156] she is initially disturbed by the idea that their flight will span an unknowable amount of time; and it is the proper Wendy who insists that having tea outweighs the notion of going on an adventure upon arriving in Neverland. This imposition of decorum and social structure is one of her outstanding maternal features in a realm where whim and fancy frequently determine the day's events. Wendy's maternal instincts are evidenced throughout the book. When the frustrated Mr Darling fails in his attempt to trick the children into taking their tonic, it is Wendy who resolves the matter by proposing they all take their medicine simultaneously; it is maternal images that Wendy first spies upon arriving in Neverland, images of 'turtles burying their eggs in the sand' and a 'wolf with her whelps';[157] upon realizing that Peter, whom she calls 'my little man',[158] has no mother, Wendy immediately runs to comfort him; and it is Wendy who knows how to connect Peter to his shadow, that is, how to make the orphan complete again. Once established as the mother in Neverland, she attends to the maternal duties of the home, hanging clothes from a string, keeping 'her nose to the pot', attempts to relegate her younger brother, Michael, to the cradle, as she 'would have a baby', and even during what she refers to as her 'breathing time', occupies herself with making new items for the boys.[159] She enforces 'strict rules about everyone being in bed by seven' and speaks 'in a voice that had to be obeyed'.[160] So effective is her imitation of the Good Mother that she inspires the lost boys to either speculate about or reconstruct depictions of the mothers they can no longer recall, and furthermore inadvertently compels her younger and less mature brothers, John and Michael, to think of her as their mother. But Wendy, too sensible and mature to succumb to Neverland's illusions, and 'nobly anxious to do her duty', insists on their remembering Mrs Darling, requiring them to take examination papers on the subject and imploring them while telling her story, 'to consider the feelings of the unhappy parents with all their children flown away'.[161]

She is a product of exposure to the nurturing and responsible model of Mrs Darling, which grounds Wendy even as it fosters her maternal attributes. Once in Neverland, Wendy is 'absolutely confident' that her parents will leave the window open for her return, 'and this gave her complete ease of mind'.[162] It is arguably the reliable stability of her domestic situation that affords her the maturity that enables her to imitate her mother so successfully, but at the same time ensures that Wendy does not submit to the fantasy played out in Neverland. That Wendy's assumption at the end of the book, for instance, is that Peter may wish to mention to her parents 'a very sweet subject',[163] evinces not only her logical approach to matters, but too an assumption on her part of the perpetuation of the kind of domestic structure of marriage and family from which she comes.

Despite this capacity to imitate the mother figure to such a successful degree, Wendy's motherhood remains in her mind merely provisional, imaginary, perhaps a foreshadowing of her future self. This is the crucial difference between Wendy, who hails from the ideal Victorian family, and characters like Sara Crewe and Mary Lennox, who do not. Unlike the other girls, Wendy's mimicry is not a requisite part of some healing process or a propitious appeal to an emblem of stability. She may temporarily effect her own orphanic condition by leaving her home, but this state is not at all substantive; it merely permits her the agency to play mother without the need of benefiting from it, and springs more from the notion of perpetuating the model from which she came rather than of recreating an imitation of that ideal out of some orphanic desperation.

Sara Crewe also exhibits the kind of selflessness inherent in the imitation of mother figures, though, as we will see with Mary, in the case of orphans who do not come from ideal domestic situations, such imitation results from maternal influence of a magical nature. Though her mother has died during childbirth, it is evident that a kind of magic akin to Lilias's spiritual presence motivates Sara to acquire maternal attributes. Indeed, Sara regards her dead mother as present in some spectral way, stating, 'I am sure she comes out sometimes to see me – though I don't see her'.[164] It is arguably this sense of her mother's attentiveness from beyond the grave, for instance, that drives Sara, upon seeing that Lottie has no mother, to immediately sympathize with the little girl and proclaim, 'I will be your mama' and 'We will play that you are my little girl'; furthermore, she explains, 'Emily shall be your sister'.[165] As Sara becomes Lottie's 'young adopted mother' and Lottie 'her adopted child'[166], Sarah establishes a provisional family construction similar to those formulated by Peter, Mary and Colin.

Despite Mary's initial apathy, the Magic aligned with Lilias and the influence of Mrs Sowerby evoke in Mary a latent maternal capacity. Madelon Gohlke points out Mary's 'intuitive and sympathetic response' to Colin, who 'is hurting like herself'.[167] I would elaborate on this notion by crediting the powerful maternal forces with which Mary comes into contact once at Misselthwaite with evoking this previously untapped attribute. Certainly once having discovered Lilias's garden and been the recipient of Mrs Sowerby's benevolence, Mary displays qualities that had heretofore remained buried. When she holds a motherless lamb, Mary is 'too full of strange joy to speak'; she offers to read to Colin and to 'pat your hand and stroke it and sing something quite low' to help him sleep; she quells the hysterics of his hypochondria so that 'Colin's aches and tiredness were forgotten'.[168] When Mary bends over to kiss a new clump of crocuses, she mimics Lilias, whom Ben Weatherstaff remarks would kiss roses. So decisively does Mary assume a maternal manner that Mrs Sowerby tells her, 'I'll warrant tha'rt like thy mother'.[169]

Arguing against the popular interpretation that Colin displaces Mary throughout the final third or so of the novel, I think it vital to acknowledge Mary's contribution to the regeneration and reconciliation of which Colin surely would have otherwise been incapable.[170] Indeed, Mary effectively replaces the mother whose absence so contributes to Colin's wounded orphanic condition, emphasized in the revelation of his mother's hidden portrait at the moment that Mary steps into the space Lilias would have occupied had she survived. As with Sara's mother's spectral observations, the mother-spirit transcends even death to ensure the perpetuation of the maternal ideal.

Domestic Disturbances and Alternate Realms

In each of the categories of this study I have pointed out the domestic space as that locus of inclusion and belonging toward which the orphan typically tends and attainment of which usually serves as his or her primary purpose, and have in the process noted the home's status as under constant threat of imbalance and fracture.[171] At times the home even fails to be a refuge or to offer the reliable accommodation. This persistent state of potential or even inevitable collapse served to underscore the vital role in society of the institution in question, while at the same time presenting a challenge to the orphan to contrive a provisional surrogate for that institution in the event of its dissolution. In the Edwardian children's fantasies in consideration here, the domestic space is either threatened, dislocated or does not exist, necessitating that the orphan endeavor to fabricate an imitative alternative to countervail the lack of an actual home.

Edwardian children's fiction offer treatments of a special, even magical space for the orphan that to some extent provides what his or her reality cannot.[172] Whereas in earlier children's fiction the ideal home exists as a potential locality of acceptance and belonging that motivates the orphan, in Edwardian children's fiction the orphan exacts the formulation of alternative places that provide for him or her the attributes traditionally associated with the domestic space, forging a mimic of that form which he or she would be otherwise ostracized.[173] The orphan thus becomes to some degree independent of the adult world; the child develops a kind of individuality and agency perhaps not heretofore experienced. Jill Muller points out, for example, that the success of the children in *The Secret Garden* is largely contingent on the application of their own will and capabilities, and Phyllis Bixler finds part of the appeal of the novel its portrayal 'of the life children share away from adults'.[174] I would clarify that it is from notably apathetic or even dangerous adults from whom the Edwardian orphan endeavors to extract him or herself, and that those adults who convey a positive, affirming demeanor inspire or even assist with the creation of the alternate space. While children's fiction naturally exhibits imaginative aspects, the Edwardian orphan notably utilizes fantasy to create a space specifically to escape a harmful or deficient reality, to exact a sense of control over the dilemma of orphanhood. When, for instance, Mary first enters the garden, 'she felt as if she had found a world all her own'.[175] This sense of isolation, rather than being one of loneliness, is instead one of freedom whereby she acquires some command over her circumstances for the first time in her life.

Peter Pan begins by establishing the Darling household as possessing a sense of normalcy and structure overseen by an attendant mother and father. Despite the children's partially insouciant play, there is a notable order and stability to their domestic situation. Mr Darling's proclamation to his wife that 'you and I starve, and our children will be flung into the streets'[176] is probably more attributable to the hysterics by which he is characterized and which permit the narrator to make sport of the figure of the patriarch; and insinuation that Wendy may not be kept 'as she was another mouth to feed' and comments such as 'the children stood around to see their fate decided'[177] are more evidence of the author's preference for hyperbole than an actual concession that the Darling home is on the verge of ruin. Such comments actually serve to convey the importance of the home and its perpetuity, suggesting as they do the tragic nature of a child's expulsion from it. They also effectively foreground the abandonment of Peter by his mother and the orphan status of the lost boys. As much a context of emotional family exchanges as it is, particularly when contrasted with the fractious and tenuous constructions devised in Neverland, the Darling household stands as a substantial domestic model.

Significantly, this relative equilibrium becomes compromised when the Darling parents depart from the home for a night out, leaving the space vulnerable to Peter, who almost immediately insinuates himself into the circle of children. Initially there to experience belonging vicariously through listening to Mrs Darling's telling of the Cinderella story, Peter misplaces his shadow, the loss of which signifies the incompleteness of his orphanhood, and the retrieval of which is only made possible by his substitute mother, Wendy. One of the outstanding themes of *Peter Pan* is the question as to whether or not a mother will leave the window open for her child; unlike Mrs Darling, who insists that the window remain open for the duration of her children's absence, Peter's mother not only closes the window while he is away, but actually permits another boy to take his place. This notion of simultaneous abandonment and exclusion shapes Peter, generating the orphanic anxiety that determines his actions and demeanor, which makes even more disconcerting the manner in which Peter's infiltration of the Darling home and subsequent excision of its children perpetuates the kind of domestic inversion and aberration that damaged him; for his attempt to acquire a mother actually reenacts the divestment of the home, resulting in its fragmentation and threatening its status as the locus of constancy, fidelity and belonging.

Once he has dispossessed the Darling home of its children, however, Peter's first order of business, and that of his congress of orphan boys, is to establish for Wendy a crude model of the space the disturbance of which he has just effected. 'Let us build a house around her',[178] Peter orders the boys, at which point they actually disassemble their own house in order to construct a new one.[179] Their former, notably motherless, household is replaced by a mean caricature, which, despite its lack of proper domestic accoutrements, is nonetheless to some degree made more complete once overseen by a maternal figure who immediately does what she can to conform the space to her conceptions of domesticity. When Michael complains about being too old to be relegated to the status of the baby of the house, Wendy states the necessity of having a baby in a cradle, as it is 'such a nice homely thing to have about a house'.[180] In addition, echoing her mother's request for her children to patronize their father, Wendy is referred to as 'far too loyal a housewife to listen to any complaints about father [Peter]'.[181] The same kind of domestication of an otherwise unruly space reoccurs upon Peter's trespassing onto Hook's ship to retrieve the kidnapped children; once Hook is disposed of, Wendy recasts the captain's cabin into a provisional home for the boys, for instance, when she 'got them to bed in the pirates' bunks'.[182]

Peter Pan provides an example of the fantasy that does not merely exist as what Braybrooke calls 'a charming picture of a child's mind';[183] rather, Neverland exceeds the imaginative and acquires the status of alternate reality. Differentiations between the real and the imagined are consistently confused in the novel,[184] and it does appear initially that the dream-like content of Peter's world assumes as viable a state of reality as that of England. As though an improvement over the foibles of Peter's forlorn earlier existence, Neverland permits the orphan to establish a mock family without the perceived limitations of an actual family, an actuality unbridled by physical boundaries. Roger Lancelyn Green notes, for instance, that Neverland allows one 'to fly, to run away from the responsibilities of the grown-up, to fight without being hurt, to kill without shedding blood or causing pain, to flirt with death the unrealized'.[185] Read this way, Neverland indeed seems emblematic of the epicurean Edwardian paradigm, an escapist but untenable foray into denial. And just as the garden party was doomed to end, Neverland proves a dismal and failed concoction that cannot properly endure and is ultimately incapable of adequately standing in the stead of the Darling household. Tellingly, Barrie once stated that the 'wrecked island' of which he often wrote, with the passing years became more and more 'sinister'.[186] Seemingly capable of reconciling the orphan state as it may appear to be, the imitation domestic space in *Peter Pan* proves incredibly tenuous, and vulnerable to intrusion and dismantling.

For example, in order to kidnap the children, Hook, Smee and Starkey inflict upon Peter's contrived home the same kind of divestment that the latter perpetrated onto the Darlings'; and the house the lost boys construct for Wendy becomes their prison when Hook appropriates it as a conveyance to transport the children to his ship; and the ship, despite the addition of a mock maternal figure, is appropriated by Peter, who usurps Hook's command. There exists, then, an irreconcilable deficit that is merely transferred from one locus to the next. Ultimately, the provisional domestic space, the imitation of the actual home, cannot bear the implications thrust upon it by the orphans responsible for its fabrication. In the course of time, it fails, necessitating that its inhabitants either relocate, as the lost boys do, to an authentic, and therefore more stable, home, or relapse, as does Peter, to the orphan condition to which he appears to be damned.

Similarly, the attic to which Sara, in *A Little Princess*, is consigned is a cold and inhospitable contrast to the material comfort she has known up that point. What she calls 'another world' is comprised of a whitewashed roof that is 'dingy and had fallen off in places'; the grate is rusty, the bed hard, the room a storage place for 'pieces of furniture too much worn to be used downstairs'.[187] This initially intolerable space Sara transforms with her imagination into an inviting and comfortable semblance of an ideal home, complete with a sofa, a shelf of books, a fur rug before a fire, pictures on the wall, a lamp, a table for tea, a kettle 'singing'.[188] But this contrivance is mere creativity that serves only temporary reprieve; the reality is deprivation, starvation and the constant threat of Miss Minchin's intrusion into and disruption of Sara's invention. Sara therefore is preoccupied with and desires inclusion into what she refers to as 'the Large Family', the elements of which are the components of the ideal family, including a father, mother and grandmother in addition to eight jubilant children who are 'always doing something enjoyable'.[189] They are, with living, loving parents and exuberant siblings, the epitome of all that Sara lacks, and a far more stable alternative to her imaginative contentions.

The incredible imaginative capacity Sara possesses is displayed throughout the novel. For Sara, to whom '[e]verything's a story', the art of pretending 'was the joy of her life', without which, 'I don't believe I could live'.[190] This penchant for fantasy usually emerges as a compensatory tactic. Her creativity serves as a coping mechanism similar to that of Pan's formulation of Neverland and Mary and Colin's establishment of the secret garden. The first indication of this creative energy is the instance that her doll, Emily, is real, 'a kind of good witch who could protect her',[191] a notion she stresses more emphatically once her father leaves her. Sara, who admits to Ermengarde that 'when I play I make up stories and tell them to myself', states in regard to Emily, 'At least I *pretend* I believe she can [walk]', an exercise 'that makes it seem as if it were true'.[192] Upon comforting the distraught orphan Lottie, Sara's words function 'rather like a fairy story, but it was all so real to her own imagination'.[193] So convincing are the elements of Sara's stories that she 'quite made Lottie see them, too'.[194] When relegated to the attic Sara claims, 'I will pretend this is part of a war', and that 'if I pretend it is a place in a story', she can endure her state.[195] She pictures herself a prisoner in the Bastille, Miss Minchin as the jailer, and Becky 'the prisoner in the next cell'.[196] When lying awake, hungry and cold in the attic, she imagines that the rain is 'saying something nice', that the rusty grate was 'polished and there was a fire in it', and even refers to the space as 'really a beautiful room'.[197] Perhaps the most notable instance of Sara's coping skill is her attempt to transform the attic into a banquet hall. A red shawl becomes a table-cloth; a mere 'glance of admiration' images 'a nice red rug'; small white handkerchiefs serve as golden plates; the flowers from an old hat are 'garlands for the feast'; and the soapdish an alabaster centerpiece covered with roses that become gems.[198] As with the fragility inherent in Neverland, however, Sara's attic fantasy proves similarly irresolute against the reality of Miss Minchin's intrusion, subsequent dispersal of the gathering, and sending of Sara to bed without supper to cry herself to sleep.

Likewise, in *The Secret Garden*, the two houses in which Mary finds herself are emotionally barren places, antitheses of the inclusive and affirming ideal family structure. Little is described about her home in India, but that it is notably loveless, her parents apathetic to the point of cruelty. Her Uncle Craven is equally indifferent, as inattentive to Mary as he is to his own son. In addition to the lack of familial affection that characterizes these houses is the remarkable representation of the architectural space as an emblem of emotional deficiency. Mary's accommodations, though supplied with fire and food, are the proposed boundaries of her agency; she is informed, 'you must keep to them'.[199] Misselthwaite proves as formidable architecturally as it does emotionally. The mansion is rendered as a labyrinthine prison of sorts, with 'near a hundred rooms in it, though most of them's shut up and locked'.[200] The rooms are accessed by traversing 'a broad staircase and down a long corridor and up a short flight of steps and through another corridor and another'; wandering the house, Mary enters a door into 'a long corridor and it branched into other corridors and it led her up short flights of steps which mounted to others again' marked by 'door and doors'; when seeking the sounds made by Colin, Mary searches '[d]own this passage and then to the left, and then up two broad steps, and then to the right again'.[201] If the Gothic space of Misselthwaite is in some way emblematic of the emotional imprisonment effected by Mary's disinterested mother, the beneficent machinations of Lilias prove more dominant, leading Mary simultaneously deeper into the labyrinth into which she bears what I read as a maternal light toward the son-figure, Colin, to whom Mary will become a mother figure, and in doing so, reconcile the damage of her own orphan condition.

In her depiction of Misselthwaite as forlorn domestic space, Burnett employs the device, noted in chapter 3, of the orphan surrounded by a façade of material elements that imply the comfort and perceived tranquility of the ideal domestic space. Like Hyde, Griffin and Helen, the sociopathic Colin is encircled by creature comforts which but mask an arrogant, vacuous existence. A 'bright fire on the hearth' warms 'a very beautiful room indeed'; there are 'rich colors in the rugs and hangings and pictures and books on the walls which made it [Colin's room] look glowing and comfortable'.[202] I find it interesting too to point out the contrast between the crudity of the lost boys' gimcrack house built for Wendy and the sophistication and style of the fastidious, and notably family-less, Tinkerbell's separate quarters. What the lost boys lack in cookery and furniture, they arguably compensate for with generosity and sincerity. Tinkerbell, on the other hand, possesses none of these qualities, and there seem to me plausible connections between the notably possessive, sociopathic and often cruel fairy, Colin Craven, and figures like those discussed in chapter 3. Neither Colin nor Tinkerbell's surrounding themselves with the accoutrements of domesticity can conceal the egoism and maliciousness that characterize these faulted, often menacing orphans. In the context of the Edwardian period, Barrie and Burnett's admonishment seems a caveat against the seduction of material wealth that is incapable of assuaging the orphan state. Thus, only upon Colin's interior regeneration and reconciliation with his father might Misselthwaite serve as a potential emblem of entirety and integration, and enable Colin, upon their resolution, to proclaim without apprehension, 'Father – to the house'.[203]

As though to emphasize the inability of monetary wealth to provide the necessary attributes intrinsic to loving but notably less affluent families like the Sowerby's, Burnett infuses into the narrative images of content, tranquil animal families such as the mice Mary finds nestled up against their mother, 'who didn't look lonely at all'.[204] Likewise, the robin that leads Mary to the garden key acquires a mate at the same time Mary and Dickon begin recreating the garden that will become their imitative domestic space. Mary tells Colin that she and Dickon pretend that 'we were missel thrushes and it was our nest', and Dickon tells the robin, 'Us is nest-buildin' too'.[205] Furthermore, they begin to refer to their space in terms that liken it to a household, going as far in their imitation of the ideal home as to consider finding a deep little hollow 'where you could build a sort of tiny oven with stones and roast potatoes and eggs in it'.[206] Synchronous with these animals, whose instinctive activity is naturally to form family groups, Mary, with the assistance of Dickon, creates a welcoming, nurturing, if imaginative, alternative to the cold and lifeless mansion.

When Mary states to Dickon in reference to the garden, 'I am the only one who wants in to be alive',[207] she displays the maternal potential Lilias's spirit and Mrs Sowerby's affection access and subsequently foster.[208] Mary initially attempts to create such a space for herself in the desolate gardens of her Indian home and the rector's residence, where she 'pretended' to make a flowerbed.[209] Both are failed endeavors to generate a nurturing environment. But once Mary discovers Lilias's abandoned garden, and is compelled by both mother figures toward a nurturing disposition, the garden is reconstituted as a mimic domestic space, with Mary as mother, Dickon as father, and Colin as son.[210] The secret garden provides a *hortus conclusus*, the geoponic space wherein one may assume an identity inaccessible to them in the context of reality. For the orphans of *The Secret Garden*, it offers an opportunity to create the family structure that both Mary and Colin lack. The garden serves as the antithesis of Misselthwaite; open yet secluded, it allows an agency the Gothic labyrinth of the manor cannot. Only within the context of the garden is Mary able to overcome the damage of her orphanic condition by assuming her maternal identity and may Colin regenerate in the capacity of son-figure. In contrast to the manor, the secret garden permits an optional world of potential where '[t]housands of lovely things grow' and 'there are thousands of little creatures all busy building nests and making holes and burrows and chippering or singing or squeaking to each other'.[211] The garden is an area of contrived home-building and communication far more conducive to relationship than the loneliness and silence of Misselthwaite; it is a celebratory place of life and well-being, and, moreover, a place where the imitative family may endeavor to regenerate and heal the orphanic condition.

Conclusion

The notion of creative energy is applied to various degrees in these texts, but always to the same effect. Sara merely pretends her predicament to be better than it actually is; Mary exacts her energies to reshape the garden into an alternative to the desolate mansion; and Neverland, fantastical as it is, becomes an actual physical alternative to the reality of England. In each case, the orphan has enlisted his or her magical inventive ability to at least temporarily escape the reality of orphanhood, an ability that is notably determined and influenced by maternal figures that exist on the narrative's periphery. The orphans here typify the anxieties of the Edwardian period, contriving an unsustainable, insular paradigm inspired by the tradition embodied in the Good Mother, and at odds with its impending engagement with the modern world.

7
Conclusion

An examination of the orphan as depicted in genre fiction of the fin-de-siècle yields insight into what occurs when the ideal family, into which the orphan had traditionally aspired to be incorporated, moves from being seen as an attainable reality to a questionable fiction. Once a cultural cornerstone of almost mythic proportions, a standard of Victorian order and morality, the family, toward the end of the nineteenth century, had in various philosophical and literary areas fallen into question, was portrayed as an inhibitive and suppressive environment and at times even regarded as corrupting and threatening. During the early and middle periods of the century, when the family ideal was exalted, venerated as advantageous and essential, the figure of the orphan, exiled from that ideal, served as a powerful convention alluding to financial state, class, reform and other social issues associated with the industrialization that helped shape the nineteenth-century family. By the advent of the fin-de-siècle, however, with the erosion of confidence in the family as a place of reassurance and totality, portraits of orphanhood acquired a less promising, more unsettling and in some cases even monstrous nature, and furthermore spoke to anxieties more specific to the century's end. Oliver Twist gave way to Renfield; Jane Eyre was replaced by Helen Vaughn; Pip yielded to Jim Hawkins. Without the potential of the family's remedial and integrative context, the orphan was compelled to formulate his or her own compensatory circumstances. This pursuit may involve the mimicry of other, more notably cohesive peers, the appeal to potential surrogate parental figures, or the establishing of imitative familial structures. It may even take on a defiant, fractious and destructive distinction.

And it is really this remarkable reaction to the absence of the family with which this book has been concerned. Even as fin-de-siècle genre fiction exhibits the period's doubts regarding the family ideal, it equally belies the panic the lack of the family generates, and displays an abiding psychic need for the security, stability and identity intrinsic to the ideal, however farfetched or unrealistic it may have been. Locating this tendency in the period's orphan narratives demonstrates the persistence of an appeal to the traditional world embodied by the ideal family, from which the Victorians felt themselves increasingly estranged and to which they frequently looked back with a demonstrable sense of loss. The fin-de-siècle orphan consistently displays, whether intentionally or not, a basic need for familial associations, repeatedly engaging in the quest for assimilation and self-definition, enduring even deficient father and cruel mother figures, while the fiction of the period presents time and again the disastrous effects of exclusion from or denial of the advantages of the family. Even in circumstances where the happy ending, culminating in the discernment of lineage, marital union or the acquisition of financial independence, might no longer be considered a justifiable, credible possibility, the impetus of such a resolution remains. The unreconciled orphan state is characterized as lamentable and inadequate, impoverished by a dearth of familial attributes; and the disruptive and irredeemable orphan is notably removed, his or her ruinous intents ultimately thwarted by order and morality, any aberrant substitutive provision proving unsustainable and self-destructive.

The choice to conclude this book with an analysis of Edwardian children's fiction emerges from my reading of this genre as more overtly acknowledging the necessity of the family ideal. If the last decades of the nineteenth century were typified by incredulity, apprehension and even hostility in regard to the concept of the family, such a pretense was attended by a telling undercurrent of deprivation and need. Edwardian children's fiction, on the other hand, unapologetically confirms a return to the happy ending, offering portraits of converted, reliable fathers, acclamatory recognition of the mother's influence, and the orphan's assumption into a domestic space that has been rediscovered as viable, curative and, moreover, possible.

Discerning fin-de-siècle genre fiction's enduring, if at times subtle, even unconscious, preoccupation with the orphan condition and its intricate pertinence to familial constructs provides insight into the late-Victorian and Edwardian periods, but may also contribute to readings of later twentieth-century texts as well. Identifying the orphan's persistent desire for the context of the family may, for example, complement – or complicate – notions of integration and individuation in texts like Joyce's *Ulysses*, where Stephen Dedalus, so intent on defining himself on his own terms, clearly fails to do so beyond the context of the provisional family presumably to be found in the Bloom household. The propensity of modern Gothic writers like Stephen King to portray the family in a constant state of fracture and insinuating embodiments of evil into the urban domestic space are a development of the fin-de-siècle narrative of the rebellious and malevolent orphan, whose eventual elimination exhibits an underlying recognition of the sanctity of the family, exterior threats to which must be annihilated. The orphan's persistent determination, even in impractical circumstances, to locate reliable, morally substantial parental figures may influence reception of traumatic, disrupted familial dynamics of the lost mother, the domineering father, even the incestuous sibling, in a writer like Virginia Woolf. Relegation of the colonial subject to the status of orphan and the trope of the colonizer as embodiment of parental authority foregrounds the convention of severance from the family and subsequent reconstruction of provisional family systems in post-colonial texts like Abdulrazak Gurnah's *Paradise*. And locating in Edwardian children's fiction an appeal to the mother and the regeneration of the father underscore the plight of the orphans in fantasies like J. K. Rowling's *Harry Potter* series or Lemony Snicket's *A Series of Unfortunate Events*. Finally, analysis of the presentation of the orphanic state and its relevance to perceptions of the family may ultimately prompt a reassessment of the turn-of-the-century as less a degenerative, decadent and philosophically hostile era, and more a poignant period grappling with the existential implications of self-definition beyond the identifying context of the family.

Notes

1: Introduction

1 The term 'the long nineteenth century' was coined by British Marxist author Eric Hobsbawm as being 1789–1914. Hobsbawm lays out his theories in *The Age of Revolution, 1789–1848; The Age of Capital, 1848–1875;* and *The Age of Empire, 1875–1914.*

2 Mallet notes, for example, that the 'picturesque elements' of Kipling's *Kim* 'distinguish [the novel] from the realistic fiction of the nineteenth century'. See Philip Mallet, *Rudyard Kipling: A Literary Life* (New York: Palgrave Macmillan, 2003), p. 119. Nicholas Daly remarks that post-1880 romance and Gothic fiction has a connection with escapism and that 'experiential reality was undergoing a fundamental mutation, and that the phantasmagorias of modern, global consumer society were closer to the dream than to nineteenth-century realism'. See *Modernism, Romance, and the* Fin-de-Siècle: *Popular Fiction and British Culture, 1880–1914* (Cambridge: Cambridge University Press, 1999), p. 161.

3 Jackson Holbrook, *The Eighteen Nineties* (London: Grant Richards, 1913), p. 62.

4 Tillet (1860–1943) was a Christian Socialist and founder and secretary of the National Transport Workers' Federation; Churchill (1874–1965) was Liberal Party secretary in 1911 and served as prime minister during the Second World War.

5 C. N. Manlove, 'Charles Kingsley, H. G. Wells, and the machine in Victorian fiction', *Nineteenth-Century Literature*, 48/2 (September 1993), 212–39 (214).

6 See, for example, N. Auerbach, 'Incarnations of the orphan', *ELH*, 42/3 (autumn 1975), 359–419.

7 Thomas Hardy, *Jude the Obscure* (New York: W. W. Norton and Company, 1978), p. 70.

8 F. P. Rigg, '(De)Constructing the patriarchal family: Mary Louisa Molesworth and the late nineteenth-century children's novel', in Andrea O'Reilly Nerrera et al. (eds), *Family Matters in the British and American Novel* (Bowling Green, OH: Bowling Green State University Popular Press, 1997), pp. 97–114 (p. 113).

9 O. Wilde, 'The Star Child', in *The Happy Prince and Other Short Stories* (London: J. M. Dent and Sons Ltd., 1968), pp. 135–57 (pp. 140, 142, and 143).

10 Marah Gubar, *Artful Dodgers: Reconceiving the Golden Age of Children's Literature* (New York and Oxford: Oxford University Press, 2009), pp. viii and 4.

11 Humphrey Carpenter, *Secret Gardens: A Study of the Golden Age of Children's Literature* (Boston: Houghton Mifflin Company, 1985), p. 17.

12 Seth Lerer, *Children's Literature: A Reader's History From Aesop to Harry Potter* (Chicago and London: University of Chicago Press, 2008), p. 255.

13 U. C. Knoepflmacher, *Ventures into Childland: Victorians, Fairy Tales, and Femininity* (Chicago and London: Chicago University Press, 1988), p. 46; J. Muller, 'Introduction', in *The Secret Garden* by Francis Hodgson Burnett (New York: Barnes and Noble Classics, 2005), pp. xv–xxxi (pp. xvii and xxi).

14 Rose Lovell-Smith writes that the Gothic is 'a way of encompassing or imaging . . . extremes of emotional experience and mental aberration brought about by extraordinary connections and/or disconnections between characters often of the same household or family'. See 'On the Gothic beach: a New Zealand reading of house and landscape in Margaret Mahy's *The Tricksters*', in Anna Jackson et al. (eds), *The Gothic in Children's Literature: Haunting the Borders* (New York and London: Routledge, 2008), pp. 93–115. (p. 109).

15 See Mighall and Hurley, below, in particular. Their notion of the body as the site of turmoil sets late-century Gothic apart from first-wave Gothic texts such as those of Radcliffe, which tend to relegate anxieties onto foreign entities in foreign lands.

16 Robert Mighall, *A Geography of Victorian Gothic Fiction* (Oxford: Oxford University Press, 1999), p. 130.

17 Kelly Hurley, *The Gothic Body* (Cambridge: Cambridge University Press, 1996), p. 5. Hurley acknowledges that her use of the term 'abhuman' is borrowed from William Hope Hodgson's novel *The Night Land* (London: Eveleigh Nash: 1912)

18 John Reed, *Victorian Conventions* (Ohio: Ohio University Press, 1975), p. 258.
19 Ibid., p. 263.
20 Kate Ferguson Ellis, *The Contested Castle: Gothic Novels and the Subversion of Domestic Ideology* (Urbana and Chicago: University of Illinois Press, 1989), p. 192.
21 Laura Peters, *Orphan Texts: Victorian Orphans, Culture and Empire* (Manchester and New York: Manchester University Press, 2000), p. 75.
22 Auerbach, 'Incarnations', 403.
23 Peters, *Orphan Texts*, p. 27.
24 M. Vicinus, '"Helpless and unfriended": nineteenth-century domestic melodrama', *New Literary History*, 13/1, On Convention: I (autumn 1981), 127–143 (132).
25 Auerbach, 'Incarnations', 415.
26 Ibid., 410.
27 Reed, *Victorian Conventions*, pp. 252 and 266.
28 Auerbach, 'Incarnations', 395.
29 Christine Van Boheemen, *The Novel as Family Romance: Language, Gender, and Authority from Fielding to Joyce* (Ithaca and London: Cornell University Press, 1987), p. 102.
30 Morse Peckam, *Beyond the Tragic Vision* (New York: George Braziller, 1962), p. 108.
31 Dianne F. Sadoff, *Monsters of Affection: Dickens, Eliot, and Bronte on Fatherhood* (Baltimore and London: The John Hopkins University Press, 1982), pp. 12 and 22.
32 Gail Marshall, *The Victorian Novel* (London: Arnold, 2002), p. 23.
33 Vicinus, 'Helpless and unfriended', 139.
34 Baruch Hochman and Ilja Wachs, *Dickens: The Orphan Condition* (Cranbury, NJ: Fairleigh Dickinson University Press, 1999), p. 17.
35 Auerbach, 'Incarnations', 416.
36 M. S. E. Bonifer, 'Like a motherless child: the orphan figure in the novels of nineteenth-century American women writers, 1850–1899' (unpublished PhD thesis, Indiana University of Pennsylvania, 1995), pp. iv, 2 and 4. Deborah D. Rogers mentions Radcliffe's 'Matrophobic Gothic', which emphasizes the daughter's conflicts with self and disjunction, and whose inadequate mothers are 'rescued by maternal reconciliation'; she furthermore discusses the daughter's need to 'disidentify' with the mother figure, whose failure is often associated with victimization of sorts. See *The Matrophobic Gothic and Its*

Legacy: Sacrificing Mothers in the Novel and in Popular Culture (New York: Peter Lang, 2007), pp. 15 and 52.

37 Auerbach, 'Incarnations', 398.

38 Robin Gilmour, *The Novel in the Victorian Age* (London: Edward Arnold, 1986), p. 2; Marshall, *Victorian Novel*, p. 114.

39 Gilmour, *The Novel in the Victorian Age*, p. 149.

40 Carol Senf, *Dracula: Between Tradition and Modernism* (New York: Twayne Publishers, 1998), p. 6.

41 Stephen Arata, *Fictions of Loss in the Victorian Fin de Siècle* (Cambridge: Cambridge University Press, 1996), pp. 1 and 2; Daly, *Modernism, Romance, and the* Fin-de-Siècle, p. 30. For other considerations of late Victorian anxieties, see also Byron, Hurley, Kitson and Marshall.

42 Bernard Bergonzi, *The Early H. G. Wells: A Study of the Scientific Romances* (Manchester: Manchester University Press, 1961), pp. 17 and 18.

43 Marshall, *The Victorian Novel*, pp. 117 and 114.

44 Bergonzi, *The Early H. G. Wells*, p. 19.

45 Walter Pater, *Studies in the History of the Renaissance* (London: Macmillan and Co., 1873), p. 233.

46 Bergonzi, *The Early H. G. Wells*, p. 24.

47 Glennis Byron, 'Gothic of the 1890s', in David Punter (ed.), *A Companion to the Gothic* (Oxford and Malden, MA: Blackwell Publishers, 2000), pp. 132–42 (p. 133).

48 Kelly Hurley, 'British Gothic fiction', in Jerrold E. Hogle (ed.), *The Cambridge Companion to Gothic Fiction* (Cambridge: Cambridge University Press, 2002), pp. 189–207 (pp. 190, 195 and 106); Hurley, *Gothic Body*, p. 5.

49 Marshall, *The Victorian Novel*, p. 118.

50 Byron, 'Gothic of the 1880s', p. 133.

51 Andrea Kaston Tange, *Architectural Identities: Domesticity, Literature, and the Victorian Middle Classes* (Toronto, Buffalo and London: University of Toronto Press, 2010), p. 5.

52 Hurley, 'British Gothic fiction', p. 199.

53 Marshall, *The Victorian Novel*, pp. 113 and 122.

54 Ibid., pp. 124 and 128.

55 Hurley, 'British Gothic fiction', pp. 192, 196 and 197.

56 Gilmour, *The Novel in the Victorian Age*, p. 149.

57 Senf, *Dracula: Between Tradition and Modernism*, p. 6.

58 R. M. Polhemus, 'The favorite child: *David Copperfield* and the scriptural issue of the child-wives', in Murray Baumgarten and H. M. Daleski (eds), *Homes and Homelessness in the*

Victorian Imagination (New York: AMS Press, 1998), pp. 3–20 (p.4).

59 Tange, *Architectural Identities*, p. 5; P. McCarthy, 'Making for home: David Copperfield and his fellow travelers', in Murray Baumgarten and H. M. Daleski (eds), *Homes and Homelessness in the Victorian Imagination* (New York: AMS Press, 1998), pp. 21–32 (p. 23).

60 Polhemus, 'The favorite child', p. 4.

61 K. Reynolds, 'Changing families in children's fiction', in M. O. Grenby and Andrea Immel (eds), *The Cambridge Companion to Children's Literature* (Cambridge: Cambridge University Press, 2009), pp. 193–208 (pp. 193 and 197–9).

62 E. Sicher, 'Bleak homes and symbolic houses: at-homeness and homelessness in Dickens', in Murray Baumgarten and H. M. Daleski (eds), *Homes and Homelessness in the Victorian Imagination* (New York: AMS Press, 1998), pp. 33–49 (p.34).

63 Sicher, 'Bleak homes', p. 34; Polhemus, 'The favorite child', p. 5.

64 Carpenter, *Secret Gardens*, pp. 86 and 87.

65 Byron, 'Gothic of the 1890s', p. 132.

66 Marshall, *The Victorian Novel*, p. 108.

2: Renfield's 'Agonized Confusion'

1 S. L. Gladden, 'Dracula's earnestness: Stoker's debt to Wilde', in Jack Lynch (ed.), *Critical Insights:* Dracula *by Bram Stoker* (California and New Jersey: Salem Press, 2010), pp. 153–67 (p. 162).

2 Carol Senf, *Dracula: Between Tradition and Modernism* (New York: Twayne Publishers, 1998), p. 63; Nur Elmessiri, 'Burying eternal life in Bram Stoker's *Dracula*: the sacred age of reason', *Alif Journal of Comparative Poetics*, 14 (1994), 101–35 (105); Royce MacGillivray, 'Bram Stoker's Spoiled Masterpiece', in Carol Senf (ed.), *The Critical Response to Bram Stoker's* Dracula (Westport, CT and London: Greenwood, 1993), pp. 61–8 (pp. 66–7).

3 Burton Hatlen, 'The return of the repressed/oppressed in Bram Stoker's *Dracula*', in Margaret L. Carter (ed), *Dracula and the Critics* (Ann Arbor, MI and London: UMI Research Press, 1988), pp. 117–35 (p. 122); B. E. McDonald, 'Recreating the world: the sacred and the profane in Bram Stoker's *Dracula*', in Jack Lynch (ed.), *Critical Insights:* Dracula *by Bram Stoker* (Pasadena, CA and Hackensack, NJ: Salem Press, 2010),

pp. 87–137; Allen, Brooke, 'Introduction', *Dracula* by Bram Stoker (New York: Barnes and Noble Classics, 2003), pp. xiii–xxix (p. xvii).

4 Bram Stoker, *Dracula* (Boston and New York: Bedford/ St Martin's Press, 2002), p. 91.

5 William Hughes, *Bram Stoker Dracula: A Reader's Guide to Essential Criticism* (New York: Palgrave, 2009), p. 44.

6 Mark M.Hennely, Jr, '*Dracula*: the gnostic quest and Victorian wasteland', in Margaret L. Carter (ed), *Dracula and the Critics* (Ann Arbor, MI and London: UMI Research Press, 1988), pp. 79–92 (p. 85).

7 Also known as Multiple Personality Disorder. I would like to acknowledge Jennifer Floyd Brown, MS, LPC, for her contribution to this chapter.

8 For a Lacanian reading of Van Helsing, see Philip Martin, who states that the doctor and philosopher 'represents the test of the socially "normal" world which the characters in the book represent' ('The vampire in the looking glass: reflection and projection in Bram Stoker's *Dracula*', in Clive Bloom et al. (eds), *Nineteenth-Century Suspense* (New York: Harper and Row, 1988), pp. 80–92 (p. 82).

9 Lombroso would have diagnosed Renfield as 'epileptic'. He states that the epileptic individual 'at one time afflicted with loss of willpower and amnesia, and incapable of formulating the simplest notion, will shortly afterwards give expression to original ideas and reason logically' (Cesare Lombroso, *Criminal Man* (Montclair, NJ: Patterson Smith, 1972). When Dr Hennessey approaches Renfield about his rating of the men on the carrier's cart, he is 'lead to believe that he was completely oblivious of the affair' (Stoker, *Dracula*, p. 168).

10 Allen, 'Introduction', pp. xvii–xviii. Klinger notes that Renfield is of 'strong intellectual character' and is 'highly educated and articulate', but also regards him as 'selfish, secretive, obsessive, morbidly excitable, and prone to violent acts' (Leslie S. Klinger (ed.), *The New Annotated Dracula* by Bram Stoker (New York: W. W. Norton & Company, 2008), p. xlviii.

11 Stoker, *Dracula*, pp. 231 and 232.

12 Ibid., pp. 270 and 91.

13 Ibid., p. 133.

14 Ibid., p. 258

15 Ibid., p. 119.

16 Ibid., pp. 133, 125 and 126.

17 Ibid., p. 125

18 Ibid., pp. 119 and 167.

19 Ibid., pp. 259 and 279.

20 Robert Mighall notes that the Count's 'eponymous figure is strangely absent from the narrative for most of the novel. He makes a few fleeting appearances, is given very few lines (most of which are mediated through others' testimonies) and is largely the object of other characters' recollections, observations, and theorizings' (*A Geography of Victorian Gothic Fiction* (Oxford: Oxford University Press, 1999), p. 239). Kelly Hurley writes that characters like Dracula 'exist across multiple categories of being and conform cleanly to none of them' (*The Gothic Body* (Cambridge: Cambridge University Press, 1996), p. 24). Despite his being from Transylvania, the Count is able to speak notably good English, has knowledge of English culture and commerce and is able to assimilate into English society. But Dracula's ability to assume some degree of acceptability in London does not completely divorce him from his status as foreign or criminal other: 'Count Dracula is not just identified as a Lombrosian criminal type, his very features mark him out as criminally degenerate: his protruding teeth, pointed ears, and hairy hands are telling signs' (Gina Lombroso Ferrero, *Criminal Man, according to the Classification of Cesare Lombroso* (New York and London: G. P. Putnam's and Sons, 1911, pp. xv, 15, 17 and 40), quoted in S. Eltis, 'Corrupting of the blood and degeneration of the race: *Dracula* and policing the borders of gender', in John Paul Riquelme (ed.), *Dracula* by Bram Stoker (Boston, MA: Bedford/St Martin's, 2002), pp. 450–65. (p. 455)). Harker's description of the Count's 'marked physiognomy' creates an image of a particularly foreign being, with his 'aquiline' face, 'lofty domed forehead', profuse growth of hair, 'massive' eyebrows and 'bushy hair that seemed to curl in its own profusion'; Harker also mentions the disturbing 'peculiarly sharp white teeth [that] protruded over the lips' and ears that are 'extremely pointed'; the Count's fingers are 'broad and squat', while 'there were hairs in the centre of the palm' of his hands, and his fingernails are 'long and fine, and cut to a sharp point' (Stoker, *Dracula*, pp. 42 and 43). Harker's depiction categorizes Dracula not as the Englishman he may endeavour to imitate, but more as a type of disturbingly foreign being. He is an amalgamation of different perceptions of him. Stylistically, then, Dracula is rendered 'a composite of otherness that manifests itself as the horror essential to dark, foreign, and perverse

bodies' (Judith Halberstam, *Skin Shows: Gothic Horror and the Technology of Monsters* (Durham, NC: Duke University Press, 1995), pp. 89–90. Elmessiri states that the Count 'has spent so much time guarding the frontier against the dark, barbaric outsider, that he has become such an outsider, a metaphoric Turk' (Elmessiri, 'Burying eternal life in Bram Stoker's *Dracula*', 125). Dracula's fractious elements, while including imitation of western modes, are largely indicative of his easternness, and generally define him as 'other'. As Elmessiri continues, 'Dracula is physically, psycho-sexually an Other; in his likeness both to the coal miners or working classes and absentee landlords or aristocracy, he is socially an Other; and, finally . . . he is culturally and metaphysically an Other. He represents "otherness" itself' (Elmessiri, 'Burying eternal life in Bram Stoker's *Dracula*', 124).

21 Hogle, Jerrold E., 'The ghost of the counterfeit', in David Punter (ed.), *A Companion to the Gothic* (Oxford and Malden, MA: Blackwell Publishers Ltd, 2000), pp. 293–304 (p. 296).

22 David Seed notes that 'Seward and Harker are members of the medical and legal professions; Lord Arthur Godalming is the liberal aristocrat; Quincey Morris (in effect a courtesy Englishman) is a man of action and a protector of frontiers' ('The narrative method of *Dracula*', *Nineteenth-Century Fiction*, 40 (1985), 61–75 (72). John L. Greenway refers to the group of heroes as 'an emblem of the Victorian establishment' ('Seward's folly: *Dracula* as critique of "normal science"', *Stanford Literature Review*, 3 (fall 1986), 213–30 (73). S. L. Varnado states that Stoker intended these representatives of Victorian England not as fully realized individuals, 'but rather as sharply etched representatives of the rational structure surrounding the occult' (*Haunted Presence: The Numinous in Gothic Fiction* (Tuscaloosa, AL and London: University of Alabama Press, 1987), p. 105).

23 If the American Quincey may be added to this list, the Dutchman Van Helsing may as well. While he is not English, and arguably not even completely western, Van Helsing's efforts, like those of the Quincey, are executed in the service of Victorian England.

24 Hennely notes that Renfield is 'a native zoophagist or vampire, one alive and unwell in London before the "foreign" Dracula is ever smuggled ashore' ('*Dracula:* the gnostic quest and Victorian wasteland', p. 85). Klinger writes of Renfield's 'own particular form of vampirism' and states that the patient's

'mania or zeal for the consummation of life is his own conception' (Klinger (ed.), *Dracula*, p. 129 n 43).

25 See, for example, Greenway's 'Seward's folly: *Dracula* as critique of "normal science"'.

26 Stoker, *Dracula*, p. 279.

27 Ibid., p. 258.

28 Ibid., pp. 259 and 248.

29 Ibid., pp. 239 and 248.

30 Ibid., p. 236.

31 Ibid., p. 169.

32 Ibid., pp. 368 and 281. In addition to a corresponding act of noble martyrdom, one other, perhaps wildly speculative but nevertheless interesting, aspect is the contrasting notion of both characters' collusion with Dracula. Renfield, of course, permits Dracula to enter the asylum to victimize Mina. Franco Moretti suggests numerous indications that Morris is actually in league with Dracula; Clive Leatherdale notes Morris's nightly visits to the woods, supposedly to report to the Count; Leslie S. Klinger claims that when it appears that Van Helsing knows too much, Morris tries to kill him, that Morris actually leads the party to the rats, and he notes that Morris is the last to see Renfield alive (Klinger, *Dracula*, p. 344 n. 49, where he refers to Franco Moretti, 'Dialectic of fear', in *Signs Taken For Wonders: Essays in the Sociology of Literary Forms*, trans. Susan Fischer, David Forgacs and David Miller (rev. edn, London: Verso, 1988), 83–108, as well as Clive Leatherdale (ed.), *Bram Stoker's Dracula Unearthed* (Westcliff-on-Sea: Desert Island Books, 1998).

33 Stoker, *Dracula*, pp. 91, 126 and 121.

34 Ibid., pp. 169, 82 and 121. Great strength is sometimes associated with mental illness. In his introduction to *Criminal Man*, Lombroso comments on the 'apparently superhuman abilities of some criminals' (Riquelme, John Paul, 'Contextual illustrations and documents', in John Paul Riquelme (ed.), *Dracula* by Bram Stoker (Boston, MA and New York: Bedford/ St Martin's Press, 2002), pp. 370–406 (p. 374)). He refers, for instance, to the famous brigand Viella, who 'possessed such extraordinary agility, that he had been known to scale steep mountain heights bearing a sheep on his shoulders' (quoted in Riquleme, 'Contextual illustrations and documents', p. 388). In *The Essential Dracula,* Wolf notes that the 59-year-old Renfield readily scales the wall of the asylum, whereas the 29-year-old Seward requires a ladder (quoted in Klinger, *Dracula*, p. 170 n. 48).

35 Stoker, *Dracula*, pp. 132 and 169.

36 Athena Vrettos states that women seemed to have more of a propensity for madness than men: 'While male lunatics were just as likely to be linked to hereditary forms of insanity, the larger number of women diagnosed with mental disorders in the nineteenth century seemed to indicate a specifically female propensity for madness'; she also notes 'women's greater tendency toward emotional excess and irrational behavior and thought' ('Victorian psychology', in Patrick Brantlinger and William B. Thesing (eds), *A Companion to the Victorian Novel* (Oxford: Blackwell, 2002), pp. 67–83 (p. 77).

37 Rosemary Ellen Guiley, *The Encyclopedia of Vampires, Werewolves, and Other Monsters* (New York: Checkmark Books, 2005), p. 241; Robert Miles, 'Ann Radcliffe and Matthew Lewis', in David Punter (ed.), *A Companion to the Gothic* (Oxford and Malden, MA: Blackwell Publishers Ltd, 2000), pp. 41–57 (p. 42).

38 Stoker, *Dracula*, p. 125.

39 Kitson, Peter J., 'The Victorian Gothic', in William Baker and Kenneth Womack (eds), *A Companion to the Victorian Novel* (Westport, CT: Greenwood Press, 2002), pp. 163–76 (p. 173).

40 Stoker, *Dracula*, p. 121.

41 Varnado points out that the asylum to which Renfield is confined 'suggests the scientific and the rational, on the one hand, and the alien and the nonrational, on the other' (*Haunted Presence*, p. 106).

42 Elmessiri makes note of the manner in which *Dracula* 'continually draws attention, sometimes to the point of tedium, to the mechanical processes that brought it into being' ('Burying eternal life in Bram Stoker's Dracula', p. 104). The novel, of course, begins by noting the manner in which the papers comprising the narrative 'have been placed in sequence' (Stoker, *Dracula*, p. 26).

43 Seed states that 'the exchange and accumulation of information literally is resistance to [Dracula]' ('The narrative method of *Dracula*, p. 73).

44 Harker, for example, famously attempts to describe the bucolic elements around him prior to his stay in Castle Dracula, in a manner that nearly renders the scene as a diorama or museum piece observed through western eyes. Seed states that Harker 'constantly tries to normalize the strange into the discourse of the nineteenth-century travelogue' ('The narrative method of *Dracula*, p. 64).

45 Stoker, *Dracula*, pp. 54 and 276.
46 Hatlen, 'The return of the repressed/oppressed in Bram Stoker's *Dracula*', p. 127.
47 Stoker, *Dracula*, pp. 135 and 90.
48 Ibid., p. 90.
49 Nordau references Lombroso's 'graphomaniacs', the category under which the latter classifies 'those semi-insane persons who feel a strong impulse to write' (quoted in Riquelme, 'Contextual illustrations and documents', p. 393).
50 Stoker creates a linguistic connection here between Renfield and Seward, the doctor remarking on the same page that 'only yesterday . . . my whole life ended with my new hope, and . . . I began a new record' (p. 92). At another point, Seward writes of his patient: 'Am I to take it that I have anything in common with him, so that we are, as it were, to stand together?' (p. 125).
51 Stoker, *Dracula*, pp. 92, 132 and 275.
52 Klinger suggests that Seward is either not a good doctor, or that he may not even be a legitimate doctor at all. Klinger notes several instances where Seward's actions are 'dense' and that in the novel are several accounts where Seward's actions are atypical of a medical man, such as an unpublished passage which features him taking a gun with him to retrieve the escaped Renfield (Klinger (ed.), *Dracula*, pp. 178 n 24 and 185 n 52). In 'Seward's folly: *Dracula* as a critique of "normal science"', Greenway also reads Seward's science as erroneous and unavailing.
53 See Riquelme's unnumbered footnote, which states that the term *sanguine* is 'often used to refer to the hopeful, confident temperament and ruddy complexion of a person whose controlling humor, or bodily fluid, is blood' and that *choleric* refers to the 'irascible and angry' (Stoker, *Dracula*, p. 82).
54 Stoker, *Dracula*, p. 155.
55 Ibid., p. 82.
56 Ibid.
57 Elmissiri, 'Burying eternal life in Bram Stoker's *Dracula*', 125.
58 Stoker, *Dracula*, pp. 90 and 239.
59 Ibid., pp. 90, 89 and 92.
60 Ibid., pp. 91 and 92.
61 Bacil F., Kirtley, '*Dracula*, the monastic chronicles and Slavic folklore', in Margaret L. Carter (ed.), *Dracula and the Critics* (Ann Arbor, MI and London: UMI Research Press, 1988),

pp. 11–17 (p. 15); Hatlen, 'The return of the repressed/oppressed in Bram Stoker's *Dracula*', p. 127.

62 Stoker, *Dracula*, p. 250.

63 Hughes, *Bram Stoker Dracula*, p. 6.

64 Hatlen, 'The return of the repressed/oppressed in Bram Stoker's *Dracula*', p. 127.

65 Hebblethwaite, 'Introduction' to *Dracula* by Bram Stoker (London: Penguin Classics, 2006), pp. xxxiii–xxxiv; John Paul Riquelme, 'Introduction: biographical and historical contexts', *Dracula* by Bram Stoker, p. 12). Riquelme states that Stoker drew on cultural anxieties that were particularly strong at the end of the nineteenth-century, combining the 'dark menace [of Gothic] with exotic materials', which allowed him to speak to issues relating to 'home and homeland concerning anthropological questions about the definition of the human' ('Introduction', p. 12).

66 Lombroso made the connection as well between criminality and the savagery associated with Otherness. He states that criminal man has a tendency not only 'to extinguish life in the victim, but to mutilate the corpse, tear its flesh, and drink its blood'; he cites the example of Verzeni, a criminal convicted of sadism and rape, 'who showed the cannibalistic instincts of primitive anthropophagists and the ferocity of beasts of prey' (*Criminal Man*, quoted in Riquelme, 'Contextual illustrations and documents', p. 388). Lombroso also cites certain criminals' 'bestial physical characteristics, and their tendency toward cannibalism and the drinking of blood' (Riquelme, 'Contextual illustrations and documents', p. 374). There may also be a link between Renfield's association with imperialism and his madness. Ken Gelder states that in *Dracula,* '[c]onsumption in the novel is an obsession which leads to madness' (*Reading the Vampire* (London and New York: Routledge, 1994), p. 83). Scott Brewster claims that 'vampirism and madness are inseparable in the text' ('Seeing things: Gothic and the madness of interpretation', in David Punter (ed.), *A Companion to the Gothic* (Oxford and Malden, MA: Blackwell Publishers Ltd, 2000), pp. 269–80 (p. 287).

67 Stoker, *Dracula's Guest and Other Weird Stories with The Lair of the White Worm* (London: Penguin Classics, 2006), pp. 158 and 191.

68 Quoted in Hughes, *Bram Stoker Dracula*, p. 4.

69 Ibid., p. 16.

70 Stoker, *Dracula*, p. 82.

71 Valente, Joseph, *Dracula's Crypt: Bram Stoker, Irishness, and the Question of Blood* (Urbana, IL and Chicago: University of Illinois Press, 2009), p. 113.
72 Stoker, *Dracula*, pp. 90, 92, 93, 132 and 238.
73 Ibid., p. 271
74 Ibid., pp. 120 and 125.
75 Ibid., p. 272.
76 Ibid., p. 125.
77 Valente, '*Dracula's Crypt*', p. 116.
78 Stoker, *Dracula*, pp. 91 and 271.
79 Ibid., pp. 274, 273, 272 and 259.
80 Ibid., p. 277, 279 and 273.
81 Klinger states that once he supplies them with his information, the vampire hunters 'abandon Renfield to die' (*Dracula*, p. 388 n. 20). Guiley notes that Renfield's 'actual death takes place offstage' (*The Encyclopedia of Vampires, Werewolves, and Other Monsters*, p. 242).
82 Armstrong, Nancy, 'Gender and the Victorian novel', in Deirdre David (ed.), *The Cambridge Companion to the Victorian Novel* (Cambridge: Cambridge University Press, 2001), pp. 97–124 (p. 119).
83 Ann McWhir remarks that Mina 'evidently has little time for romantic dreaming, only for work, concern, and responsibility' ('Pollution and redemption in *Dracula*', *Modern Language Studies*, 17/3 (summer 1987), 31–40 (31).
84 Stoker, *Dracula*, pp. 228, 75, 196 and 336.
85 Ibid., p. 240.
86 Ibid., p. 325.
87 Kathy Casey, 'Note', in *Dracula* by Bram Stoker (Mineola, NY: Dover Publications Inc., 2000), pp. iii–iv (p. iv).
88 Stoker, *Dracula*, p. 170.
89 Ibid., p. 306.
90 Ibid., p. 236.
91 Ibid., p. 237.
92 Ibid., p. 239.
93 Ibid., p. 229.
94 Ibid.
95 Kitson, 'The Victorian Gothic', p. 173.
96 Stoker, *Dracula*, p. 238.
97 Ibid., p. 239.
98 Ibid., p. 248.
99 Ibid., p. 251.
100 Ibid., pp. 273–4; ibid., p. 273.

101 Maurice Richardson recommends a Freudian reading of the Count, seeing him as a 'huge father-figure'. See his 'The psychoanalysis of ghost stories', *Twentieth Century*, 166 (1959), 419–31. Astle reads Renfield as a rebellious son to the father figure posed by Dracula ('Dracula as totemic monster: Lacan, Freud, Oedipus and history', *SubStance*, 8/4, issue 25 (1979), 98–105.

102 E. Fontana, 'Lombroso's Criminal Man and Stoker's *Dracula*', *Victorian Newsletter*, 66 (fall 1984), 25–7 (25–6).

3: Rebellious Orphans

1 Like a number of other critics, Mark Kanzer and Karl Miller among them, I read Hyde as a son figure, created by Jekyll. I furthermore read Hyde as intending to effect his own orphan state through various actions this chapter discusses, not the least of which is the elimination, the patricide, of his father-creator, Jekyll. Hammond makes note of the structural similarity between *Dr Jekyll and Mr. Hyde* and Wells's *The Invisible Man* and notes Wells's debt to Stevenson. See *A Robert Louis Stevenson Companion* (New York: Macmillan Publishing Company, 1984), pp. 117 and 125.

2 Karl Miller, *Doubles: Studies in Literary History* (Oxford: Oxford University Press, 1985), p. 211.

3 Havelock Ellis wrote in 1896, for example, that Thomas Hardy offered 'the reality of marriage clearly recognized as something wholly apart from the mere ceremony with which our novelists have usually identified it'. See 'Concerning *Jude the Obscure*', *Savoy Magazine* [Oct 1896], quoted in the Norton edition of Thomas Hardy, *Jude the Obscure* (New York: W. W. Norton and Company, 1978) pp. 393–4. In *The Haunted Study* (London: Secker & Warburg, 1989), Peter Keating mentions H. G. Wells's personal enthusiasm for the breakdown of the family in Victorian life.

4 Irving S. Saposnik, *Robert Louis Stevenson* (New York: Twayne Publishers, 1974), p. 101.

5 L. Dryden, ' "City of dreadful night": Stevenson's Gothic London', in Richard Ambrosini and Richard Dury (eds), *Robert Louis Stevenson: Writer of Boundaries* (Madison, Wisconsin: University of Wisconsin Press, 2006), pp. 253–64 (p. 253).

6 B. Allen, 'Introduction', *Dracula* by Bram Stoker (New York: Barnes and Noble Classics, 2003), pp. xiii–xxix (p. xxiii).

7 A. Jefford, 'Dr Jekyll and Professor Nabokov: Reading a reading', in Andrew Noble (ed.), *Robert Louis Stevenson* (London: Vision Press, 1983), pp. 47–72 (pp. 62–3); Miller, *Doubles*, p. 268.

8 K. B. Linehan, ' "Closer than a wife": the strange case of Dr Jekyll's significant other', in William B. Jones (ed.), *Robert Louis Stevenson Reconsidered* (Jefferson, NC and London: McFarland and Company, Inc. Publishers, 2003), pp. 85–100 (p. 88); Briggs, Julia, *The Rise and Fall of the English Ghost Story* (London: Faber, 1977), pp. 70 and 73.

9 Stevenson, Robert Louis, *The Strange Case of Dr Jekyll and Mr Hyde and Other Stories* (New York: Barnes and Noble Classics, 2003), p. 24.

10 Ibid., p. 67.

11 Ibid.

12 M. Kanzer, MD, 'The self analytic literature of Robert Louis Stevenson', in Harry Geguld (ed.), *The Definitive* Dr Jekyll and Mr. Hyde *Companion* (New York and London: Garland Publishing, Inc., 1983), pp. 118–26 (p. 123); Miller, *Doubles*, p. 211.

13 Stevenson, *Strange Case*, p. 70.

14 On an interesting biographical note that extends beyond the scope of this study, William Veeder states that Stevenson 'hates fathers for being overbearing but he hates them still more for being weak' ('Children of the night: Stevenson and patriarchy', in William Veeder and Gordon Hirsh (eds), *Dr Jekyll and Mr Hyde After One Hundred Years* (Chicago: University of Chicago Press, 1988), pp. 107–60). J. Calder states, 'Louis's impatience with his father's anguished guilt' was 'operating in *Jekyll and Hyde*' (*Robert Louis Stevenson: A Life Study* (New York and Toronto: Oxford University Press, 1980), p. 222).

15 Lynn Pykett, 'Sensation and the fantastic in the Victorian novel', in Deirdre David (ed.), *The Cambridge Companion to the Victorian Novel* (Cambridge: Cambridge University Press, 2001), pp. 192–211 (p. 207). Linehan states that Stevenson himself valued the support system of '[i]ntimate friends, family members, and most of all well-loved spouses' in combating ones' faults ('Closer than a wife', p. 96).

16 Stevenson, *Strange Case*, p. 6.

17 Ibid.

18 Ibid., p. 13.

19 Ibid., p. 22.

20 Linehan, 'Closer than a wife', pp. 93 and 97.

21 Stevenson, *Strange Case*, p. 77.

22 Kanzer states that Stevenson may have had dreams of a patricidal nature that 'evoke more than the unconscious fantasies of the means by which an inheritance may be acquired' ('The self analytic literature of Robert Louis Stevenson', p. 122). Miller writes that in *Jekyll and Hyde* emerge 'images of disobedience dreamed by a loyal son' (*Doubles*, p. 213).

23 Stevenson, *Strange Case*, p. 12.

24 Ibid., p. 66.

25 Ibid., p. 63.

26 Ibid., pp. 46, 64 and 65.

27 Ibid., p. 74.

28 Dryden discusses '[m]etropolitan anxiety about criminal activity', which she states 'goes to the heart of the domestic sphere in the modern gothic novel, where the urban monster leaves the streets of low-life London to attack citizens in or near their own homes' ('City of dreadful night', p. 258).

29 Stevenson, *Strange Case*, pp. 12 and 19.

30 Ibid., p. 27.

31 Ibid., p. 48.

32 Ibid., p. 48.

33 Various critics have speculated that Hyde's 'unspeakable' nocturnal activities are generally of a sexually deviant nature, ranging from visiting prostitutes, the blurring of gender roles, homosexual encounters and rape. See, for example, Saposnik, *Robert Louis Stevenson*, pp. 94–5, and J. V. Rago, '*Dr Jekyll and Mr Hyde*: a "men's narrative" of hysteria and containment', in Richard Ambrosini and Richard Dury (eds), *Robert Louis Stevenson: Writer of Boundaries* (Madison, WI: University of Wisconsin Press, 2006), pp. 275–85 (pp. 275 and 285 n. 1).

34 Stevenson, *Strange Case*, p. 29.

35 Ibid., p. 64 (emphasis mine).

36 Ibid., p. 25.

37 Ibid., p. 26.

38 By the nineteenth century, the cane had replaced the sword as an essential accessory of a European gentleman's ensemble.

39 Stevenson, *Strange Case*, p. 23.

40 Ibid., p. 17.

41 R. Dury, 'The hand of Hyde', in William B. Jones, Jr (ed.), *Robert Louis Stevenson Reconsidered* (Jefferson, NC and London: McFarland and Company, Inc. Publishers, 2003), pp. 101–16 (p. 110); R. Tymms, 'Doubles in literary

psychology', in Harry Geguld (ed.), *The Definitive* Dr Jekyll and Mr Hyde *Companion* (New York and London: Garland Publishing, Inc., 1983), pp. 77–94 (p. 78). Hyde implies deicide as well; R. J. Walker writes that Hyde's blasphemous annotations are his way of 'symbolically killing God by defacing Jekyll's "pious work"' ('Pious works: aesthetics, ethics, and the modern individual in Robert Louis Stevenson's *Dr Jekyll and Mr Hyde*', in R. Ambrosini and R. Dury (eds), *Robert Louis Stevenson: Writer of Boundaries*, pp. 265–74 (p. 272).

42 Stevenson, *Strange Case*, p. 78.

43 Jefford, 'Dr Jekyll and Professor Nabokov', p. 59.

44 Stevenson, *Strange Case*, p. 14.

45 Ibid., pp. 59 and 60.

46 In theory, at least; clearly, Jekyll succumbs to the temptation to step out of the societal order which his status as Victorian professional implies. Utterson, likewise, is morally ambiguous in some instances. The point is that their status as professionals bears an assumed morality which was thought to accompany the wealth and intelligence of the professional class.

47 Rago calls Hyde 'fundamentally different', an 'anarchist of the city streets of London' ('*Dr Jekyll and Mr. Hyde*: a "men's narrative" of hysteria and containment', p. 275). Dury notes that Hyde exists both as 'the socially excluded' and as 'the threat to established authority' ('The hand of Hyde', p. 105).

48 As did some of his contemporaries, Wells saw the institution of the family as overbearing and restrictive, so it is not surprising to find within his work a character whose primary function is to sever himself from familial and social structures in order to further his own individual pursuits. One interesting aspect of this, however, is that, despite being responsible for his own orphanhood and seeming emblematic of such modernist individualism, Griffin ultimately suffers from his orphan condition and serves as an argument for the values and benefits for which the ideal family stood.

49 H. G. Wells, *The Time Machine* and *The Invisible Man* (New York: Barnes and Noble Classics, 2003), p. 161.

50 Ibid., pp. 187 and 188.

51 Ibid., p. 107.

52 Wells's use of Whitsuntide as providing a context in which Griffin's exile is even more pronounced. Whit Monday, with its gathering of the community to commemorate Whitsunday, the seventh Sunday after Easter, commemorates the descent of

the Holy Spirit at Pentecost, the event whereat Christ's disciples were endowed with the ability to communicate with people in various tongues. This notion of surmounting barriers to communication creates a contrast to the self-concerned and recalcitrant Griffin.

53 Wells, *The Time Machine* and *The Invisible Man*, pp. 174 and 175.
54 Ibid., p. 175.
55 Ibid., p. 175.
56 Ibid., p. 174.
57 Ibid., p. 175.
58 Ibid., pp. 178 and 211.
59 Ibid., p. 189.
60 Ibid., p. 188.
61 Ibid., pp. 195 and 200 (emphasis mine).
62 Ibid., p. 190.
63 Note that, as a younger student, Griffin 'won the medal for chemistry' (p. 161) at University College, but later falls to the temptation of utilizing science for his corrupt intentions. Contrast this with the more ethical Kemp, whose thoughts, when we first encounter him, revolve around the publication of his work, which he hopes 'would earn him . . . the fellowship of the Royal Society' (p. 152). Kemp seeks involvement, acknowledgement and validation from others, as opposed to the antisocial and self-concerned Griffin. Kemp even implores Griffin: 'Don't be a lone wolf. Publish your results; take the world – take the nation at least – into your confidence' (p. 203).
64 Norman Mackenzie and Jeanne Mackenzie, *H. G. Wells* (New York: Simon and Schuster, 1973), pp. 126 and 127; Robert M. Philmus, *Into the Unknown: The Evolution of Science Fiction from Francis Godwin to H. G. Wells* (Berkeley and Los Angeles: University of California Press, 1970), p. 103; Richard Hauer Costa, *H. G. Wells* (New York: Twayne Publishers, 1967), p. 31. Each of these critics charts Griffin's decline.
65 Wells, *The Time Machine* and *The Invisible Man*, p. 183.
66 Ibid., p. 144.
67 Glen Cavaliero states that Machen's best work 'transcends hermeticism, presenting a view of the world that is basically Christian and sacramental' (*The Supernatural in English Fiction* (Oxford: Oxford University Press, 1995), p. 79).
68 Wesley D. Sweetser claims that 'no more dedicated advocate of tradition, of individuality, of spirituality, of romance and

mystery exists than Arthur Machen' (*Arthur Machen* (New York: Twayne, 1964), p. 139).

69 Arthur Machen, *The Great God Pan* and *The Hill of Dreams* (Mineola, NY: Dover Publications, Inc., 2006), p. 1.

70 See 'Arthur Machen: the mystery of the universe', in S. T. Joshi, *The Weird Tale* (Austin: University of Texas Press, 1990), pp. 12–41. Joshi speaks of Machen's 'battle against naturalism' and compulsion 'to undertake a systematic rearguard opposition to the course of modern civilization as it is possible to imagine' (p. 14).

71 B. Nash, 'Arthur Machen among the Arthurians', in Charles Alva Hoyt (ed.), *Minor British Novelists* (Carbondale and Edwardsville: Southern Illinois University Press, 1967), pp. 108–20 (pp. 112 and 120); Briggs, *Rise and Fall*, p. 75.

72 Vladimir Lossky states that on the cross, Christ 'unites paradise, the dwelling place of the first men before the fall, with the terrestrial reality where the fallen descendents of the first Adam now dwell' and 'unit[es] the created to the uncreated' (*The Mystical Theology of the Eastern Church* (Crestwood, NY: St Vladimir's Seminary Press, 1976), p. 137.

73 Quoted in Cavaliero, *The Supernatural in English Fiction*, p. 78.

74 Nash, 'Arthur Machen among the Arthurians', p. 112.

75 I do not regard Raymond as Helen's father. His role in her creation is simply to administer the experiment that permits Pan to impregnate her.

76 In the context of Christian theology, this would relegate Helen to the lower status of an animal, a soulless, purely physical being. The underlying statement that Machen seems to be making here, of course, is that human beings who do not address their spirituality are likened to animals, whose behaviours are more determined by base desires and instinct.

77 This, of course, is not to imply that Mary's union with Pan is necessarily morally acceptable; but my focus here is Helen's orphanhood, not the means of her conception.

78 Edward Wagenknect states that the sin with which Machen is concerned 'is an offense against the nature of things' (*Seven Masters of Supernatural Fiction* (New York: Greenwood Press, 1991), p. 105).

79 Robert Mighall is one critic who is hesitant to make this assumption, claiming problems in the effort 'to uncover a sexual "meaning" that the text cannot express'; whereas other authors of the period used 'rhetoric of horror (talking of

monsters, vampires and pests)' to figure sexuality, Mighall argues that Machen 'frames the diabolical with the erotic' and furthermore remarks that late nineteenth-century sexology Gothicized 'contemporary deviants' by regarding them as 'vampires', and pathologized monsters 'by reclassifying them as perverts' (*A Geography of Victorian Gothic Fiction* (Oxford: Oxford University Press, 1999), pp. 202, 207 and 235).

80 Kelly Hurley, *The Gothic Body* (Cambridge: Cambridge University Press, 1996), p. 13; Joshi, *The Weird Tale*, p. 21; Mighall cites the Creation Classics quote on p. 199.

81 Quoted in L. Sprague de Camp, *H. P. Lovecraft, A Biography* (New York: Barnes and Noble, 1975), p. 301.

82 See St Paul's references to the mystical body of Christ: 1 Cor 12:12–31; Col 1:18, 2:18; Eph 1:22–3, 3:17 and 4:13.

83 Philmus notes, for instance, that Wells stresses 'the social matrix of Griffin's action' (*Into the Unknown*, p. 100).

84 The disturbed domestic space has biographical roots in Machen. In his introduction to *The Great God Pan*, he touches on one of the evocative images that was to influence his work in his description of the house Bertholy, near his homeplace. Calling the white house in the distance 'one of the many symbols of the world of wonder that were afforded to me', Machen notes the mysterious effect the house had on him; 'It became as it were', he continues, 'a great word in the secret language by which the mysteries were communicated' (*The Great God Pan* and *The Hill of Dreams*, p. 3). He elaborates on this mode of communication where, in *Elusiana* and *Beneath the Barley*, he wrote of 'the art of the veil, which reveals what it conceals' (quoted in Joshi, *The Weird Tale*, p. 234 n. 1). For Machen, images like Bertholy and the Roman ruins of Isca Silurum near his birthplace at Caerleon-on-Usk, Wales, were not only evidence of history, but reminders of the spiritual world which coexists with the material. Within this fascination with such evocative architectural models of his sacramental world-view was his disparagement over the manner in which his homeplace was being swallowed up by industrialization. In *Far Off Things* (1922), he refers to the place of his birth as 'the vision of an enchanted land' and in *Things Near and Far* (1923) called it 'a little white city in dream'; by 1926, though, he wrote that his town had become 'an agonizing spectacle', and that progress had reduced it to '*uffern du*' [black inferno]. See George C. Schoolfield, *A Baedeker of Decadence: Charting a Literary*

Fashion, 1884–1927 (New Haven and London: Yale University Press, 2005), pp. 198–9.

85 Machen, *The Great God Pan* and *The Hill of Dreams*, p. 26.

86 Ibid., p. 54.

87 Stevenson, *Strange Case*, p. 28.

88 Ibid., p. 18.

89 Wells, *The Time Machine* and *The Invisible Man*, pp. 118, 223 and 224.

90 Machen, *The Great God Pan* and *The Hill of Dreams*, p. 28.

91 Ibid., pp. 55 and 19.

92 Stevenson, *Strange Case*, p. 65.

93 Machen, *The Great God Pan* and *The Hill of Dreams*, pp. 48 and 31.

94 Ibid., pp. 54 and 56.

95 Ibid., p. 66.

96 Ibid., p. 66.

97 Stevenson, *Strange Case*, p. 65.

98 It is interesting and perhaps telling that rebellion and individualism will become notably tolerated and even admired in later, modernist fiction.

4: The Orphaning Island

1 There are numerous critical assessments of the island as a literary convention that exceed the scope of this study. Ruddick, for example, addresses the island trope of British science fiction; Thompson and Keenan's collection focuses particularly on Irish fiction's sensibilities concerning the use of literary islands; Weaver-Hightower's focus is primarily on islands of empire and their relation to postcolonial issues. There is, to my knowledge, no study on the island as an orphanic space.

2 With the exception of the occasional attendant wife or daughter, the fin-de-siècle castaway is a notably male figure, an emblem of normative notions of masculinity.

3 J. E. Cirlot, *A Dictionary of Symbols* (New York: Philosophical Library, Inc., 1962), p. 281; Rene Guenon, *Le Roi du monde* (Paris: Galimard, 1950), p. 28.

4 Heinrich Zimmer, *Form of Art and Yoga in the Indian Cult Image* (Berlin: Bibliothek Suhrkamp, 1926), p. 60.

5 Carl Jung, *Psychology of the Transference* (London: Pantheon Books, 1954), p. 33.

6 Peter Hunt, *An Introduction to Children's Literature* (Oxford and New York: Oxford University Press, 1994), p. 56.

7 Harold Bayley, *The Lost Language of Symbolism*, 2 vols (London: Ernest Benn Limited, 1957), ii, p. 225.
8 See chapter X, 'Monsters, sea serpents and enchanted islands', Horace Palmer Beck, *Folklore and the Sea* (Middletown, CT: Wesleyan University Press, 1973).
9 Ibid., pp. 270–1.
10 Bayley, *The Lost Language of Symbolism*, pp. 323 and 238.
11 Frank McConnel, *The Science Fiction of H. G. Wells* (New York: Oxford University Press, 1981), p. 106.
12 H. G. Wells, *The Island of Dr Moreau* (Minneapolis, MN: Filiquarian Publishers, LLC, 2007), p. 6.
13 Robert Kiely, *Robert Louis Stevenson and the Fiction of Adventure* (Cambridge, MA: Harvard University Press, 1965), p. 81.
14 Robert Louis Stevenson, *Treasure Island* (New York: Barnes and Noble Classics, 2005), p. 11.
15 J. M. Barrie, *Peter Pan* (New York: Barnes and Noble Classics, 2005), p. 38.
16 B. S. Oldsey and Stanley Weintraub, 'Golding's deliberately obscure setting', in David Bender et al. (eds), *Readings on* Lord of the Flies (San Diego, CA: Greenhaven Press, 1997), pp. 112–15 (p. 113).
17 Nicholas Ruddick, *Ultimate Island: On the Nature of British Science Fiction* (Westport, CT and London: Greenwood Press, 1993), p. 62. Ruddick discusses various symbolic possibilities of the island, ranging from its function as 'a threatened or an actual incursion into private space, represented by the Island-nation, home territory, or insular self'; as 'the individual psyche of bourgeois Western man' or 'a world within a world, each man an island unto himself, swimming through seas of archipelagos'; and 'a locus of Darwinian struggle' (pp. 109, 157 and 165). His discussion includes metaphorical islands as well as actual ones, and their recurring use in British science fiction. His consideration of the tropical island, however, is of interest to us here.
18 Batya Weinbaum, *Islands of Women and Amazons: Representations and Realities* (Austin, TX: University of Texas Press, 1999), pp. 161 and 168. Pauline Dewan states: 'Because islands are spatially removed from the rest of the world, they can be places of opposition or contrast to their mainland counterparts' and that island inhabitants 'develop modes of living that are diametrically opposed to accustomed ones elsewhere' (*The House as Setting, Symbol, and Structural Motif in*

Children's Literature (Lewiston, Queenston and Lampeter: The Edwin Mellen Press, 2004), p. 165).

19 John Peck notes that as Victorians attempted to absorb the implications of evolutionary concepts, 'it is the sea, the traditional symbol of chaos' that provided a most effective symbol for this burgeoning awareness and its attendant anxieties (*Maritime Fiction: Sailors and the Sea in British and American Novels, 1719–1917* (New York: Palgrave, 2001), p. 144).

20 From Mathew Arnold's 'To Marguerite', l. 24.

21 Nathalie Jaeck, 'Conrad's and Stevenson's logbooks and "paper boats": attempts at textual wreckage', in Linda Dryden et al. (eds), *Robert Louis Stevenson and Joseph Conrad: Writers of Transition* (Lubbock, TX: Texas Tech University Press, 2009), pp. 39–51 (pp. 39 and 40).

22 Peck writes of the sense of control that the British navy of the Victorian period conveyed and which contrasted with both the sense of being overwhelmed by technological advancement on the land as well as the chaotic implications of the sea itself. He notes of the Victorians that 'there was a sense of a more complex world, a world where the individual was increasingly in the service of the machine rather than being in control' (p. 128). He argues that the sea offered a sense of control to Victorians who otherwise felt that technological advancement led to anxiety; on the sea, for instance, one might feel dominion to some extent as operator of a ship. It is when that control is wrested from the individual through shipwreck, by being marooned, or simply by being lost, and he or she is cast away and put into the orphanic condition, that is the focus of this study. Interestingly, Peck locates in the condition of being castaway a sense of freedom from the implications of society. Being stranded on an island permitted a kind of freedom from such servitude; it afforded the potential for liberty from the restrictions and sense of attachment to society. Perhaps in order to emphasize this point, we may note Peck's description of the constricted and oppressive environment of *Heart of Darkness*, which contrasts with the openness of the ocean and the island: 'There is none of the sense of liberation that is conventionally present in a maritime story: the river, with the jungle on both sides, is oppressive; there is no freedom of movement, only obstacles' (p. 174).

23 It is from *Robinson Crusoe* that the term 'Robinsonade' derives to describe the story of a castaway.

24 Weaver-Hightower remarks that, despite differences in focus of island tales from the fifteenth to the nineteenth century, 'the remarkable narrative consistency of the stories suggests psychosocial significance in addition to historical impact' (*Empire Islands: Castaways, Cannibals, and Fantasies of Conquest* (Minneapolis and London: University of Minnesota Press, 2007), p. xiv). Her *Empire Islands* is an excellent treatment of island literature in regard to imperial and jingoistic concerns.

25 Seth Lerer, *Children's Literature: A Reader's History From Aesop to Harry Potter* (Chicago and London: University of Chicago Press, 2008), p. 131.

26 Crusoe essentially enacts a gesture of symbolic patricide in the denial of his father and his virtually orphaning himself with a severance from his family that is fraught with orphanic characteristics.

27 Weaver-Hightower, *Empire Islands*, p. xvii.

28 Michael Seidel, Robinson Crusoe: *Island Myths and the Novel* (Boston: Twayne Publishers, 1991), p. 38.

29 Lerer poses the simple question which must be answered: 'When cast adrift, do you create society and family . . . or not?' (*Children's Literature*, p. 149).

30 Weaver-Hightower, *Empire Islands*, p. xxvii; K. Hebblethwaite, 'Creating wildmen in one's own image: maroons, Darwin and the question of humanity', in Mary Shine Thompson and Celia Keenan (eds), *Treasure Islands: Studies in Children's Literature* (Dublin: Four Courts Press, 2006), pp. 24–32 (p. 24).

31 Both Hebbelthwaite and Weaver-Hightower discuss the "Wildman" character.

32 Ayerton first appears in Verne's *In Search of the Castaway* (1867–8), where he elects being marooned in lieu of being handed over to British authorities for his treasonous activities.

33 Jules Verne, *The Mysterious Island* (New York: Charles Scribner's Sons, 1920), p. 278.

34 Stevenson, *Treasure Island*, p. 102.

35 Ibid.

36 The notion that Ayerton's descent into Wildman status is connected with an inherent criminality is discussed by Weaver-Hightower in *Empire Islands*.

37 A. Fowler, 'Parables of adventure: the debatable novels of Robert Louis Stevenson', in Ian Campbell (ed.), *Nineteenth-Century Scottish Fiction* (Manchester: Carcanet New Press, 1979), pp. 114–15.

38 Stevenson, *Treasure Island*, pp. 236 and 237.
39 J. Wilson, 'Landscape with figures', in Andrew Noble (ed.), *Robert Louis Stevenson* (London and Ottawa, New Jersey: Vision and Barnes and Noble, 1983), pp. 73–95 (pp. 92–3).
40 Wells, *The Island of Dr Moreau*, p. 162.
41 Ruddick, *Ultimate Island*, p. 64.
42 Wells, *The Island of Dr Moreau*, p. 175.
43 Ibid., p. 181.
44 Ibid., pp. 183 and 184.
45 Ibid., p. 183.
46 Ibid., pp. 182 and 181.
47 Ibid.,, p. 182.
48 Ruddick refers to 'the Wellsian project', which serves 'to violate the complacency of the literal and figurative Islander' (*Ultimate Island*, p. 167).
49 See Weaver-Hightower's chapter 'Disciplined islands: white fatherhood, homosocial masculinity, and law', pp. 43–90. Citing *Masterman Ready*, Weaver-Hightower remarks that 'the characters that maintain their self-control . . . survive the wreck, while those who lose their self-control . . . are consumed by the raging waters' (p. 44). She goes on further to discuss the need for the castaway to control the appetites of the body as well as the emotional turmoil that accompanies being cast away.
50 Lerer traces this convention from the works of Captain Marryat to those of H. Rider Haggard.
51 J. Richards, 'Introduction', in Jeffrey Richards (ed.), *Imperialism and Juvenile Literature* (Manchester and New York: Manchester University Press, 1989), pp. 1–11 (pp. 2 and 3).
52 R. G. Kelly, 'Terms for order in some late nineteenth century fiction for children', *Children's Literature*, 1, 58–61 (59).
53 A. Bogen, '"The Island come true" ': *Peter Pan*, Wild Cat Island, and the lure of the real', *Treasure Islands: Studies in Children's Literature*, in Mary Shine Thompson and Celia Keenan (eds) (Dublin: Four Courts Press, 2006), pp. 53–61 (p. 54).
54 Jean-Jacques Rousseau, *Emile, or On Education*, trans. Allan Bloom (New York: Basic Books, 1979), p. 188.
55 Weaver-Hightower, *Empire Islands*, p. xxvi.
56 Mary Louise Pratt, *Imperial Eyes: Travel Writing and Transculturation* (London: Routledge, 2007), p. 197.

57 Johann Wyss, *The Swiss Family Robinson* (New York: Grosset and Dunlap Publishers, 1949), p. 87.
58 Ibid., p. 388.
59 Daniel Defoe, *The Life and Surprising Adventures of Robinson Crusoe, of York, Mariner*, ed. J. Donald Crowley, Oxford English Novels series (London: Oxford University Press, 1972), pp. 101 and 102.
60 Ibid., pp. 53 and 57.
61 Seidel states that, for the civilized man, 'making himself at home is not a luxury but a necessity' (Robinson Crusoe: *Island Myths and the Novel*, p. 59). One is reminded of Hyde's surrounding himself with homely accoutrements to form a kind of façade of domesticity, or of Griffin's desperate attempt in Omnium's to imitate the home. These examples decry the orphan's underlying, if at times disavowed, need for some type of home, provisional, artificial, or otherwise.
62 Robert Michael Ballantyne, *The Coral Island* (New York: Garland, 1977), pp. 47–8.
63 Ibid., pp. 15 and 72.
64 Marah Gubar, *Artful Dodgers: Reconceiving the Golden Age of Children's Literature* (New York and Oxford: Oxford University Press, 2009), p. 70.
65 Stevenson, *Treasure Island*, pp. 20, 27 and 29.
66 Gubar, *Artful Dodgers*, p. 74.
67 H. James, 'Robert Louis Stevenson', in *Century Magazine*, reprinted in J. Smith's *Henry James and Robert Louis Stevenson: A Record of Friendship and Criticism* (London: Rupert Hart-Davis, 1948), quoted in Gubar, *Artful Dodgers*, p. 87.
68 C. McCracken-Flesher, 'Introduction', in *Treasure Island* by Robert Louis Stevenson (New York: Barnes and Noble Classics, 2005), pp. xi–xix (p. xi).
69 In some editions, Cyrus Harding's last name is Smith.
70 Robert Louis Stevenson, *Kidnapped* (New York: Barnes and Noble, 2006), p. 88.
71 Kiely, *Robert Louis Stevenson and the Fiction of Adventure*, p. 84.
72 Stevenson, *Kidnapped*, p. 89.
73 Ibid., p. 91.
74 Ibid.
75 Ibid., pp. 87, 88, 88–9 and 90.
76 Ibid., p. 90.
77 Wells, *The Island of Dr Moreau*, pp. 53, 55, 57, 59 and 62.

78 Ibid., pp. 27, 153 and 45.
79 Ibid., pp. 43, 45 and 113.
80 Ibid., p. 44.
81 Ibid.,, p.75.
82 Ibid., p. 77.
83 Ibid., p.80.
84 Stevenson, *Treasure Island*, p. 42.
85 Stevenson, *Kidnapped*, pp. 8 and 9.
86 Kingston translated into English both Verne's *Mysterious Island* and *Swiss Family Robinson.*
87 See chapter 8, 'Adventures at sea', Peck, *Maritime Fiction.*
88 D. Denisoff, 'Consumerism and Stevenson's misfit masculinities', in Richard Ambrosini and Richard Dury (eds), *Robert Louis Stevenson: Writer of Boundaries* (Madison, WI: University of Wisconsin Press, 2006), pp. 286–98 (p. 289); Edwin M. Eigner, *Robert Louis Stevenson and the Romantic Tradition* (Princeton, NJ: Princeton University Press, 1966), p. 89; Weaver-Hightower, *Empire Islands*, p. xvi.
89 Angus Fletcher refers to him as 'shrewd, and well-equipped psychologically' ('Introduction', *Treasure Island* by Robert Louis Stevenson (New York: Barnes and Noble, 2005), pp. xv–xli (p. xvi). McCracken-Flesher writes that David is '[m]ore knowing than Scott's Waverly, with lower expectations than Pip, skeptical of yet sympathetic to Uncle Ebenezer, less capable than Robinson Crusoe, much less poetic than Alan, and not ready to be an Odysseus' ('Introduction', p. xvi).
90 Conceptions of Moreau as godlike figure can be found in Jack Williamson, *H. G. Wells: Critic of Progress* (Baltimore, MD: The Mirage Press, 1973). Bernard Bergonzi notes that Wells called the novel 'a theological grotesque' (*The Turn of the Century: Essays on Victorian and Modern English Literature* (New York: Barnes and Noble Books, 1973), p. 99. Weaver-Hightower's reading of Moreau as father-type is more focused on notions of irresponsible imperialism. She argues, for instance, that the novel displays the results of irresponsible 'colonial fathers who lose their discipline or abuse their power' as well as the fate of 'children who don't follow the law of the father' (*Empire Islands*, p. 89).
91 Wells, *The Island of Dr Moreau*, p. 106.
92 Ibid., p. 110.
93 Ibid., pp. 135 and 136.
94 Ibid., p. 105.
95 Ibid., p. 103. Ruddick refers to the figure of Prospero as a

precedent of Moreau in that the power derived from his knowledge permits his control over others on the island and states that Wells's novel as the paradigmatic work in that regard.

96 Wells, *The Island of Dr Moreau*, pp. 38 and 68.
97 Ibid., p. 118.
98 Ibid., pp. 21 and 117.
99 Ibid., p. 117.
100 Ibid.
101 Ibid.
102 Compare M'ling's appeal to justice with the reaction of the Wolf-man, for instance, who, with 'the exultation of hunting', pursues the Leopard-man for the thrill of the hunt.
103 Wells, *The Island of Dr Moreau*, pp. 143 and 145.
104 Wilkie Collins, *The Moonstone* (New York: The Modern Library, 2001), p. 26.
105 Wells, *The Island of Dr Moreau*, p. 17.
106 Ibid.
107 Ibid., p. 22.
108 Ibid., pp. 38, 39, 45, 40, 46, 86, 128 and 152.
109 This aspect of David's experience allies *Kidnapped* more with traditional depictions of orphans, with David's condition remedied to some extent with the reclamation of his rightful fortune. The majority of late-century island narratives, though, do not permit the orphan this kind of reconciliation and fulfillment.
110 Peck, *Maritime Fiction*, p. 117.
111 Stevenson, *Treasure Island*, p. 48.
112 I pursue this tendency of Stevenson's further in my unpublished paper '"A promise of intellect and refinement": Robert Louis Stevenson's silencing of the Victorian professional', which was presented at the Locating Stevenson Conference at the University of Stirling, July 2010.
113 Louisa Villa remarks that Stevenson 'does seem to go out of his way to underscore the moral unreliability of the older generation as compared to the sane moral fiber of their sons' ('Quarreling with the father', in Richard Ambrosini and Richard Dury (eds), *Robert Louis Stevenson: Writer of Boundaries* (Madison, WI: University of Wisconsin Press, 2006), pp. 109–20 (p. 115).
114 Stevenson, *Treasure Island*, p. 48.
115 See Saposnik's commentary concerning these characters, *Robert Louis Stevenson*, pp. 107–8.

116 R. Hampson, 'Maps, class, and sexuality', in Linda Dryden et al. (eds), *Robert Louis Stevenson and Joseph Conrad: Writers of Transition* (Lubbock, TX: Texas Tech University Press, 2009), pp. 140–55 (p. 147); Saposnik, *Robert Louis Stevenson*, p. 108.
117 Stevenson, *Treasure Island*, p. 118.
118 Peck states that Stevenson 'displays a fondness for presenting disfigured or maimed bodies' (*Maritime Fiction*, p. 155).
119 Stevenson, *Treasure Island*, p. 28.
120 For what it's worth, Davy states that Alan is 'unwearedly kind' to him.
121 Stevenson, *Treasure Island*, p. 62.
122 Peck, *Maritime Fiction*, p. 130.
123 Stevenson, *Treasure Island*, pp. 59 and 189.
124 Eigner notes interesting structural similarities between *Kidnapped* and Twain's *Huckleberry Finn*, noting that they both involve a newly rich orphan threatened by a greedy male figure, being kidnapped by a relative who attempts to murder the orphan, an escape and circumstances that lead to the orphan's being assumed dead, isolation on a near-shore island and a journey in an older man's company.
125 Stevenson, *Treasure Island*, pp. 31 and 37.
126 Stevenson, *Kidnapped*, p. 12.
127 Although this study limits itself to *Treasure Island* and *Kidnapped*, it is noteworthy to mention that in Stevenson's *The Black Arrow* (1888), Richard Shelton is estranged from his former guardian, Sir Daniel Brackley, who has murdered Richard's father; Richard comes to rely on Ellis Duckworth, a Robin-Hood type somewhat akin to Alan Breck.

5: Orphans of Empire

1 Jeffrey Richards, *Visions of Yesterday* (London: Routledge and Kegan Paul, 1973), p. 11. Allen J. Greenberger, *The British Image of India: A Study in the Literature of Imperialism, 1880–1960* (Oxford: Oxford University Press, 1969), p. 13.
2 Henry Seton Merriman (Hugh Stowell Scott), *Flotsam: The Story of a Life* (New York: Longmans, Green, and Co., 1986), p. 7. J. Richards, 'With Henty to Africa', in Jeffrey Richards (ed.), *Imperialism and Juvenile Literature* (Manchester and New York: Manchester University Press, 1989), pp. 72–106 (p. 100). Richards refers to L. P. Curtis, *Anglo Saxons and Celts* (Bridgeport: The Conference on British Studies, 1968).

3 John Pocock, *Rider Haggard and the Lost Empire* (London: Weidenfeld and Nicolson, 1993), pp. 6 and 10.

4 Piers Brenden, *Imminent Edwardians: Four Figures Who Defined Their Age: Northcliffe, Balfour, Parkhurst, Baden-Powell* (Missoula, MT: Pimlico, 2003), p. 215.

5 Lawrence James, *The Rise and Fall of the British Empire* (New York: St Martin's Griffin, 1994), p. 289.

6 Said's *Orientalism* (1978) and Spivak's 'Three Women's Texts and a Critique of Imperialism' (*Critical Theory* (1985)) are often credited with initiating the reading of nineteenth-century fiction as perpetuating imperial ideologies. Brantlinger's *Rule of Darkness* (1988) and Perera's *Reaches of Empire: The English Novel from Edgeworth to Dickens* (1991) also see the period's literature as intrinsically reaffirming those ideologies.

7 Daniel Brown, *Desire and Contradiction: Imperial Visions and Domestic Debates in Victorian Literature* (Manchester, UK: Manchester University Press, 1990), p. viii.

8 Martin Green, *Deeds of Adventure, Deeds of Empire* (London: Routledge and Kegan Paul, 1980), p. xi. Brantlinger pursues other genres as well: 'Adventure and domesticity, romance and realism, are the seemingly opposite poles of a single system of discourse, the literary equivalents of imperial domination abroad and liberal reform at home'. See *Rule of Darkness: British Literature and Imperialism, 1830–1914* (Ithaca: Cornell UP, 1988), p. 12.

9 Wendy Roberta Katz, *Rider Haggard and the Fiction of Empire: A Critical Study of British Imperial Fiction* (Cambridge: Cambridge University Press, 1987), p. 153; Piers Brenden, *The Decline and Fall of the British Empire, 1781–1997* (New York: Aflred A. Knoff, 2008), p. 154.

10 Brenden, *The Decline and Fall of the British Empire*, p. 154.

11 A. J. Greenburger, *The British Image of India*, p. 3. Greenburger refers to p. 46 of L. W. Growing, *An Autobiography of the Years 1904–1911* (London: 1961). Brenden notes that Kipling himself stated that swaggering was a duty incumbent on the Briton. See *The Decline and Fall of the British Empire*, p. 149.

12 See 'Knowing the Oriental' in Edward Said, *Orientalism* (New York: Vintage Books, 1979), pp. 31–49.

13 G. A. Henty, *At the Point of the Bayonet: A Tale of the Mahratta War* (New York: Charles Scribner's Sons, 1901), p. 4.

14 Rudyard Kipling, *The Jungle Books* (New York: Barnes and

Noble Classics, 2004), p. 229. This edition publishes both *The Jungle Book* and *The Second Jungle Book* together.

15 L. Makman, 'Introduction', in Rudyard Kipling, *The Jungle Books* (New York: Barnes and Noble Classics, 2004), pp. xv–xli (p. xxvi).

16 John McLeod, *Beginning Post-colonialism* (Manchester, UK: Manchester University Press, 2000), pp. 39-50.

17 Richards, 'With Henty to Africa', p. 89.

18 James, *The Rise and Fall of the British Empire*, p. 292. James refers to A. F. Mockler-Ferryman, *Up the Niger: Narrative of Major Claude Macdonald's Mission to the Niger and Benue Rivers* (London: G. Philip and Son, 1892), pp. 3–4.

19 See Diana Fuss, *Essentially Speaking* (New York: Routledge, 1989), for discussion of the Empire's tendency to cast native peoples into one stereotypical category to ease the process of colonization.

20 M. Daphne Kutzer, *Empire's Children: Empire and Imperialism in Classic British Children's Books* (New York and London: Garland Publishing Inc., 2000), p. 16; Zohreh T. Sullivan, *Narratives of Empire: The Fictions of Rudyard Kipling* (Cambridge: Cambridge University Press, 1993), p. 2.

21 Said, *Orientalism*, p. 42; McLeod, *Beginning Post-colonialism*, pp. 39–50.

22 H. Rider Haggard, *King Solomon's Mines* (New York: Barnes and Noble Classics, 2004), p. 106.

23 H. Rider Haggard, *She* (Oxford and New York: World's Classics, 1991), pp. 17–18.

24 Most affairs in these narratives are usually between a white male and a native female, such as Good's relationship with Foulata or Leo's with Ustane, but these unions are inevitably doomed, typically ending with the female's death, and that usually in a sacrificial manner.

25 Nicholas Daly, *Modernism, Romance, and the* Fin-de-siècle: *Popular Fiction and British Culture, 1880–1914* (Cambridge: Cambridge University Press, 1999), p. 57.

26 Interestingly, while this kind of heroic, paternal figure was a consistent convention of literature of the New Imperialism, island narratives of the same period, which are discussed in chapter 4, demonstrate apprehension and doubt about the feasibility of this figure.

27 Laura Chrisman, *Rereading the Imperial Romance: British Imperialism and South African Resistance in Haggard,*

Schreiner and Plaatje (Oxford: Clarendon Press, 2000), pp. 46 and 48.

28 Kipling, *The Jungle Books*, p. 105.

29 Bhabha discusses hybridity as 'a mixture of two social languages within the limits of a single utterance, an encounter, within the arena of an utterance, between two different linguistic consciousnesses, separated by an epoch, by social differentiation, or by some other factor'. See Homi K. Bhabha, *The Location of Culture* (London: Routledge, 1995), p. 85.

30 One of Bhabha's assertions is that truth and authenticity should be replaced by ambiguity in order to avoid this kind of polemic.

31 Kipling, *The Jungle Books*, p. 107.

32 Ibid., p. 113.

33 Ibid., p. 116.

34 Ibid., p. 112.

35 Greenberger, *The British Image of India*, p. 5.

36 Robert Dixon, *Writing the Colonial Adventure: Gender, Race and Nation in Anglo-Australian Popular Fiction, 1875–1914* (Cambridge, UK: Cambridge University Press, 1995), pp. 1 and 3.

37 Stephen Arata, *Fictions of Loss in the Victorian fin-de-siècle.* (Cambridge: Cambridge University Press, 1996), p. 151. Ian Baucom, *Out of Place: Englishness, Empire, and the Locations of Identity* (Princeton, NJ: Princeton University Press, 1999), p. 38.

38 Norman Mackenzie and Jeanne Mackenzie, *H.G. Wells* (New York: Simon and Schuster, 1973), p. 253.

39 Brantlinger, *Rule of Darkness*, pp. 20–3; Dixon, *Writing the Colonial Adventure*, p. 2.

40 Brantlinger, *Rule of Darkness*, p. 43.

41 James, *The Rise and Fall of the British Empire*, p. 206.

42 Greenberger, *The British Image of India*, p. 11.

43 Henty, *At the Point of the Bayonet*, pp. 31 and 32.

44 Haggard, *King Solomon's Mines*, p. 16.

45 Ibid., p. 36.

46 Ibid., p. 103.

47 Ibid., pp. 36 and 103.

48 Ibid., p. 141.

49 Ibid., p. 141.

50 Ibid., p. 140.

51 Haggard, H. Rider, *She* (Oxford and New York: World's Classics, 1991), p. 8.

52 Ibid., pp. 8 and 46.
53 Ibid., p. 8.
54 Ibid., p. 8
55 Ibid., p. 140.
56 Ibid., p, 20.
57 Ibid., pp. 211 and 212.
58 Ibid., p. 65.
59 Ibid., p. 101.
60 Ibid., p. 21.
61 Ibid., pp. 75 and 115. Leo's confidence can be attributed to his British lineage; however, it should be pointed out that, despite his academic capabilities, he is something of a dolt.
62 Ibid., p. 101.
63 Leo's evident reincarnation from Kalikrates would seem to position him as well as racially superior to the natives in Ayesha's entourage and therefore endow him with an ancestral superiority comparable to his Englishness.
64 Suvendrini Perena, *Reaches of Empire: The English Novel from Edgeworth to Dickens* (New York and Oxford: Columbia University Press, 1991), p. 12.
65 P. Brantlinger, 'Race and the Victorian Novel', in Deirdre David (ed.), *The Cambridge Companion to The Victorian Novel* (Cambridge: Cambridge University Press, 2001), pp. 149–68 (p. 160).
66 K. Bhaskava Rao, *Rudyard Kipling's India* (Norman, OK: Oklahoma University Press, 1967), p. 25.
67 Sullivan, *Narratives of Empire*, p. 148.
68 Philip Mallet, *Rudyard Kipling: A Literary Life* (New York: Palgrave Macmillan, 2003), p. 118. Mallet also states, 'Even the external threat posed by the Russians, although it has to be resisted, is never felt to be serious' (p. 18).
69 Joseph Bristow, *Empire Boys: Adventures in a Man's World* (London: HarperCollins Academic, 1991), pp. 198 and 203; Kutzer, *Empire's Children*, p. 15.
70 Sullivan, *Narratives of Empire*, p. 28.
71 Rudyard Kipling, *Kim* (New York: Barnes and Noble Classics, 2003), p. 3.
72 Bristow, *Empire Boys*, p. 198.
73 Ibid., p. 209.
74 John McBratney, *Imperial Subject, Imperial Space: Rudyard Kipling's Fiction of the Native-Born* (Columbus, OH: The Ohio State University Press, 2002), p. 107.
75 Bhabha states that mimicry is 'one of the most elusive and

effective strategies of colonial power and knowledge'. See *The Location of Culture*, p. 85.

76 Kipling, *Kim*, p. 116.

77 McBratney, *Imperial Subject, Imperial Space*, p. 127.

78 Sullivan, *Narratives of Empire*, p. 148.

79 Kipling, *Kim*, p. 123.

80 McBratney, *Imperial Subject, Imperial Space*, pp. 122 and 123.

81 Ibid., p. 126.

82 Kipling, *The Jungle Books*, p. 280. Rudyard Kipling, *Many Inventions* (New York: D. Appleton and Company, 1899), p. 232. Kipling's 'In the Rukh' is the one Mowgli story that does not appear in *The Jungle Books*. Though published in *Many Inventions* (1893), prior to the composition of *The Jungle Books*, it is chronologically the last Mowgli story.

83 Ibid., p. 218.

84 Philip Mason, *Kipling: The Glass, the Shadow and the Fire* (New York: Harper and Row, 1915), p. 168.

85 Kipling, *The Jungle Books*, p. 183.

86 Ibid., p. 17.

87 Ibid., pp. 218, 347, 347 and 362; Kipling, *Many Inventions*, p. 259; Kipling, *The Jungle Books*, p. 218.

88 Kipling, *The Jungle Books*, p. 361.

89 Ibid., p. 78.

90 Ibid., pp. 74 and 77.

91 Ibid., p. 16.

92 Ibid., pp. 36 and 46.

93 Ibid., p. 61.

94 Ibid., pp. 278 and 60.

95 Ibid., p. 64.

96 Ibid., p. 275.

97 Mason refers to Mowgli as imagining 'the heroic white man among a thousand natives, who recognize his hateful superiority because he is immune from their magic'. See *Kipling: The Glass, the Shadow and the Fire*, p.168.

98 Makman, 'Introduction', p. xxix.

99 Kipling, *The Jungle Books*, p. 24.

100 Eliot L. Gilbert, *The Good Kipling: Studies in the Short Story* (Oberlin, OH: Ohio University Press, 1970), p. 72.

101 Kipling, *Many Inventions*, p. 223.

102 Ibid., pp. 236 and 253.

103 Ibid., pp. 236 and 239.

104 Ibid., p. 232.

105 Ibid., p. 230.
106 Ibid., p. 278.
107 Merriman, *Flotsam: The Story of a Life*, pp. 17 and 33.
108 Ibid., p. 40.
109 Ibid., p. 24.
110 Ibid., p. 105.
111 Ibid., p. 127.
112 Homer T. Cox, *Henry Seton Merriman* (New York: Twayne Publishers, 1967), p. 75. Cox refers to Edward Oliver, 'A Sense of Duty', in *Talking of Books*, *London Times* (Oct 3, 1957).
113 Merriman, *Flotsam: The Story of a Life*, pp. 63 and 64.
114 Ibid., pp. 77, 260 and 335.
115 Ibid., p. 5.
116 It should be noted that Harry's abuse of authority should not be mistaken for criticism of the imperial mission. Merriman, like Haggard and other contemporary adventure writers, advocated the work of the Empire and 'the masterfulness of the dominant race' (p. 19). Merriman's focus seems instead to be a psychological study of a self-destructive orphan.
117 Merriman, *Flotsam: The Story of a Life*, p. 6.
118 Ibid., pp. 16 and 19.
119 Ibid., p. 104 and 198.
120 Ibid., p. 178.
121 Ibid., p. 100.

6: Orphans in Haunted Arcadia

1 I refer throughout this chapter to J. M. Barrie, *Peter Pan* (New York: Barnes and Noble Classics, 2005). Barrie's *The Little White Bird* (1902) is an earlier version of Peter's story, including his time as a baby. The play *Peter Pan* premiered on 27 December 1904. In 1906, Barrie published six chapters of *The Little While Bird* as *Peter Pan in Kensington Gardens*. In 1911 he modified the story into a longer novel, *Peter and Wendy,* which is known now as *Peter Pan.*
2 Jacqueline Rose, *The Case of Peter Pan or the Impossibility of Children's Fiction* (Philadelphia: University of Pennsylvania Press, 1993), pp. 4 and 1.
3 Lerer writes of the years between the death of Queen Victoria in 1901 and the events in Sarajevo as 'the great tea party'. See *Children's Literature: A Reader's History From Aesop to Harry Potter* (Chicago and London: University of Chicago Press, 2008), p. 253. Nicolson writes of Edwardian young

men 'about to be slaughtered' who 'feasted, unconscious of all but the moment'. See *The Perfect Summer: England 1911, Just Before the Storm* (New York: Grove Press, 2006), p. 1. She furthermore remarks that there were 'unmistakable signs of perfection overreaching itself' and notes 'a sense of urgency' about the summer of 1911, 'as if time was running out' (p. 2).

4 Francis Hodgson Burnett, *A Little Princess* (New York: Barnes and Noble Classics, 1995), p. 100.

5 Mary Louisa Molesworth, *The Palace in the Garden* (London: Hatchard, Piccadilly, 1887), p. 90.

6 R. Helson, 'The Psychological Origins of Fantasy for Children in Mid-Victorian England', *Children's Literature*, 3. (Philadelphia: Temple University Press, 1974), pp. 66–76, p. 68; D. Roberts, 'The Paterfamilias of the Victorian Governing Classes', in Anthony S. Wohl (ed.), *The Victorian Family* (London: Croon Helm, 1978), pp. 59–80 (pp. 62–5).

7 J. Manheimer, 'Murderous Mothers: The Problem of Parenting in the Victorian Novel', *Feminist Studies*, 5/3 (Autumn, 1979), 530–46 (532).

8 M. S. E. Bonifer, 'Like A Motherless Child: The Orphan Figure in the Novels of Nineteenth-Century American Women Writers, 1850–1899' (unpublished PhD thesis, Indiana University of Pennsylvania, 1995), 10.

9 Barbara Thaden, *The Maternal Voice in Victorian Fiction: Rewriting the Patriarchal Family* (New York: Garland, 1997), p. 45.

10 Hirsch even claims that dead or absent mothers provide 'the only positive maternal figures' of Victorian novels. See *The Mother/Daughter Plot: Narrative, Psychoanalysis, Feminism* (Bloomington: Indiana University Press, 1989), p. 47.

11 Thaden, *The Maternal Voice in Victorian Fiction*, p. 18.

12 There are exceptions to any critical generalization. Thaden notes, for instance, that Bella Wilfer of *Our Mutual Friend* and Amelia Sedley and Lady Jane of *Vanity Fair* seem content.

13 R. B. Anolik, 'The Missing Mother: The Meanings of Maternal Absence in the Gothic Mode', *Modern Language Studies*, 33/1/2 (Spring-Autumn, 2003), 25–43 (p. 27); M. S. E. Bonifer, 'Like a Motherless Child', p. 170 n. 4; Phyllis A. Roth, *Bram Stoker* (Boston: Twayne Publishers, 1982), p. 39.

14 Anolik, 'The Missing Mother', p. 30.

15 Thaden sees detachment from the mother as actual freedom from 'the bonds of domesticity and convention'. See *The Maternal Voice in Victorian Fiction*, p. 21; Reed refers to the

'bondage of parental direction'. See *Victorian Conventions* (Ohio: Ohio University Press, 1975), p. 252.

16 Manheimer, 'Murderous Mothers', pp. 520 and 530; Thaden, *The Maternal Voice in Victorian Fiction*, p. 35.

17 Manheimer suggests that the Terrible Mother figure is a referendum against a society she sees as imposing the miseries of motherhood, a society she claims is incapable of justifying its perpetuation. Motherhood 'drains the self of all possibilities of self-interest, sexuality, and activity outside the home'. Manheimer looks dimly upon the negation of the self-intrinsic to the nurturing of another. While Dickens extols the concept of the Good Mother, Manheimer states that this ideal is 'an exercise in self-mutilation'. She notes, for example, that for all her cheery motherhood, Esther is incapable of rescuing the truant Richard or the sickened Jo or her own mother, Lady Dedlock, 'from the ravages of an inhumane social system'. Manheimer focuses on Esther's selfhood, and states that her sacrifice is a casualty of her 'lack of self-interest', which she reads as speaking to the general suppression of women. Ultimately, she aligns the abandonment of motherly duties with the strength of resisting the sacrificial aspect of motherhood. Her idea is that Mrs Jellyby's rigidity and negligence is a laudable avoidance of the kind of self-effacement Esther employs, 'a corrective to the disfigurement which the Victorian ideal of motherhood required'. Furthermore, Manheimer sees Hetty, of *Adam Bede*, is a 'serious threat' to the order of the traditional world, challenges, among other things, 'the stability of the community' and the 'sanctity of the family'. See 'Murderous Mothers', pp. 545, 539, 538, 540, and 543).

18 H. Murray, 'Francis Hodgson Burnett's *The Secret Garden*: The Organ(ic)ized World', *Touchstones: Reflections of the Best in Children's Literature*,1(1985) 30–43 (p. 34).

19 In her discussion of Wendy, Wullschlager includes her in 'a group of idealized . . . mothers who appear in English fiction for the next two decades'. See *Inventing Wonderland: The Lives and Fantasies of Lewis Carroll, Edward Lear, J. M. Barrie, Kenneth Grahame, and A. A. Milne* (New York: The Free Press, 1995), p. 130. Barrie and Burnett are certainly emblematic of this trend.

20 J. M. Barrie, *Peter Pan* (New York: Barnes and Noble Classics, 2005), pp. 10 and 11.

21 Ibid., p. 11.

22 Ibid., p. 17.

23 Ibid., p. 140.
24 Ibid., p. 144.
25 Frances Hodgson Burnett, *The Secret Garden* (New York: Barnes and Noble Classics, 2005), pp. 193, 195 and 211.
26 Ibid., p. 27.
27 Ibid., pp. 60 and 144.
28 Ibid., p. 213.
29 Ibid., p. 191.
30 Ibid., p. 76.
31 Helson makes note of the convention in nineteenth-century fantasy of magical women paired with a child 'who represents the nurturant unconscious'. See 'The Psychological Origins of Fantasy for Children in Mid-Victorian England', p. 72, of which Lilias and Dickon are examples.
32 Burnett, *The Secret Garden,* p. 195.
33 Ibid., p. 168.
34 Ibid., p. 168.
35 Ibid., p. 108.
36 Ibid., p. 205.
37 Ibid., p. 210.
38 Ibid., p. 205.
39 Wullschlager calls Mr Darling 'the more powerful symbol of father figure that a child wants to vanquish'. See *Inventing Wonderland*, p. 112.
40 Barrie, *Peter Pan*, p. 8.
41 Ibid., pp. 10 and 22.
42 Ibid., p. 149.
43 Ibid., p. 142.
44 Burnett, *The Secret Garden*, p. 18.
45 Ibid., p. 215.
46 Ibid., p. 135.
47 Ibid., p. 218.
48 Ibid., p. 189. Phyllis Bixler points out that Colin 'unconsciously lives out a perverse combination of his father's fears and wishes'. See *The Secret Garden: Nature's Magic* (New York: Twayne Publishers, 1996), p. 45.
49 Thaden, *The Maternal Voice in Victorian Fiction*, p. 13.
50 Ibid., p. 9. Thaden cites John Bowlby's *Maternal Care and Mental Health* (New York: Schocken Books, 1966).
51 B. D'Amato, 'Mary Shelley's *Frankenstein*: an orphaned author's dream and journey toward integration', *Modern Psychoanalysis*, 34/1 (2009), 117–35 (p. 118).
52 U. C. Knoepflmacher, *Ventures into Childland: Victorians,*

Fairy Tales, and Femininity (Chicago and London: Chicago University Press, 1988), p. 187.

53 Patrick Baybrooke, *J. M. Barrie: A Study in Fairies and Mortals* (New York: Haskell House Publishers, Ltd., 1971), p. 120.

54 Tellingly, as though to emphasize Peter's reliance on female figures, we are told that the lore of the island Peter has taught the lost boys he learned from Tinkerbell and Tiger Lily.

55 Barrie, *Peter Pan*, p. 144.

56 Humphrey Carpenter, *Secret Gardens: A Study of the Golden Age of Children's Literature* (Boston: Houghton Mifflin Company, 1985), p. 186.

57 Barrie, *Peter Pan*, p. 31.

58 Ibid., p. 115.

59 Wullschlager, *Inventing Wonderland*, p. 109. She also states that a marked shift occurred around 1880 'from an emphasis on the child as moral icon, emblem of purity, to a craze for the child as funloving playboy hero' (p. 109).

60 Walter Pater, *Studies in the History of the Renaissance* (London: Macmillan and Co., 1873), p. 210.

61 Alison Lurie, *Don't Tell the Grownups: Subversive Children's Literature* (Boston, Toronto, and London: Little, Brown and Company, 1990), p. 124.

62 Barrie, *Peter Pan*, p. 135.

63 Ibid., p. 68.

64 Tim Morris, *You're Only Young Twice: Children's Literature and Film* (Urbana and Chicago: University of Illinois Press, 2000), p. 118.

65 See Barrie, *Peter Pan*, p.162 n. 8 for Billone's commentary.

66 Barrie, *Peter Pan*, p. 25.

67 Ibid., p. 25.

68 Ibid., p. 135.

69 Carpenter observes what he calls Peter's knowledge 'that he is not a 'real' person'. See *Secret Gardens*, p. 179).

70 Barrie, *Peter Pan*, p. 95.

71 Ibid.

72 Ibid., p. 91.

73 Ibid., p. 94.

74 Ibid., p. 140.

75 Ibid., p. 94.

76 Ibid., pp. 119, 127 and 133.

77 There seems a substantial similarity between the instability of Peter's fractious, orphanic demeanor and the overall fragility and tenuous nature of fairies, beings formed from the

shattered first laugh of the first baby and liable to dying from the very utterance of unbelief from a child.

78 Barrie, *Peter Pan*, p. 25.
79 Ibid., p. 64.
80 Ibid., p. 71.
81 Ibid., p. 73.
82 Ibid., p. 127.
83 Ibid., pp. 151, 79 and 85.
84 Ibid., p. 147.
85 There is in the novel an interesting correlation between orphanhood and the changing of names. Once deprived of the context of family, Michael claims to have thought of naming himself 'Redhanded Jack', while John contemplates becoming 'Blackbeard Joe'. Immediately after the death of Hook, the lost boys assume pirate identities. Tootles, for example, becomes the bo'sun, thrashing the others with a rope's end and chewing tobacco, while 'Captain Pan' refers to the boys as 'the scum of Rio and the Gold Coast' (Barrie, *Peter Pan*, p. 139).
86 Barrie, *Peter Pan*, pp. 52, 114 and 52.
87 Ibid., pp. 55, 82 and 109.
88 Ibid., pp. 55 and 56.
89 Ibid., pp. 52 and 126.
90 Ibid., p. 134.
91 Ibid., p. 82.
92 Ibid., p. 133.
93 Ibid., p. 83.
94 Ibid., p. 123.
95 Ibid., p. 131.
96 Ibid., p. 132.
97 Ibid., pp. 82, 137 and 115.
98 Ibid., p. 120.
99 Ibid., p. 81.
100 Ibid., p. 115.
101 Lerer, *Children's Literature*, p. 260.
102 Barrie, *Peter Pan*, p. 121.
103 Ibid., pp. 52 and 121.
104 Ibid., p. 111.
105 Ibid., p. 121.
106 Ibid., pp. 109 and 121.
107 Ibid., p. 52.
108 Ibid., p. 137.
109 Ibid., p. 52.
110 Burnett, *A Little Princess*, p. 150.

111 Ibid., p. 173.
112 Ibid., p. 40.
113 Ibid., pp. 116 and 117.
114 Ibid., pp. 85 and 97.
115 Ibid., pp. 95 and 82.
116 Ibid., pp. 87 and 219.
117 Ibid., p. 88.
118 Burnett, *The Secret Garden*, pp. 78, 80 and 146.
119 Ibid., p. 80.
120 Ibid., pp. 87, 80 and 124.
121 Ibid., pp. 87 and 81.
122 Ibid., pp. 150 and 200.
123 Ibid., pp. 155, 78 and 97.
124 Ibid., p. 143.
125 Ibid., pp. 159–60.
126 Ibid., p. 162.
127 Nicolson writes of the Edwardians as '[g]orgeous, decorative and dumb' living a life of 'tedium' (see inset between pp. 82 and 83) and states that they were 'growing restless and complacent'. See *The Perfect Summer: England 1911, Just Before the Storm* (New York: Grove Press, 2006), p. 2.
128 Burnett, *The Secret Garden*, pp. 7, 15 and 17.
129 Ibid., p. 14.
130 Ibid., p. 125.
131 Ibid., p. 123.
132 Ibid., pp. 80 and 89.
133 Ibid., p. 157.
134 Ibid., p. 150.
135 Ibid., p. 130.
136 Ibid., pp. 104, 138 and 131.
137 Ibid., p. 104.
138 Ibid., pp. 103, 179 and 104.
139 Ibid., p. 179.
140 See L. Vallone, 'Ideas of Difference in Children's Literature', in M. O. Greaby and Andrea Immel (eds), *The Cambridge Companion to Children's Literature* (Cambridge: Cambridge University Press, 2009), pp. 174–89. Vallone discusses such characters as Clara Sesemann of Johanna Spyri's 1881 novel *Heidi*.
141 Burnett, *The Secret Garden*, p. 152.
142 Ibid., p. 152.
143 Ibid., p. 154.
144 Ibid., p. 166.

145 Ibid., p. 185.
146 Ibid., p. 168.
147 Ibid., pp. 191 and 168.
148 Ibid., pp. 175 and 172.
149 Ibid., p. 187.
150 Ibid., p. 202.
151 Ibid., p. 225.
152 Ibid., p. 184.
153 Ibid., p. 226.
154 Burnett, *A Little Princess*, p. 114.
155 Barrie, *Peter Pan*, p. 150.
156 Ibid., pp. 152 and 117.
157 Ibid., p. 42.
158 Ibid., p. 26.
159 Ibid., pp. 71 and 70.
160 Ibid., pp. 77 and 90.
161 Ibid., pp. 72 and 99.
162 Ibid., p. 71.
163 Ibid., p. 149.
164 Burnett, *A Little Princess*, p. 37.
165 Ibid., p. 38.
166 Ibid., pp. 100 and 38.
167 M. S. Gohlke, 'Re-Reading *The Secret Garden*', *College English*, 41/8 (April 1980), pp. 984–2 (p. 895).
168 Burnett, *The Secret Garden*, pp. 154, 120, 109 and 147.
169 Ibid., p. 211.
170 Gunther states that Mary attains a 'transcendence of ego' that Colin cannot achieve, and notes the crucial role her 'wisdom and effort' and 'passionate and selfless effort' play in Colin's development. See '*The Secret Garden* Revisited', *Children's Literature in Education*, 25/3 (1994), 159–68 (pp. 165 and 166).
171 Dewan lists various threats to domestic spaces, ranging from wild animals or birds, various forces of nature, threatening individuals, ghosts or goblins, physical or mental illness, and bombs. See *The House as Setting, Symbol, and Structural Motif in Children's Literature*, p. 91.
172 In his discussion of space in children's fiction, Watson states that writing about children 'brings into play an irresistible imperative to define "magical" space'. See 'The Possibilities of Children's Fiction', in Morag Styles, Eve Bearne, and Victor Watson (eds), *After Alice: Exploring Children's Literature* (London and New York: Cassell, 1992), pp. 11–24 (p.11).

Smedman discusses Burnett's portrayal of the garden as permitting the children to experience time and space in a special way. See 'Springs of Hope: Recovery of Primordial Time in "Mythic" Novels for Young Readers', *Children's Literature*, 16 (1988), 91–107.

173 Dewan refers to 'the traditional elements such as security, love and protection that characterize the ideal family home'. See *The House as Setting, Symbol, and Structural Motif in Children's Literature*, p. 191.

174 J. Muller, 'Introduction' to Francis Hodgson Burnett, *The Secret Garden* (New York: Barnes and Noble Classics, 2005), pp. xv–xxxi (p. xxi); Bixler, *The Secret Garden: Nature's Magic*, p. 5.

175 Burnett, *The Secret Garden*, p. 66.

176 Barrie, *Peter Pan*, p. 19.

177 Ibid., pp. 8 and 19.

178 Ibid., p. 63.

179 We find a similar imitation of a domestic space in *Peter Pan in Kensington Gardens*, though to a different effect. When the young girl Maimie Mannering remains in the garden after its closing to see Peter, and the fairies there find her sleeping in the snow, they resolve to construct a house around her. The house eventually disappears, at which point a naked Peter appears to comfort Maimie. Geduld reads this as an emblem of 'an immaculate childbirth: the house (womb) shrivels as the naked newborn infant arrives'. See *James Barrie* (New York: Twayne Publishers Inc., 1971), p. 61.

180 Barrie, *Peter Pan,* p. 93.

181 Ibid., p. 90.

182 Ibid., p. 138.

183 Baybrooke, *J. M. Barrie*, p. 120.

184 A. Billone, 'Introduction' to J. M. Barrie, *Peter Pan* (New York: Barnes and Noble Classics, 2005), pp. xv–xxviii (p. xxi).

185 Roger Lancelyn Green, *J. M. Barrie* (New York: Henry Z. Walck Incorporated, 1961), p. 39.

186 Billone, 'Introduction', p. xxvii.

187 Burnett, *A Little Princess*, p. 86.

188 Ibid., *A Little Princess*, p. 105.

189 Ibid., pp. 114–15.

190 Ibid., pp. 112, 56 and 111.

191 Ibid., p. 119.

192 Ibid., pp. 24 and 25.

193 Ibid., p. 37.

194 Ibid., p. 105.
195 Ibid., pp. 92 and 98.
196 Ibid., p. 99.
197 Ibid., p. 105.
198 Ibid., pp. 181, 182 and 183.
199 Burnett, *The Secret Garden*, p. 22.
200 Ibid., p. 16.
201 Ibid., pp. 22, 46 and 99. Misselthwaite qualifies as what Anolik calls 'the conventional Gothic space', one that is 'darkly empty and mysterious', and which Anolik reads as representative of an oppressive maternal body out of which the daughter endeavors to extract herself. Gunther interprets the house in the same way.
202 Ibid., p. 113.
203 Ibid., p. 226.
204 Ibid., p. 49.
205 Ibid., pp. 106 and 129.
206 Ibid., p. 196.
207 Ibid., p. 83.
208 The kindergarten movement, which was based on the writings of Friedrich Froebel, proposed the benefits of outdoor activity, clean air and exposure to sunshine, 'in an environment in which nature is celebrated but controlled' (Muller, 'Introduction', p. xxv). Burnett gave to charities supporting his educational methods. Froebel shared with Rousseau the nostalgic notion of an idealized country folk and a romanticized concept of the rural poor. In *Emile,* Rousseau stated that a child should be given a garden to cultivate and described children as young plants to be carefully tended.
209 In her discussion of the employment of gardens as loci of regeneration in children's literature, Gwyneth Evans notes that 'girls who seek out or create the gardens do so out of a profound loneliness and sense of alienation, stemming largely from the loss of a relationship with their mothers'. See 'The Girl in the Garden: Variations on a Feminine Pastoral', *Children's Literature Association Quarterly*, 19 (1994), 20–4 (20–1). Linda T. Parsons sees the seclusion of the garden as 'analogous to the power of the mother'. See '"Otherways" into the Garden: Re-Visioning the Feminine in *The Secret Garden*', *Children's Literature in Education*, 33 (2002), 247–66 (p. 258–9). Anne Silver refers to the garden as 'part of women's private domestic space' that was 'conceptualized as female spaces in nineteenth century England'. See 'Domesticating Brontë's Moors:

Motherhood in *The Secret Garden*', *The Lion and the Unicorn*, 21/2 (1997), 193–203 (p. 2).

210 This arrangement is no doubt temporary; both Muller and Bixler notes Colin's eventual rise to status of head of Misselthwaite and probably Dickon's future employer. For the duration of the novel, at least, the garden provides a classless area.

211 Burnett, *The Secret Garden*, p. 115.

Bibliography

Allen, Brooke, 'Introduction' to Bram Stoker, *Dracula* (New York: Barnes and Noble Classics, 2003), pp. xiii–xxix.

Anolik, R. B., 'The Missing Mother: The Meanings of Maternal Absence in the Gothic Mode', *Modern Language Studies*, 33/1/2 (Spring-Autumn, 2003), 25–43.

Arata, Stephen, *Fictions of Loss in the Victorian Fin de Siècle*. (Cambridge, UK: Cambridge University Press, 1996).

Armstrong, Nancy, 'Gender and the Victorian novel', in Deirdre David (ed.), *The Cambridge Companion to the Victorian Novel* (Cambridge: Cambridge University Press, 2001), pp. 97–124.

Astle, R., 'Dracula as totemic monster: Lacan, Freud, Oedipus and history', *SubStance*, 8/4, issue 25 (1979), 98–105.

Auerbach, N., 'Incarnations of the Orphan', *ELH*, 42/3 (Autumn, 1975), 359–419.

Barrie, J. M., *Peter Pan* (New York: Barnes and Noble Classics, 2005).

Ballantyne, Robert Michael, *The Coral Island* (New York: Garland, 1977).

Baucom, Ian, *Out of Place: Englishness, Empire, and the Locations of Identity* (Princeton, NJ: Princeton University Press, 1999).

Baybrooke, Patrick, *J. M. Barrie: A Study in Fairies and Mortals* (New York: Haskell House Publishers Ltd., 1971).

Bayley, Harold, *The Lost Language of Symbolism*, 2 vols (London: Ernest Benn Limited, 1957).

Beck, Horace Palmer, *Folklore and the Sea* (Middletown, Connecticut: Wesleyan University Press, 1973).

Bergonzi, Bernard, *The Turn of the Century: Essays on Victorian and Modern English Literature* (New York: Barnes and Noble Books, 1973).

Bergonzi, Bernard, *The Early H. G. Wells: A Study of the Scientific Romances* (Manchester, UK: Manchester University Press, 1961).

Bhabha, Homi K., *The Location of Culture* (London: Routledge, 1995).
Billone, A., 'Introduction' to J. M. Barrie, *Peter Pan* (New York: Barnes and Noble Classics, 2005), pp. xv–xxviii.
Bixler, Phyllis, *The Secret Garden: Nature's Magic* (New York: Twayne Publishers, 1996).
Bogen, A., '"The Island come true"': *Peter Pan*, Wild Cat Island, and the lure of the Real', in Mary Shine Thompson and Celia Keenan (eds), *Treasure Islands: Studies in Children's Literature* (Dublin: Four Courts Press, 2006), pp. 53–61.
Bonifer, M. S. E., 'Like A Motherless Child: The Orphan Figure in the Novels of Nineteenth-Century American Women Writers, 1850–1899' (unpublished PhD thesis, Indiana University of Pennsylvania, 1995).
Brantlinger, P., 'Race and the Victorian Novel', in Deirdre David (ed.), *The Cambridge Companion to The Victorian Novel* (Cambridge: Cambridge University Press, 2001), pp. 149–68.
Brantlinger, Patrick, *Rule of Darkness: British Literature and Imperialism, 1830–1914* (Ithaca: Cornell University Press, 1988).
Brenden, Piers, *The Decline and Fall of the British Empire, 1781–1997* (New York: Aflred A. Knoff, 2008).
Brenden, Piers, *Imminent Edwardians: Four Figures Who Defined Their Age: Northcliffe, Balfour, Parkhurst, Baden-Powell* (Missoula, MT: Pimlico, 2003).
Brewster, S., 'Seeing Things: Gothic and the Madness of Interpretation', in David Punter (ed.), *A Companion to the Gothic* (Oxford and Malden, MA: Blackwell Publishers Ltd, 2000), pp. 269–80.
Briggs, Julia, *The Rise and Fall of the English Ghost Story* (London: Faber, 1977).
Bristow, Joseph, *Empire Boys: Adventures in a Man's World* (London: HarperCollins Academic, 1991).
Brown, Daniel, *Desire and Contradiction: Imperial Visions and Domestic Debates in Victorian Literature* (Manchester, UK: Manchester University Press, 1990).
Burnett, Frances Hodgson, *The Secret Garden* (New York: Barnes and Noble Classics, 2005).
Burnett, Francis Hodgson, *A Little Princess* (New York: Barnes and Noble Classics, 1995).
Byron, G.,'Gothic of the 1890s', in David Punter (ed.), *A Companion to the Gothic.* (Oxford and Malden, MA: Blackwell Publishers, 2000), pp. 132–42.
Calder, Jenni, *Robert Louis Stevenson: A Life Study* (New York and Toronto: Oxford University Press, 1980).

Carpenter, Humphrey, *Secret Gardens: A Study of the Golden Age of Children's Literature* (Boston: Houghton Mifflin Company, 1985).

Casey, Kathy, 'Note', in *Dracula* by Bram Stoker (Mineola, NY: Dover Publications Inc., 2000), pp. iii–iv.

Cavaliero, Glen, *The Supernatural in English Fiction* (Oxford: Oxford University Press, 1995).

Chrisman, Laura, *Rereading the Imperial Romance: British Imperialism and South African Resistance in Haggard, Schreiner and Plaatje* (Oxford: Clarendon Press, 2000).

Cirlot, J. E., *A Dictionary of Symbols* (New York: Philosophical Library Inc., 1962).

Collins, Wilkie, *The Moonstone* (New York: The Modern Library, 2001).

Costa, Richard Hauer, *H. G. Wells* (New York: Twayne Publishers, 1967).

Cox, Homer T., *Henry Seton Merriman* (New York: Twayne Publishers, 1967).

Daly, Nicholas, *Modernism, Romance, and the* Fin-de-Siècle: *Popular Fiction and British Culture, 1880–1914* (Cambridge: Cambridge University Press, 1999).

D'Amato, B., 'Mary Shelley's *Frankenstein*: an orphaned author's dream and journey toward integration', *Modern Psychoanalysis*, 34/1 (2009), 117–35.

Daniel Defoe, *The Life and Surprising Adventures of Robinson Crusoe, of York, Mariner*, ed. J. Donald Crowley, Oxford English Novels series (London: Oxford University Press, 1972).

de Camp, L. Sprague, *H. P. Lovecraft, A Biography* (New York: Barnes and Noble, 1975).

Denisoff, D., 'Consumerism and Stevenson's Misfit Masculinities', in Richard Ambrosini and Richard Dury (eds), *Robert Louis Stevenson: Writer of Boundaries* (Madison, Wisconsin: University of Wisconsin Press, 2006), pp. 286–98.

Dewan, Pauline, *The House as Setting, Symbol, and Structural Motif in Children's Literature* (Lewiston, Queenston, and Lampeter: The Edwin Mellen Press, 2004).

Dixon, Robert, *Writing the Colonial Adventure: Gender, Race and Nation in Anglo-Australian Popular Fiction, 1875–1914* (Cambridge, UK: Cambridge University Press, 1995).

Dryden, L., '"City of dreadful night": Stevenson's Gothic London', in Richard Ambrosini and Richard Dury (eds), *Robert Louis Stevenson: Writer of Boundaries* (Madison, Wisconsin: University of Wisconsin Press, 2006), pp. 253–64.

Dury, R., 'The hand of Hyde', in William B. Jones, Jr. (ed.), *Robert Louis Stevenson Reconsidered* (Jefferson, NC and London: McFarland and Company Inc. Publishers, 2003), pp. 101–16.

Eigner, Edwin M., *Robert Louis Stevenson and the Romantic Tradition* (Princeton, New Jersey: Princeton University Press, 1966).

Ellis, Kate Ferguson, *The Contested Castle: Gothic Novels and the Subversion of Domestic Ideology* (Urbana and Chicago: University of Illinois Press, 1989).

Elmessiri, Nur, 'Burying Eternal Life in Bram Stoker's *Dracula*: The Sacred Age of Reason', *Alif Journal of Comparative Poetics*, 14 (1994), 101–35.

Eltis, S., 'Corrupting of the Blood and Degeneration of the Race: *Dracula* and Policing the Borders of Gender', in Bram Stoker, *Dracula*, ed. John Paul Riquelme (Boston: Bedford/St Martin's, 2002), pp. 450–65.

Evans, G., 'The Girl in the Garden: Variations on a Feminine Pastoral', *Children's Literature Association Quarterly*, 19 (1994), 20–4.

Ferrero, Gina Lombroso, *Criminal Man According to the Classification of Cesare Lombroso* (New York and London: G. P. Putnam's Sons, 1911).

Fletcher, Angus, 'Introduction' to Robert Louis Stevenson, *Treasure Island* (New York: Barnes and Noble Classics, 2005), pp. xi–xix (p. xi).

Fontana, E., 'Lombroso's Criminal Man and Stoker's *Dracula*', *Victorian Newsletter*, 66 (Fall 1984), 25–7.

Fowler, A., 'Parables of Adventure: The Debatable Novels of Robert Louis Stevenson', in Ian Campbell (ed.), *Nineteenth-Century Scottish Fiction* (Manchester: Carcanet New Press, 1979).

Fuss, Diana, *Essentially Speaking* (New York: Routledge, 1989).

Geduld, Harry M., *James Barrie* (New York: Twayne Publishers Inc., 1971).

Gelder, Ken, *Reading the Vampire* (London and New York: Routledge, 1994).

Gilbert, Eliot L., *The Good Kipling: Studies in the Short Story* (Oberlin, OH: Ohio University Press, 1970).

Gilmour, Robin, *The Novel in the Victorian Age* (London: Edward Arnold, 1986).

Gladden, S. L., 'Dracula's Earnestness: Stoker's Debt to Wilde', in Jack Lynch (ed.), *Critical Insights:* Dracula *by Bram Stoker* (Pasadena, CA and Hackensack, NJ: Salem Press, 2010), pp. 153–67.

Gohlke, M. S., 'Re-Reading *The Secret Garden*', *College English*, 41/8 (April 1980), pp. 984–02.

Green, Martin, *Deeds of Adventure, Deeds of Empire* (London: Routledge and Kegan Paul, 1980).

Green, Roger Lancelyn, *J. M. Barrie* (New York: Henry Z. Walck, Incorporated, 1961).

Greenberger, Allen J., *The British Image of India: A Study in the Literature of Imperialism, 1880–1960* (Oxford: Oxford University Press, 1969).

Greenway, John L., 'Seward's Folly: *Dracula* as Critique of "Normal Science"', *Stanford Literature Review*, 3 (Fall 1986), 213–30.

Gubar, Marah, *Artful Dodgers: Reconceiving the Golden Age of Children's Literature*. (New York and Oxford: Oxford University Press, 2009).

Guenon, Rene, *Le Roi du monde* (Paris: Galimard, 1950).

Guiley, Rosemary Ellen, *The Encyclopedia of Vampires, Werewolves, and Other Monsters* (New York: Checkmark Books, 2005).

Gunther, A., '*The Secret Garden* Revisited', *Children's Literature in Education*, 25/3 (1994), 159–68.

Haggard, H. Rider, *King Solomon's Mines* (New York: Barnes and Noble Classics, 2004).

Haggard, H. Rider, *She* (Oxford and New York: World's Classics, 1991).

Halberstam, Judith, *Skin Shows: Gothic Horror and the Technology of Monsters* (Durham, NC: Duke University Press, 1995).

Hammond, J. R., *A Robert Louis Stevenson Companion* (New York: Macmillan Publishing Company, 1984).

Hampson, R., 'Maps, Class, and Sexuality', in Linda Dryden et al. (eds), *Robert*

Louis Stevenson and Joseph Conrad: Writers of Transition (Lubbock, Texas: Texas Tech University Press, 2009), pp. 140–55.

Hardy, Thomas, *Jude the Obscure* (New York: W. W. Norton and Company, 1978).

Hatlen, Burton, 'The Return of the Repressed/Oppressed in Bram Stoker's *Dracula*', in Margaret L. Carter (ed.), *Dracula and the Critics* (Ann Arbor, MI and London: UMI Research Press, 1988), pp. 117–35.

Hebblethwaite, K., 'Creating wildmen in one's own image: maroons, Darwin and the question of humanity', in Mary Shine Thompson and Celia Keenan (eds), *Treasure Islands: Studies in Children's Literature* (Dublin: Four Courts Press, 2006), pp. 24–32.

Hebblethwaite, K., 'Introduction' to *Dracula* by Bram Stoker (London: Penguin Classics, 2006), pp. xi–xxxix.

Helson, R., 'The Psychological Origins of Fantasy for Children in Mid-Victorian England', *Children's Literature*, 3 (Philadelphia: Temple University Press, 1974), pp. 66–76.

Hennely, Jr., Mark M., '*Dracula*: The Gnostic Quest and Victorian Wasteland', in Margaret L. Carter (ed.), *Dracula and the Critics* (Ann Arbor and London: UMI Research Press, 1988), pp. 79–92.

Henty, G. A., *At the Point of the Bayonet: A Tale of the Mahratta War* (New York: Charles Scribner's Sons, 1901).

Hirsch, Marianne, *The Mother/Daughter Plot: Narrative, Psychoanalysis, Feminism* (Bloomington: Indiana University Press, 1989).

Hochman, Baruch and Ilja Wachs, *Dickens: The Orphan Condition* (Cranbury, NJ: Fairleigh Dickinson University Press, 1999).

Hogle, Jerrold E., 'The ghost of the counterfeit', in David Punter (ed.), *A Companion to the Gothic* (Oxford and Malden: Blackwell Publishers Ltd, 2000), pp. 293–304.

Holbrook, Jackson, *The Eighteen Nineties* (London: Grant Richards, 1913).

Hughes, William, *Bram Stoker Dracula: A Reader's Guide to Essential Criticism* (New York: Palgrave, 2009).

Hunt, Peter, *An Introduction to Children's Literature* (Oxford and New York: Oxford University Press, 1994).

Hurley, K., 'British Gothic fiction', in Jerrold E. Hogle (ed.), *The Cambridge Companion to Gothic Fiction* (Cambridge: Cambridge University Press, 2002), pp. 189–207.

Hurley, Kelly, *The Gothic Body* (Cambridge: Cambridge University Press, 1996).

Jaeck, N., 'Conrad's and Stevenson's Logbooks and "Paper Boats": Attempts at Textual Wreckage', in Linda Dryden et al. (eds), *Robert Louis Stevenson and Joseph Conrad: Writers of Transition* (Lubbock, Texas: Texas Tech University Press, 2009), pp. 39–51.

Jackson, Holbrook, *The Eighteen Nineties* (London: Grant Richards, 1913).

James, Lawrence, *The Rise and Fall of the British Empire* (New York: St Martin's Griffin, 1994).

Jefford, A., 'Dr Jekyll and Professor Nabokov: Reading a Reading', in Andrew Noble (ed.), *Robert Louis Stevenson.* (London: Vision Press, 1983), pp. 47–72.

Joshi, S. T., *The Weird Tale* (Austin: University of Texas Press, 1990).

Jung, Carl, *Psychology of the Transference* (London: Pantheon Books, 1954).

Kanzer, MD, M., 'The Self Analytic Literature of Robert Louis Stevenson', in Harry Geguld (ed.), *The Definitive* Dr Jekyll and

Mr Hyde *Companion* (New York and London: Garland Publishing Inc., 1983), pp. 118–26.

Karsavina, Lev Platonovich, *The Holy Fathers and Doctors of the Church* (Paris, 1926).

Katz, Wendy Roberta, *Rider Haggard and the Fiction of Empire: A Critical Study of British Imperial Fiction* (Cambridge: Cambridge University Press, 1987).

Keating, Peter, *The Haunted Study* (London: Secker & Warburg, 1989).

Kelly, R. G., 'Terms for Order in Some Late Nineteenth Century Fiction for Children', *Children's Literature*, 1, 58–61.

Kiely, Robert, *Robert Louis Stevenson and the Fiction of Adventure* (Cambridge, MA: Harvard University Press, 1965).

Kipling, Rudyard, *The Jungle Books* (New York: Barnes and Noble Classics, 2004).

Kipling, Rudyard, *Kim* (New York: Barnes and Noble Classics, 2003).

Kipling, Rudyard, *Many Inventions* (New York: D. Appleton and Company, 1899).

Kirtley, Bacil F., '*Dracula,* the Monastic Chronicles and Slavic Folklore', in Margaret L. Carter (ed.), *Dracula and the Critics* (Ann Arbor, MI and London: UMI Research Press, 1988), pp. 11–17.

Kitson, Peter J., 'The Victorian Gothic', in William Baker and Kenneth Womack (eds), *A Companion to the Victorian Novel* (Westport, CT: Greenwood Press, 2002), pp. 163–76.

Klinger, Leslie S. (ed.), *The New Annotated Dracula* by Bram Stoker (New York: W. W. Norton & Company, 2008).

Knoepflmacher, U. C., *Ventures into Childland: Victorians, Fairy Tales, and Femininity* (Chicago and London: Chicago University Press, 1988).

Kutzer, M. Daphne, *Empire's Children: Empire and Imperialism in Classic British Children's Books* (New York and London: Garland Publishing Inc., 2000).

Leatherdale, Clive (ed.), *Bram Stoker's Dracula Unearthed* (Westcliff-on-Sea: Desert Island Books, 1998).

Lerer, Seth, *Children's Literature: A Reader's History From Aesop to Harry Potter* (Chicago and London: University of Chicago Press, 2008).

Linehan, K. B., '"Closer than a wife": the strange case of Dr Jekyll's significant other', in William B. Jones (ed.), *Robert Louis Stevenson Reconsidered* (Jefferson, NC and London: McFarland and Company Inc. Publishers, 2003), pp. 85–100.

Lombroso, Cesare, *Criminal Man* (Montclair, NJ: Paterson Smith, 1972).

Lossky, Vladimir, *The Mystical Theology of the Eastern Church* (Crestwood, New York: St Vladimir's Seminary Press, 1976).

Lovell-Smith, R., 'On the Gothic Beach: A New Zealand Reading of House and Landscape in Margaret Mahy's *The Tricksters*', in Anna Jackson et al. (eds), *The Gothic in Children's Literature: Haunting the Borders* (New York and London: Routledge, 2008), pp. 93–115.

Lurie, Alison, *Don't Tell the Grownups: Subversive Children's Literature* (Boston, Toronto, and London: Little, Brown and Company, 1990).

MacGillivray, Royce, 'Bram Stoker's Spoiled Masterpiece', in Carol Senf (ed.), *The CriticalResponse to Bram Stoker's* Dracula (Westport, CT and London: Greenwood, 1993), pp. 61–8.

Mackenzie, Norman and Jeanne Mackenzie, *H. G. Wells* (New York: Simon and Schuster, 1973).

Machen, Arthur, *The Great God Pan* and *The Hill of Dreams* (Mineola, New York: Dover Publications Inc., 2006).

Makman, L., 'Introduction' to Rudyard Kipling, *The Jungle Books* (New York: Barnes and Noble Classics, 2004), pp. xv–xli.

Mallet, Philip, *Rudyard Kipling: A Literary Life* (New York: Palgrave Macmillan, 2003).

Manheimer, J., 'Murderous Mothers: The Problem of Parenting in the Victorian Novel', *Feminist Studies*, 5/3 (Autumn, 1979), 530–46.

Marshall, Gail, *The Victorian Novel* (London: Arnold, 2002).

Manlove, C. N., 'Charles Kingsley, H. G. Wells, and the Machine in Victorian Fiction', *Nineteenth-Century Literature*, 48/2 (Sept., 1993), 212–39 (p. 214).

Marshall, Gail, *The Victorian Novel* (London: Arnold, 2002).

Martin, Philip, 'The Vampire in the Looking Glass: Reflection and Projection in Bram Stoker's *Dracula*', in Clive Bloom et al. (eds), *Nineteenth-Century Suspense*

(New York: St Martin's Press, 1988), pp. 80–92.

Mason, Philip, *Kipling: The Glass, the Shadow and the Fire* (New York: Harper and Row, 1915).

McBratney, John, *Imperial Subject, Imperial Space: Rudyard Kipling's Fiction of the Native-Born* (Columbus, OH: The Ohio State University Press, 2002).

McCarthy, P., 'Making for Home: David Copperfield and His Fellow Travelers', in Murray Baumgarten and H. M. Daleski (eds), *Homes and Homelessness in the Victorian Imagination* (New York: AMS Press, 1998), pp. 21–32.

McConnel, Frank, *The Science Fiction of H. G. Wells* (New York: Oxford University Press, 1981).

McCracken-Flesher, C., 'Introduction' to Robert Louis Stevenson, *Treasure Island* (New York: Barnes and Noble Classics, 2005), pp. xi–xix.

McDonald, B. E., 'Recreating the World: the Sacred and the Profane in Bram Stoker's *Dracula*', in Jack Lynch (ed.), *Critical Insights:* Dracula *by Bram Stoker* (Pasadena, CA and Hackensack, NJ: Salem Press, 2010), pp. 87–137.

McGillis, Roderick. *A Little Princess: Gender and Empire* (New York: Twayne Publishers, 1996).

McLeod, John, *Beginning Post-colonialism* (Manchester, UK: Manchester U University Press P, 2000).

McWhir, Ann, 'Pollution and Redemption in *Dracula*', *Modern Language Studies*,17/3 (Summer 1987), 31–40.

Merriman, Henry Seton (Hugh Stowell Scott), *Flotsam: The Story of a Life* (New York: Longmans, Green and Co., 1986).

Mighall, Robert, *A Geography of Victorian Gothic Fiction* (Oxford: Oxford University Press, 1999).

Miles, R., 'Ann Radcliffe and Matthew Lewis', in David Punter (ed.), *A Companion to the Gothic* (Oxford and Malden, MA: Blackwell Publishers, 2000), pp. 41–57.

Miller, Karl, *Doubles: Studies in Literary History* (Oxford: Oxford University Press, 1985).

Mockler-Ferryman, A. F., *Up the Niger: Narrative of Major Claude Macdonald's Mission to the Niger and Benue Rivers* (London: G. Philip and Son, 1892).

Molesworth, Mary Louisa, *The Palace in the Garden* (London: Hatchard, Piccadilly, 1887).

Moretti, Franco, 'Dialectic of fear', in *Signs Taken For Wonders: Essays in the Sociology of Literary Forms*, trans. Susan Fischer, David Forgacs and David Miller (rev. edn, London: Verso, 1988).

Morris, Tim, *You're Only Young Twice: Children's Literature and Film* (Urbana and Chicago: University of Illinois Press, 2000).

Muller, J., 'Introduction' to Francis Hodgson Burnett, *The Secret Garden* (New York: Barnes and Noble Classics, 2005), pp. xv–xxxi.

Murray, E. B. *Ann Radcliffe* (New York: Twayne Publishers, 1972).

Murray, H., 'Francis Hodgson Burnett's *The Secret Garden*: The Organ(ic)ized World', *Touchstones: Reflections of the Best in Children's Literature*,1 (1985), 30–43.

Nash, B., 'Arthur Machen Among the Arthurians', in Charles Alva

Hoyt (ed.), *Minor British Novelists* (Carbondale and Edwardsville: Southern Illinois University Press, 1967), pp. 108–20.

Nicolson, Juliet, *The Perfect Summer: England 1911, Just Before the Storm* (New York: Grove Press, 2006).

Oldsey, B. S. and Stanley Weintraub, 'Golding's Deliberately Obscure Setting' in David Bender et al. (eds), *Readings on* Lord of the Flies (San Diego, California: Greenhaven Press, 1997), pp. 112–15.

Parsons, L. T., '"Otherways" into the Garden: Re-Visioning the Feminine in *The Secret Garden*', *Children's Literature in Education*, 33 (2002), 247–66.

Pater, Walter, *Studies in the History of the Renaissance* (London: Macmillan and Co., 1873).

Peck, John, *Maritime Fiction: Sailors and the Sea in British and American Novels, 1719–1917* (New York: Palgrave, 2001).

Peckam, Morse, *Beyond the Tragic Vision* (New York: George Braziller, 1962).

Perena, Suvendrini, *Reaches of Empire: The English Novel from Edgeworth to Dickens* (New York and Oxford: Columbia University Press, 1991).

Peters, Laura, *Orphan Texts: Victorian Orphans, Culture and Empire* (Manchester and New York: Manchester University Press, 2000).

Philmus, Robert M., *Into the Unknown: The Evolution of Science Fiction from Francis Godwin to H. G. Wells* (Berkeley and Los Angeles: University of California Press, 1970).

Pocock, John, *Rider Haggard and the Lost Empire* (London: Weidenfeld and Nicolson, 1993).

Polhemus, R. M., 'The Favorite Child: *David Copperfield* and the Scriptural Issue of the Child-Wives', in Murray Baumgarten and H. M. Daleski (eds), *Homes and Homelessness in the Victorian Imagination* (New York: AMS Press, 1998), pp. 3–20.

Pratt, Mary Louise, *Imperial Eyes: Travel Writing and Transculturation* (London: Routledge, 2007).

Pykett, Lynn, 'Sensation and the fantastic in the Victorian novel', in Deirdre David (ed.),

The Cambridge Companion to the Victorian Novel (Cambridge: Cambridge University Press, 2001), pp. 192–211.

Rago, J. V., '*Dr Jekyll and Mr. Hyde*: A "Men's Narrative" of Hysteria and Containment', in Richard Ambrosini and Richard Dury (eds), *Robert Louis Stevenson: Writer of Boundaries* (Madison, Wisconsin: University of Wisconsin Press, 2006), pp. 275–85.

Rao, K. Bhaskava, *Rudyard Kipling's India* (Norman, OK: Oklahoma University Press, 1967).

Reed, John R., *Victorian Conventions* (Ohio: Ohio University Press, 1975).

Reynolds, K., 'Changing Families in Children's Fiction', in M. O. Grenby and Andrea Immel (eds), *The Cambridge Companion to Children's Literature* (Cambridge: Cambridge University Press, 2009), pp. 193–208.

Richards, J., 'Introduction', in Jeffrey Richards (ed.), *Imperialism and Juvenile Literature* (Manchester and New York: Manchester University Press, 1989), pp. 1–11.

Richards, J., 'With Henty to Africa', in Jeffrey Richards (ed.), *Imperialism and Juvenile Literature* (Manchester and New York: Manchester University Press, 1989), pp. 72–106.

Richards, Jeffrey, *Visions of Yesterday* (London: Routledge and Kegan Paul, 1973).

Richardson, M., 'The Psychoanalysis of Ghost Stories', *Twentieth Century*, 166 (1959), 419–31.

Rigg, F. P., '(De)Constructing the Patriarchal Family: Mary Louisa Molesworth and the Late Nineteenth-Century Children's Novel', in Andrea O'Reilly Nerrera et al. (eds), *Family Matters in the British and American Novel* (Bowling Green, OH: Bowling Green State University Popular Press, 1997), pp. 97–114.

Riquelme, J. P., 'Introduction: Biographical and Historical Contexts', in John Paul Riquelme (ed.), *Dracula* by Bram Stoker (Boston and New York: Bedford/ St Martin's Press, 2002), pp. 3–21.

Riquelme, John Paul, 'Contextual Illustrations and Documents', in John Paul Riquelme (ed.), *Dracula* by Bram Stoker (Boston and New York: Bedford/ St Martin's Press, 2002), pp. 370–406.

Roberts, D., 'The Paterfamilias of the Victorian Governing Classes', in Anthony S. Wohl (ed.), *The Victorian Family* (London: Croon Helm, 1978), pp. 59–80.

Rogers, Deborah D., *The Matrophobic Gothic and Its Legacy: Sacrificing Mothers in the Novel and in Popular Culture* (New York: Peter Lang, 2007).

Rose, Jacqueline, *The Case of Peter Pan or the Impossibility of Children's Fiction* (Philadelphia: University of Pennsylvania Press, 1993).

Roth, Phyllis A., *Bram Stoker* (Boston: Twayne Publishers, 1982).

Rousseau, Jean-Jacques, *Emile, or On Education*, trans. Allan Bloom (New York: Basic Books, 1979).

Ruddick, Nicholas, *Ultimate Island: On the Nature of British*

Science Fiction (Westport, Connecticut and London: Greenwood Press, 1993).

Sadoff, Dianne F., *Monsters of Affection: Dickens, Eliot, and Bronte on Fatherhood* (Baltimore and London: The Johns Hopkins University Press, 1982).

Said, Edward, *Orientalism* (New York: Vintage Books, 1979).

Saposnik, Irving S., *Robert Louis Stevenson* (New York: Twayne Publishers, 1974).

Schoolfield, George C., *A Baedeker of Decadence: Charting a Literary Fashion, 1884–1927* (New Haven and London: Yale University Press, 2005), pp. 198–9

Seed, David, 'The Narrative Method of *Dracula*', *Nineteenth-Century Fiction*, 40 (1985), 61–75.

Seidel, Michael, Robinson Crusoe: *Island Myths and the Novel* (Boston: Twayne Publishers, 1991).

Senf, Carol, *Dracula: Between Tradition and Modernism* (New York: Twayne Publishers, 1998).

Sicher, E., 'Bleak Homes and Symbolic Houses: At-Homeness and Homelessness in Dickens', in Murray Baumgarten and H. M. Daleski (eds), *Homes and Homelessness in the Victorian Imagination* (New York: AMS Press, 1998), pp. 33–49.

Silver, A., 'Domesticating Bronte's Moors: Motherhood in *The Secret Garden*', *The Lion and the Unicorn*, 21/2 (1997), 193–203.

Smedman, M. S., 'Springs of Hope: Recovery of Primordial Time in "Mythic" Novels for Young Readers', *Children's Literature*, 16 (1988), 91–107.

Stevenson, Robert Louis, *Kidnapped* (New York: Barnes and Noble, 2006).

Stevenson, Robert Louis, *Treasure Island* (New York: Barnes and Noble Classics, 2005).

Stevenson, Robert Louis, *The Strange Case of Dr Jekyll and Mr Hyde and Other Stories* (New York: Barnes and Noble Classics, 2003).

Stoker, Bram, *Dracula's Guest and Other Weird Stories with* The Lair of the White Worm (London: Penguin Classics, 2006).

Stoker, Bram, *Dracula* (Boston and New York: Bedford/ St Martin's Press, 2002).

Sullivan, Zohreh T., *Narratives of Empire: The Fictions of Rudyard Kipling* (Cambridge: Cambridge University Press, 1993).

Sweetser, Wesley D., *Arthur Machen* (New York: Twayne, 1964).

Tange, Andrea Kaston, *Architectural Identities: Domesticity, Literature, and the Victorian Middle Classes* (Toronto, Buffalo and London: University of Toronto Press, 2010).

Thaden, Barbara, *The Maternal Voice in Victorian Fiction: Rewriting the Patriarchal Family* (New York: Garland, 1997).

Tymms, R., 'Doubles in Literary Psychology', in Harry Geguld (ed.), *The Definitive* Dr Jekyll and Mr Hyde *Companion* (New York and London: Garland Publishing Inc., 1983), pp. 77–94.

Vallone, L., 'Ideas of Difference in Children's Literature', in M. O. Greaby and Andrea Immel (eds), *The Cambridge Companion to Children's Literature* (Cambridge: Cambridge University Press, 2009), pp. 174–89.

Valente, Joseph, *Dracula's Crypt: Bram Stoker, Irishness, and the Question of Blood* (Urbana, IL and Chicago: University of Illinois Press, 2009).

Van Boheemen, Christine, *The Novel as Family Romance: Language, Gender, and Authority from Fielding to Joyce* (Ithaca and London: Cornell University Press, 1987).

Varnado, S. L., *Haunted Presence: The Numinous in Gothic Fiction* (Tuscaloosa, AL and London: University of Alabama Press, 1987).

Veeder, W., 'Children of the Night: Stevenson and Patriarchy', in William Veeder and Gordon Hirsh (eds), *Dr Jekyll and Mr Hyde After One Hundred Years* (Chicago: University of Chicago Press, 1988), pp. 107–60.

Verne, Jules, *The Mysterious Island* (New York: Charles Scribner's Sons, 1920).

Vicinus, M., '"Helpless and Unfriended": Nineteenth-Century Domestic Melodrama', *New Literary History*, 13/1, On Convention: I (Autumn, 1981), 127–43.

Villa, L., 'Quarreling with the Father', in Richard Ambrosini and Richard Dury (eds), *Robert Louis Stevenson: Writer of Boundaries* (Madison, Wisconsin: University of Wisconsin Press, 2006), pp. 109–20.

Vrettos, A., 'Victorian Psychology', in Patrick Brantlinger and William B. Thesing (eds), *A Companion to the Victorian Novel* (Oxford: Blackwell, 2002), pp. 67–83.

Wagenknect, Edward, *Seven Masters of Supernatural Fiction* (New York: Greenwood Press, 1991).

Wagenknect, Edward, *Seven Masters of Supernatural Fiction* (New York: Greenwood Press, 1991).

Walker, R. J., 'Pious Works: Aesthetics, Ethics, and the Modern Individual in Robert Louis Stevenson's *Dr Jekyll and Mr Hyde*', in Richard Ambrosini and Richard Dury (eds), *Robert Louis Stevenson: Writer of Boundaries* (Madison, Wisconsin: University of Wisconsin Press, 2006), pp. 265–74.

Watson, V., 'The Possibilities of Children's Fiction', in Morag Styles, Eve Bearne and Victor Watson (eds), *After Alice: Exploring Children's Literature* (London and New York: Cassell, 1992), pp. 11–24.

Weaver-Hightower, Rebecca, *Empire Islands: Castaways, Cannibals, and Fantasies of Conquest* (Minneapolis and London: University of Minnesota Press, 2007).

Weinbaum, Batya, *Islands of Women and Amazons: Representations and Realities* (Austin, TX: University of Texas Press, 1999).

Wells, H. G., *The Island of Dr Moreau* (Minneapolis, MN: Filiquarian Publishers, LLC, 2007).

Wells, H. G., *The Time Machine* and *The Invisible Man* (New York: Barnes and Noble Classics, 2003).

Wilde, O., 'The Star Child', in *The Happy Prince and Other Short Stories* (London: J. M. Dent and Sons Ltd.,1968), pp. 135–57.

Williamson, Jack, *H. G. Wells: Critic of Progress* (Baltimore: The Mirage Press, 1973).

Wilson, J., 'Landscape with Figures', in Andrew Noble (ed.), *Robert Louis Stevenson* (London and Ottawa, New Jersey: Vision and Barnes and Noble, 1983), pp. 73–95.

Wullschlager, Jackie, *Inventing Wonderland: The Lives and Fantasies of Lewis Carroll, Edward Lear, J. M. Barrie, Kenneth Grahame, and A. A. Milne* (New York: The Free Press, 1995).

Wyss, Johann, *The Swiss Family Robinson* (New York: Grosset and Dunlap Publishers, 1949).

Zimmer, Heinrich, *Form of Art and Yoga in the Indian Cult Image* (Berlin: Bibliothek Suhrkamp, 1926).

Index